# Microsoft Azure Virtual Desktop Guide

## Configuring and Operating Microsoft Azure Virtual Desktop (Exam AZ-140)

Arun Sabale
Balu N Ilag

**Apress®**

**Microsoft Azure Virtual Desktop Guide: Configuring and Operating Microsoft Azure Virtual Desktop (Exam AZ-140)**

Arun Sabale
New Jersey, NJ, USA

Balu N Ilag
Tracy, CA, USA

ISBN-13 (pbk): 978-1-4842-8062-1
https://doi.org/10.1007/978-1-4842-8063-8

ISBN-13 (electronic): 978-1-4842-8063-8

Managing Director, Apress Media LLC: Welmoed Spahr
Acquisitions Editor: Smriti Srivastava
Development Editor: Laura Berendson
Coordinating Editor: Shrikant Vishwakarma
Copy Editor: Kim Wimpsett

Cover designed by eStudioCalamar

Cover image designed by Pexels

Distributed to the book trade worldwide by Springer Science+Business Media LLC, 1 New York Plaza, Suite 4600, New York, NY 10004. Phone 1-800-SPRINGER, fax (201) 348-4505, e-mail orders-ny@springer-sbm. com, or visit www.springeronline.com. Apress Media, LLC is a California LLC and the sole member (owner) is Springer Science + Business Media Finance Inc (SSBM Finance Inc). SSBM Finance Inc is a **Delaware** corporation.

For information on translations, please e-mail booktranslations@springernature.com; for reprint, paperback, or audio rights, please e-mail bookpermissions@springernature.com, or visit www.apress.com/ rights-permissions.

Apress titles may be purchased in bulk for academic, corporate, or promotional use. eBook versions and licenses are also available for most titles. For more information, reference our Print and eBook Bulk Sales web page at www.apress.com/bulk-sales.

Any source code or other supplementary material referenced by the author in this book is available to readers on GitHub via the book's product page, located at https://link.springer.com/book/10.1007/ 978-1-4842-8062-1.

Printed on acid-free paper

*This book is dedicated to my parents to whom I owe everything.*

# Table of Contents

# About the Authors

**Arun Sabale** is a Microsoft Certified Azure Architect and Microsoft Certified Modern Desktop Expert. He has blogged about Azure services and automation, PowerShell, ARM, and Terraform. Arun has more than 12 years of experience with PowerShell automation and other Microsoft services and more than 6 years of experience with Azure infra design, deployment, and automation, as well as PowerShell, ARM, Terraform, and Azure DevOps. He is fascinated about coding and scripting to make techies life easy. His current role is a combination of Azure design, development, and automation. Arun is the owner and author of the PowershellTalk.com blog and regularly writes about Microsoft products and new services.

**Balu N Ilag** is a Microsoft Certified Trainer (MCT), former Microsoft MVP (2013–2019), and Microsoft Certified Solution Expert (MCSE) for communication. He currently works as a unified communication and collaboration engineer. His role is a combination of product support and customization, implementation, and strategic guidance for enterprise customers. He is fascinated by artificial intelligence (AI) and machine learning (ML) technology. He regularly writes books, blog posts, and articles on Microsoft products. He is highly motivated and engaged with the Microsoft Tech community, writing blog posts on Bloguc.com and interacting on Twitter and LinkedIn.

# About the Technical Reviewer

**Carsten Thomsen** is a back-end developer primarily but works with smaller front-end bits as well. He has authored and reviewed a number of books and created numerous Microsoft Learning courses, all to do with software development. He works as a freelancer/contractor in various countries in Europe, using Azure, Visual Studio, Azure DevOps, and GitHub. He is an exceptional troubleshooter, asking the right questions, and he enjoys working with architecture, research, analysis, development, testing, and bug fixing. Carsten is an excellent communicator with great mentoring and team-lead skills.

# Acknowledgments

Thank you to my friends, family and all individuals who supported me to start writing. My colleagues and friends have always believed in me, and I thank them for being so kind. Thank you to Microsoft for making such a good product and making product information available so individuals like me can make use of it. Finally, special thanks to everyone on my publishing team.

# Introduction

Azure Virtual Desktop (AVD) is a virtual desktop infrastructure running on the Azure platform and utilizing Azure cloud services and resources to create an infrastructure for the remote delivery of desktops. AVD has many benefits, which is why organizations worldwide have migrated essential apps and data to the cloud to achieve business stability and agility. The covid-19 pandemic forced many companies to permit remote work, and Azure Virtual Desktop is an important service that makes working remotely accessible with high-class resiliency and security. Many organizations have turned to Azure Virtual Desktop to support the new remote workforce, giving remote users a secure, easy-to-manage, productive personal computing experience with Windows 10 from the cloud. AVD adoption is expanding as are AVD support needs, and that's where this book comes into the picture.

This book will help you to understand AVD high-level architecture, AVD types (pooled/personal), the configuration and management aspects of AVD, how they are set up, and automation. Additionally, it will help you to understand how to design, implement, configure, and maintain an Azure Virtual Desktop environment for the enterprise.

Lastly, this book covers all the topics you will need to know to prepare for the Microsoft AZ-140 certification exam.

The book begins with an introduction to Azure Virtual Desktop and its design architecture. You will understand how to design an Azure Virtual Desktop, including user identities and profiles. Also, you will learn how to implement a network for Azure Virtual Desktop. The book covers the steps to create and configure host pools and session hosts so that you can understand all options and select the appropriate structure for enterprise deployment. We will also go through how to create the session host images and manage the image gallery and possible automation options. Later, we cover governing access and security in AVD along with the installation, configuration, and management of FSLogix. The book will take you through user experience settings and show you how to configure apps on a session host. You will also learn about disaster recovery and how to automate AVD management tasks. Monitoring and managing performance are included, as well as how to use AVD automation to create and delete the host pool and session host.

After reading this book, you will understand all aspects of AVD architecture, design, implementation, monitoring, and management to prepare for the AZ-140 certification exam.

# What You Will Learn

Specifically, you will learn the following in this book:

- What Azure Virtual Desktop is

- How to prepare the Azure Virtual Desktop architecture for enterprise deployment

- How to design Azure Virtual Desktop for user identities and profiles

- How to plan and implement networking for Azure Virtual Desktop

- How to plan and implement storage for Azure Virtual Desktop

- How to implement and manage FSLogix for pooled desktops

- How to create, manage, and automate operating system images with an image gallery

- How to implement FSLogix profile containers and FSLogix Cloud Cache

- How to create and configure host pools and session hosts

- How to use automation to create and configure host pools and session hosts

- How to install and configure apps on a session host including, all app publish options

- How to plan and implement business continuity and disaster recovery

- How to implement and manage OneDrive and Teams for a multisession environment

- How to monitor and manage the performance and health of Azure Virtual Desktop

AVD is a desktop and app virtualization service that resides in the cloud and can be accessed by users using any device from any location. Regardless of device type (Windows, Mac, iOS, Android, or any other device), with an HTML5 web client users can connect to the enterprise with Azure Virtual Desktop.

Most organizations are using a virtual desktop infrastructure (VDI) solution so that employees can connect to the office network while working from home. They can still use compliant machines and access internal applications and services from anywhere, but the problems with the VDI solution are scalability, cost, and lead time to get hardware and licenses.

Companies are undergoing digital transformations to become more agile, and Azure Virtual Desktop is a prime way to be flexible.

Here is a partial list of what AVD can do for you:

- Virtualize both desktops and apps and assign them to users

- Virtualize Office 365 Pro and deliver it to your end users in an optimized environment

- Reduce your capital expenditures by lessening the impact of hardware product lifecycles

- Lower costs per user by using multisession AVD (multiple users sharing a single host)

- Bring your existing Remote Desktop Services (RDS) and Windows Server desktops and apps to any computer easily

- Provide a unified and simplified management experience for your admins

- Reduce time to create a new virtual desktop without worrying about hardware/software procurement and setup

## Who Is This Book For?

If you are an IT professional, cloud administrator, support personnel, developer, DevOps engineer, architect, or consultant and want to learn about designing, implementing, and managing Azure Virtual Desktop to improve your knowledge or pass the Microsoft AZ-140 exam, then this book is for you.

# About This Book

In this book, you will learn about the cloud-based Azure Virtual Desktop from beginning topics to expert-level usage. Additionally, you will discover AVD prerequisites, learn about the high-level architecture, see how to set up different desktop types (pooled/personal), and how to set up AVD. Furthermore, you will learn how to use automation for AVD creation/deletion and autoscale up and down to save AVD costs.

Here are details about what you will learn in each chapter:

- *Chapter 1, "Introduction to Azure Virtual Desktop"*: This chapter introduces Azure Virtual Desktop including its capabilities, prerequisites, licensing, pricing, virtual desktop types (personal/pooled), and components.

- *Chapter 2, "Design the Azure Virtual Desktop Architecture"*: This chapter provides information about AVD's high-level architecture including cost-saving options, user session flow with and without an RDP shortpath, Azure platform/Azure Virtual Desktop limitations, VM sizing, network capacity requirements, operating system recommendations, DNS for AVD, Azure Virtual Desktop host pool placement, and resource groups.

- *Chapter 3, "Design for User Identities and Profiles"*: In this chapter, you will learn about all the identity options available in the Azure cloud, which identity options are best for AVD, licensing model/options, user profile storage plans, and network connectivity recommendations.

- *Chapter 4, "Implement and Manage Networking for Azure Virtual Desktop"*: In this chapter, you will learn about AVD network requirements including implementing Azure virtual network connectivity, managing connectivity to the Internet and on-premises networks from AVD, implementing and managing network security for AVD, and managing Azure Virtual Desktop session hosts by using Azure Bastion.

- *Chapter 5, "Implement and Manage Storage for Azure Virtual Desktop"*: In this chapter, you will learn about user profile storage configuration for pooled desktops. A pooled desktop is a nonpersistent desktop, which means users won't be able to get a session on the same back-end session host, so that's why we must store user profiles on remote storage account file share. FSLogix is the tool help to store user profiles on remote storage and mount it at the time of user login. You will also learn how to set up a file share for user profiles and FSLogix installation/configuration considering enterprise security.

- *Chapter 6, "Implement and Manage FSLogix"*: In this chapter, you will learn about the FSLogix tool, which is used for storing user profiles on remote storage. It is important to understand FSLogix options so that you can select the appropriate option for your requirements. In this chapter, you will look at planning, installing, and configuring FSLogix for pooled desktops and all the profile options such as containers and cloud caches to store the user profiles on remote storage.

- *Chapter 7, "Create and Manage Session Host Images"*: In this chapter, you will learn how to create an Azure Virtual Desktop image, use a shared image gallery to store custom images, and plan image update and management.

- *Chapter 8, "Create and Configure Host Pools and Session Hosts"*: In this chapter, you will learn how to create Azure Virtual Desktop hosts and host pools using the Azure portal, PowerShell, command-line interface (CLI), and Azure Resource Manager templates. Additionally, you will see how to configure host pool settings, assign users to host pools, apply OS and application updates to a running Azure Virtual Desktop host, and apply security and compliance settings to session hosts.

- *Chapter 9, "Install and Configure Apps on a Session Host"*: In this chapter, you will learn about the Azure Virtual Desktop application publishing options, including MSIX app attach, application masking, and the application RemoteApp group. All these options are different from each other, so you will look at each option in detail so that you can decide which option is better for your organization's requirements. Additionally, you will see how to set up common applications such as Teams and OneDrive, as well as browsers of your choice for Internet access.

- *Chapter 10, "Plan and Implement Business Continuity and Disaster Recovery"*: In this chapter, you will learn about planning and implementing disaster recovery for Azure Virtual Desktop and designing and configuring a backup strategy for personal desktops. You will also learn about FSLogix user profiles, MSIX packages, golden images, and restore options for all the backed-up components.

- *Chapter 11, "Monitor and Manage Performance and Health"*: In this chapter, you will learn about monitoring Azure Virtual Desktop by using the Azure Monitor native tool to see all the different components you can monitor. Additionally, you will see all the recommendations from Azure Advisor for Azure Virtual Desktop. You can customize Azure Monitor workbooks for Azure Virtual Desktop monitoring and create dashboards with a customized view required for your monitoring team.

# Getting Ready

Azure Virtual Desktop is a significant product that involves multiple Azure cloud services such as compute, network, Azure AD, and operating systems. Therefore, you must learn about Azure compute, network, and Azure AD (authentication) services that will help you on your AVD journey. For more information about Azure services and automation using PowerShell, ARM, and Terraform, you can visit `https://powershelltalk.com`. Additionally, you can contact me via `Arun.Sabale@outlook.com` for any questions or feedback.

We have covered most of the content of "Configuring and operating – Microsoft Azure Virtual Desktop - Exam AZ-140" exam, so if you are preparing for the exam or if you are planning to implement AVD in your organization, then let's get started!

# CHAPTER 1

# Introduction to Azure Virtual Desktop

This chapter introduces Azure Virtual Desktop (AVD) and its capabilities. It also covers the different virtual desktop infrastructure (VDI) platforms compared to AVD. Additionally, this chapter provides detail about AVD prerequisites, licensing, pricing, different AVD types (personal/pooled), and AVD components.

After reading this chapter, you will understand the use of Azure Virtual Desktop including its high-level components that the support team needs to manage and the best desktop options for your organization.

## What Is Azure Virtual Desktop?

Azure Virtual Desktop was previously known as Windows Virtual Desktop (WVD). AVD officially launched in September 2019, and Microsoft rebranded Windows Virtual Desktop as Azure Virtual Desktop in June 2021.

Microsoft Azure Virtual Desktop is a cloud-based virtual desktop that runs in Azure and allows end users to access organization-specific internal applications securely. Azure Virtual Desktop provides desktop and application virtualization capabilities for the enterprise with some exclusive features such as Windows 10 enterprise multisessions, which allows multiple users to concurrently connect to a remote desktop on a cloud-based virtual machine. AVD provides a familiar user experience to RDS users with optimal app compatibility and no RDS CAL licensing on Windows 10 multisessions. Windows 7 is also available with extended support so you can run your legacy apps securely and efficiently in the cloud.

© Arun Sabale and Balu N Ilag 2022
A. Sabale and B. N. Ilag, *Microsoft Azure Virtual Desktop Guide*,
https://doi.org/10.1007/978-1-4842-8063-8_1

Traditionally, deploying a VDI was often considered time-consuming and complex because of the hardware and software license procurement for VDI deployment for each region. Additionally, VDI depends on several key components including VDI brokers, database servers, session host machines, domain controllers, and more to work together seamlessly. Azure Virtual Desktop is a cloud-based VDI solution that provides all the benefits of the cloud such as easy scalability, availability, security, high availability, easy disaster recovery, and most importantly cost. The Azure Virtual Desktop service is available in most regions so you can deploy a desktop in any available region with less lead time.

The pandemic has accelerated the number of companies leveraging cloud resources; with most employees are working from home, it is difficult to accommodate the high demand for infra resources with limited on-premises infrastructure and network setup. That's where Azure Virtual Desktop is useful. Organizations can simply deploy desktops in the cloud based on the organization's requirements and following its security and compliance policies.

Azure Virtual Desktop provides a solid foundation for a cloud VDI based on Windows server and Windows desktop hosts to keep end users productive. AVD also manages the virtual desktop broker, gateway, diagnostics, and metadata for you, and you will still be able to manage/control the virtual machines, operating system, and network and make sure AVD is compliant as per the company's policies. The Azure portal is your management hub for Azure Virtual Desktop. Admins can configure network settings, add users, deploy desktop apps, and enable security with a few clicks from the Azure portal. Additionally, PowerShell and ARM templates can be used to create/configure/manage AVD host pools, workspaces, and session hosts. See Figure 1-1.

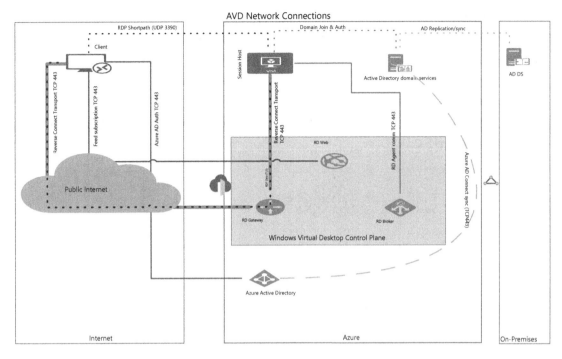

***Figure 1-1.*** *Azure Virtual Desktop control plane*

# What Does Microsoft Azure Virtual Desktop Do?

Azure Virtual Desktop is a desktop-as-a-service (DaaS) offering that allows customers to run virtual apps and desktop services from the Azure public cloud. Admins deploy the solution through the Azure portal and can leverage Azure Active Directory and a host of operating system options to deliver resources to users. Since Azure Virtual Desktop is a cloud-based solution, you don't have to worry about hardware procurement or any other license cost.

Due to the ongoing pandemic, most companies are allowing employees to work from home across the world. That's why demand for VDI/VPNs has increased, but at the same time expanding a VDI/VPN infrastructure is time-consuming, so companies started looking for alternative. Microsoft came up with a solution to allow companies to set up a VDI in the cloud on demand with multiregion support.

Azure Virtual Desktop allows admins to set up a virtual desktop in the cloud on demand and scale up and down whenever they want. Additionally, admins can use an existing operating system image with all the tools and agents installed on it or create a new image with a company-specific compliance policy, tools, and agents to create an AVD session host. AVD desktops can be joined to an existing AD domain controller so that users can use the same credential they were using earlier. AD domains also allow the enterprise to set up compliance policy on the AVD session host and use an existing patching, antivirus, and monitoring solution to manage AVD. Users can access on-premises applications over a site-to-site VPN or over ExpressRoute from Azure Virtual Desktop. See Figure 1-2.

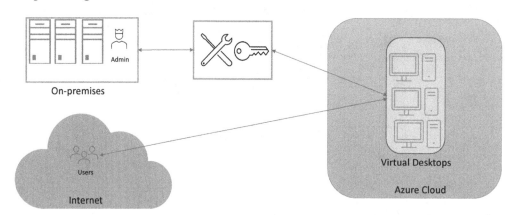

***Figure 1-2.*** *What does Azure Virtual Desktop do?*

# What Are the Benefits of Using Azure Virtual Desktop?

In the past, VDI solutions have been complex, time-consuming, expensive, and difficult to manage. Small and medium-sized businesses don't want to use VDI solutions as a large server infrastructure and dedicated team are required to manage/run VDI infrastructure on-premises. Azure Virtual Desktop makes this affordable and easier for all businesses.

These are the high-level benefits you will get compared to other VDI platforms:

- *Windows 10 multisession advantage*: Multiple users can log in and share back-end host/VM resources with a pooled host pool.

- *Office 365 Pro plus support*: Azure Virtual Desktop is optimized for Office 365.

- *Windows 7*: Azure Virtual Desktop supports Windows 7 with free extended support for legacy applications.

- *Full desktops and remote apps*: A full desktop as well as applications can be published on Azure Virtual Desktop.

- *Auto scaling*: It is easy to scale up and down in less time based on the organization demand (with automation).

- *Low lead time and fast enablement of virtual desktop*: Enable remote users in hours compared to on-prem VDI solutions.

- *Simple to deploy and configure*: You can deploy and manage virtual desktops and apps, assign users, and have access to monitoring and diagnostics. All of this is available to you in a single interface.

- *Cost effective*: Azure Virtual Desktop is a cost-effective VDI solution as you pay for the virtual machines only when your virtual desktops are running, and the management plane is managed by Microsoft without any additional cost. There is a significant cost advantage of low per user cost with a pooled host pool.

- *Flexible*: Like with all Microsoft Cloud Services, there are no contractual commitments with Azure Virtual Desktop, and the organization can easily delete virtual desktops at any time. The service itself is flexible, and it allows you to publish a full desktop experience or offer only a specific virtual application.

## Who Should Use Azure Virtual Desktop?

The Azure Virtual Desktop solution is suitable for businesses of all sizes. Many organizations are allowing their employees to work from home due to the covid-19 pandemic, and AVD is particularly useful in this case because it allows organizations to set up all the security controls on the cloud-based desktop, which can be accessed over the Internet securely. In some scenarios, AVD is useful in case organizations want their external consultants/venders to connect to organization-specific internal application/infrastructure resources.

Azure Virtual Desktop also provides an AVD shortpath feature, which allows users to connect to the AVD desktop directly (direct sight connection required). This is useful when an organization wants its intranet users to access cloud-based desktops for compliance reasons. See Figure 1-3.

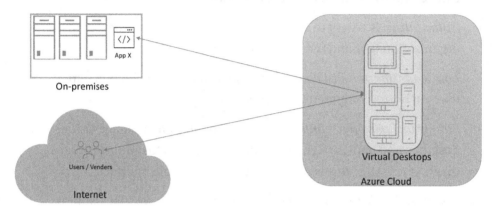

***Figure 1-3.***  *Who should use Azure Virtual Desktop?*

# What Are the Differences Between Traditional VDI and AVD DaaS?

Table 1-1 compares the differences between AVD DaaS and a traditional VDI.

***Table 1-1.*** *Differences Between Traditional VDI and AVD*

| Traditional VDI | AVD Desktop-as-a-Service |
| --- | --- |
| Fixed VM size | Scale on demand |
| Rely on AVD for Windows 10 multisession | Windows 10 multisessions supported, which helps to lower per user cost |
| Additional efforts to enable use of Office 365 | Office 365 optimized |
| Long implementation time | Fast implementation |
| Self-managed control plane (Broker, Gateway) | Control plane managed by Azure |
| Difficult and time-consuming to set up globally | Globally available and easy to set up on demand |
| Software/hardware procurement required for each additional workload; time-consuming process | On-demand procurement |
| Fix hardware/software required to set up DR | Easy to set up disaster recovery for business-critical users and user automation to scale DR on demand |
| Annual/long-term perpetual licensing/hardware procurement | Monthly or pay-as-you-go billing |

# Azure Virtual Desktop Types: Personal vs. Pooled Desktops

A personal desktop (also called a *persistent* desktop) allows users to always connect to the same session host (back-end VM in Azure). Users can modify the virtual desktop based on their preferences and save files in the desktop environment. A personal desktop solution allows the following:

- Lets users customize their virtual desktop including user-installed applications and save files within the virtual desktop

- Allows users to assign dedicated resources (CPU/memory/storage) to a specific user, which can be helpful when users are running applications requiring complex configuration

A pooled desktop solution is also called a *nonpersistent* desktop. In a pooled desktop, a load balancer sends a user session request to the currently available session host (back-end VM) depending on the load-balancing type selected for the host pool. Since the users don't always return to the same session host each time, they have a limited ability to customize the virtual desktop including additional application installation. A user profile can be stored on remote storage using FSLogix so that user will get same profile every time they log into the pooled desktop.

Table 1-2 compares the differences between pooled and personal AVD. See also Figure 1-4.

***Table 1-2.*** *Differences Between Pooled and Personal AVD*

| Pooled AVD Desktop | Personal AVD Desktop |
|---|---|
| Nonpersistent desktop. | Persistent desktop. |
| Need Windows 10 multisession OS image. | Windows 10 OS image. |
| Multiple users can share single VM. | Dedicated VM per user. |
| Per user cost will be less. | Per user cost will be higher than pooled. |
| Depth/breadth-first load balancing for user sessions. | Direct session to dedicated VM. |
| One user can use all resources (CPU, RAM) from the pooled VM as there is no per user resource restriction, and this may cause performance issue for other users on the same VM. | Dedicated resources (CPU, RAM, storage). |
| User-centric app installation required so that the app will be available for all user. | Both user/system-centric installations are supported. |
| Application needs to be installed on all VMs in the pooled host pool so that it will be available for user. | App installation on dedicated VM. |
| FSLogix required to store user profile on remote storage to keep the same profile during every login. | FSLogix is not required/mandatory. |
| Autoscaling can be added to stop /start a VM on demand and help to reduce cost. | Start VM on connect, and auto-shutdown features can be used to stop /start an AVD VM and reduce cost. |

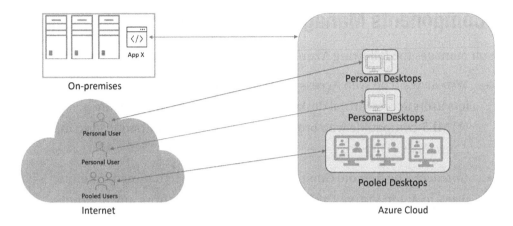

**Figure 1-4.**  *Pooled and personal virtual desktop*

# Azure Virtual Desktop Components

The Azure Virtual Desktop service architecture is similar to Windows Server Remote Desktop Services. Microsoft manages the infrastructure and brokering components, while enterprise customers manage their own desktop session host (virtual machines), networking data, and clients. See Figure 1-5.

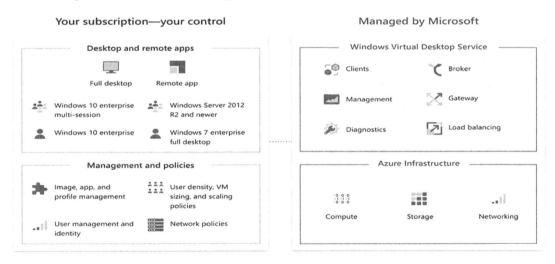

**Figure 1-5.**  *Azure Virtual Desktop control plane*

# AVD Components Managed by Microsoft

Microsoft manages the following Azure Virtual Desktop services as part of Azure:

- *Web Access*: The Web Access service within Window Virtual Desktop lets users access virtual desktops and remote apps through an HTML5-compatible web browser with multifactor authentication in Azure Active Directory.

- *Gateway*: The Remote Connection Gateway service connects remote users to Azure Virtual Desktop apps and desktops from any Internet-connected device with an Azure Virtual Desktop client. The client connects to a gateway, which then orchestrates a connection from a session host VM back to the same gateway.

- *Connection Broker*: The Connection Broker service manages user connections to virtual desktops and remote apps. The Connection Broker provides load balancing and reconnection to existing sessions.

- *Diagnostics*: Remote Desktop Diagnostics is an event-based aggregator that marks each user or administrator action on the Azure Virtual Desktop.

- *Extensibility components*: Azure Virtual Desktop includes several extensibility components. You can manage Azure Virtual Desktop using Windows PowerShell or using the provided REST APIs, which also enable support from third-party tools.

# AVD Components Managed by the User

Customers manage these components of Azure Virtual Desktop solutions:

- *Azure Virtual Network*: Azure Virtual Network lets Azure resources like VMs communicate privately with each other and with the on-premises network. You can connect an Azure Virtual Desktop to an on-premises network using a site-to-site VPN or using ExpressRoute to extend the on-premises network into the Azure cloud over a private connection for an AVD session host domain join or to access a specific application from AVD desktop.

- *Azure AD*: Azure Virtual Desktop uses Azure AD for identity and access management. On-premises domain user accounts can be synced with Azure AD, and the same account can be used for AVD authentication so that the user doesn't have to manage multiple credentials. Azure AD can also provide MFA, which is an additional layer of security when users are accessing AVD from the Internet.

- *AD DS*: Azure Virtual Desktop VMs must domain-join an AD DS service, and the AD DS must be in sync with Azure AD (via Azure AD Connect) to associate users between the two services.

- *Azure Virtual Desktop session hosts*: A host pool can have a session host (Azure VM) with the following operating systems:

  - Windows 7 Enterprise

  - Windows 10 Enterprise

  - Windows 10 Enterprise multisession

  - Windows Server 2012 R2 and above

  - Custom Windows system images (above OS) with preloaded apps, group policies, or other customizations

- *Azure Virtual Desktop workspace*: The Azure Virtual Desktop workspace or tenant is a management construct to manage and publish host pool resources.

# Before Getting Started with Azure Virtual Desktop

Azure Virtual Desktop is a desktop-as-a-service. There are some prerequisites that need to be in place before an AVD implementation:

The following requirements are needed for the use of Azure Virtual Desktop on Azure:

- Licensing (check the "Licensing" section in following Chapter 3 for details about the types of licenses available)

- Azure subscription

  - Azure Active Directory setup with Azure AD Connect to sync on-premises AD user for AVD authentication

  - Contributor and user administrator (or owner) permission with a subscription to create AVD resources and assign users to AVD

- Domain controller and DNS

  - AD must be in sync with Azure AD

  - Domain-join credentials to join an AVD VM to AD

  - DNs to resolve domain names as well as all other name resolution

  - Optional: Azure AD Domain Services (instead of a domain controller)

- Profile containers network share (Azure file share or Azure NetApp to store pooled user profiles)

- Network connectivity to on-premises

  - Networking/on-premises connectivity via ExpressRoute or a site-to-site VPN so that a VM can join to an AD domain controller for user authentication and access on-premises application from the AVD

  - Open required port and IP address (monitoring, patching and security agents, AD, DNS, other application) on a firewall between on-premises and Azure

- OS image (Windows 10 for personal and/or a Windows 10 multisession image for pooling with all agents/software installed in it)

# How Much Does Azure Virtual Desktop Cost?

Azure Virtual Desktop is a desktop-as-a-service, and most of the resources are managed by Microsoft Azure and are free. The following resources need to be considered while estimating the cost of AVD. You can use the Azure cost calculator to get the estimated cost based on the AVD desktop type (see Figure 1-6).

If you want to go with the personal desktop version, then one VM per user needs to be added in the Azure cost calculator. For a pooled desktop, you may select the number of VMs based on the total users/number of users per VM.

- *User access rights/license cost*

  - License entitlement: There is no additional cost if you have an eligible Windows, Microsoft 365, or Microsoft Remote Desktop Services (RDS) Client Access License (CAL). Check the "Licensing" section in Chapter 3 for details about the types of licenses.

- *Azure infrastructure costs*: In addition to user access, the following are the Azure components required to host Azure Virtual Desktop that have additional cost:

  - Virtual machines

  - Storage

    - Operating system (OS) storage

    - Data disk (wherever applicable)

    - User profile storage (pooled AVD)

  - Networking (user data transfer cost)

- Additional optional infrastructure costs

  - Log analytics

  - Automation account (autoscaling)

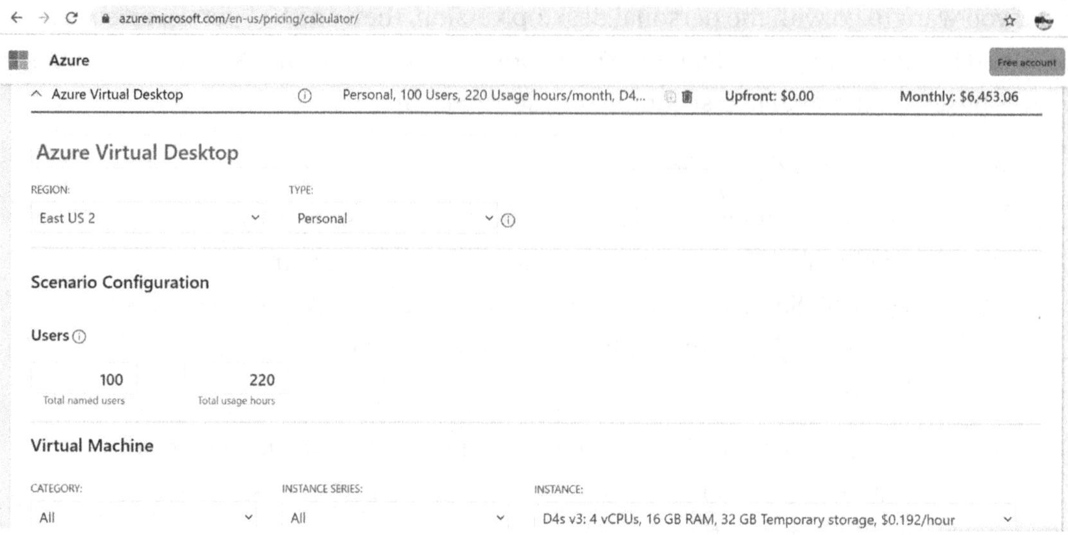

**Figure 1-6.** *Azure cost calculator*

# Summary

In this chapter, you were introduced to Microsoft Azure Virtual Desktop, including its benefits, different types of desktops, different components involved, and prerequisites needed by the support/operation team. You also learned about AVD licensing requirements, costs, and other details.

# CHAPTER 2

# Design the Azure Virtual Desktop Architecture

This chapter provides information on Azure Virtual Desktop's high-level architecture, including cost-saving options, user session flow with and without RDP shortpath, Azure platform/Azure Virtual Desktop limitations, VM sizing, network capacity requirements, operating system recommendations, DNS for Azure Virtual Desktop, Azure Virtual Desktop host pool placement, and resource groups.

You learned about the basics of Azure Virtual Desktop in Chapter 1, so let's get into the details of the Azure Virtual Desktop architecture and the user connection flow to Azure Virtual Desktop.

## Azure Virtual Desktop Architecture

Azure Virtual Desktop is a desktop and application virtualization service that runs in the Azure cloud. Figure 2-1 shows the reference architecture for Azure Virtual Desktop to build virtualized desktop infrastructure (VDI) solutions at enterprise scale. Enterprise-scale solutions generally cover 1,000 or more virtual desktops.

© Arun Sabale and Balu N Ilag 2022
A. Sabale and B. N. Ilag, *Microsoft Azure Virtual Desktop Guide*,
https://doi.org/10.1007/978-1-4842-8063-8_2

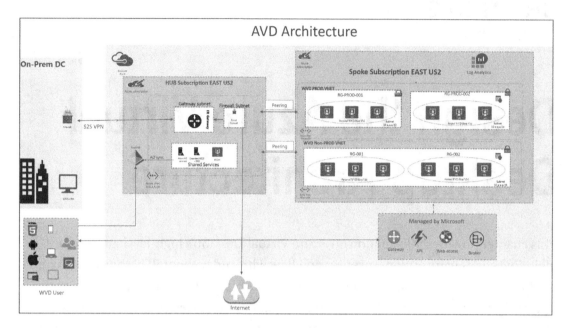

***Figure 2-1.***  *Azure Virtual Desktop high-level architecture*

This architecture diagram shows a typical architectural setup for Azure Virtual Desktop including authentication, network, and compute resources. The following are the high-level points needs to be considered in the Azure Virtual Desktop design:

- *Hub-and-spoke architecture*: It is recommended you use a dedicated virtual network and subscription for Azure Virtual Desktop resources to isolate Azure Virtual Desktop as well as avoid Azure subscription-level limitations. If it's a greenfield deployment (new to Azure), then you must consider a hub-and-spoke architecture and a dedicated hub virtual network. The following are the typical resources needed in a hub-and-spoke architecture:

  - *Hub resources*: You can use a hub virtual network per region to place all common/shared services such as an extended ADDS, DNS, SCCM, and firewall. A hub virtual network needs to be connected to an on-premises datacenter via ExpressRoute or a site-to-site VPN so that the on-premises services/application will be accessible in Azure. The hub subscription must have all the security controls in place, including a firewall to validate all outgoing traffic from the Azure virtual network's to on-premises or the Internet.

- *Spoke resources*: All the Azure Virtual Desktop resources including VMs, log analytics, and storage can be created in a spoke subscription/virtual network. It is recommended to create different subnets as well as a resource group for different types of host pools/business units. Spoke virtual networks can be peered with hub virtual networks, and user-defined routing (route table) can be configured to send all traffic via a hub virtual network firewall to on-premises or the Internet. For easy management, you must create a separate host pool for different VM sizes so that it will be easy to manage user access and advance autoscaling. Personal and pooled are the two different types of desktop options that Azure Virtual Desktop provides, so you must consider having a separate host pool for a pooled setup as well as a separate host pool for a personal setup. The Azure Virtual Desktop control plane handles web access, gateway, broker, diagnostics, and REST APIs and is managed by Microsoft, so you just have to manage AD DS and Azure AD, virtual networks, Azure Files or Azure NetApp Files, and the Azure Virtual Desktop host pools, session host, and workspaces. The Azure Virtual Desktop control plane is available in the United States (US), Europe (EU), United Kingdom (UK), and Canada (CA) regions as of September 2021; however, a host pool can exist in any other Azure region, but it will impact user performance if the control plane is not in the same or nearby region.

- *Authentication*: You can use Azure AD for Azure Virtual Desktop authentication and ADDS for domain joins of the Azure Virtual Desktop session host. You can user Azure AD Connect to integrate the on-premises Active Directory Domain Services (AD DS) with Azure Active Directory (Azure AD) so that the same credentials can be used to log in to Azure Virtual Desktop. It is recommended to extend on-premises ADDS to the Azure hub to avoid authentication traffic over a VPN or ExpressRoute.

- *Network*: Azure Virtual Desktop uses a reverse connect transport, which means you don't need any inbound connection to an Azure Virtual Desktop session host from the Azure Virtual Desktop control plane or RD client. You need specific outbound IP/ports for Azure Virtual Desktop to work in case you are planning to block the Internet on the Azure Virtual Desktop session host. Azure Virtual Desktop users can connect the Azure Virtual Desktop gateway/broker over the Internet to access the Azure Virtual Desktop app (refer to the user connection flow Figure 2-2 for details) and reverse the connect transport from the session host to the Azure Virtual Desktop gateway/broker. If you have Azure Virtual Desktop shortpath enabled, then the user session traffic can go over a private IP address (refer to the "Azure Virtual Desktop User Session Traffic Flow with RDP Shortpath" section for details).

# How Does the User Connect to Azure Virtual Desktop?

It is important to understand the user session connection flow from the Azure Virtual Desktop client to Azure Virtual Desktop so that you can consider all the session requirements in the Azure Virtual Desktop design phase and set up the network accordingly. Understanding user session flow can also help to troubleshoot the Azure Virtual Desktop access and performance issues.

The Azure Virtual Desktop client is available for all devices and operating systems so that users can log in to Azure Virtual Desktop from anywhere using any device. Connecting from Azure Virtual Desktop client to your host pool (session host) works differently with Windows Virtual Desktop than other VDI sessions. Azure Virtual Desktop uses a reverse connection, which means no inbound IP/ports are required on the session host (back-end VM) to set up the Azure Virtual Desktop connection.

Figure 2-2 shows the detail user session flow from the Azure Virtual Desktop client to Azure Virtual Desktop.

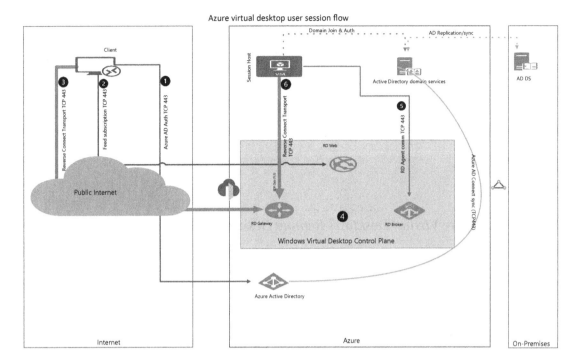

***Figure 2-2.***   *Azure Virtual Desktop user session flow*

This diagram shows a typical Azure Virtual Desktop client flow to an Azure Virtual Desktop session host.

- The user launches an RD client and enters credentials that connect to Azure AD for sign-in. If third-party MFA is enabled, then the authentication request will go to the MFA server/provider as well. Clients get a token after successful authentication (flow 1 in Figure 2-2).

- The client presents a token to Web Access to determine the resources authorized for the user from the Azure Virtual Desktop metadata; currently the Azure Virtual Desktop metadata is available in limited regions, so you must select a nearby metadata region for better performance if the metadata is not available in the region selected for Azure Virtual Desktop (flow 2 in Figure 2-2).

- The user gets the authorized resources (Azure Virtual Desktop/ application) to select in the RD client. See Figure 2-3.

**Figure 2-3.** *Azure Virtual Desktop's Remote Desktop client view*

- The user selects a resource by clicking the workspace name visible in the RD client.

- The RD client connects to the gateway and gateway contact broker from the same region (flows 3 and 4 in Figure 2-2).

- The broker orchestrates a connection from the host agent to the gateway (flows 4 and 5 in Figure 2-2).

- RDP traffic now flows between the RD client and session host VM over connections 6 and 3 shown in Figure 2-2 (only if RDP shortpath is not enabled on AVD).

  If RDP shortpath is enabled, then it establishes the direct connectivity between the Remote Desktop client and the session host. Direct connectivity reduces the dependency on the Azure Virtual Desktop gateways, improves the connection's reliability, and increases the bandwidth available for each user session.

- Once the connection flow proceeds, bidirectional communication between your session hosts/host pool will go over port HTTPS (443).

# Azure Virtual Desktop User Session Traffic Flow with RDP Shortpath

As you know, by default Azure Virtual Desktop traffic goes through the RD gateway over port 443, but that increases the dependency on the Azure Virtual Desktop control plane, and if the gateway is not in the same region as the session host, then it impacts the end-user performance. Microsoft provides an RDP shortpath option to avoid performance issues and dependency on the RD gateway. RDP shortpath needs a direct line of sight to the session host from the RD client. A direct line of sight means that firewalls aren't blocking UDP port 3390, and the client can connect directly to the session host using RDP over a private (or public) IP.

You can get a direct line of sight by using one of the following technologies:

- ExpressRoute

- A site-to-site or point-to-site VPN

- Public IP address assignment on the session host (not recommend)

Figure 2-4 gives a high-level overview of the RDP shortpath network connection.

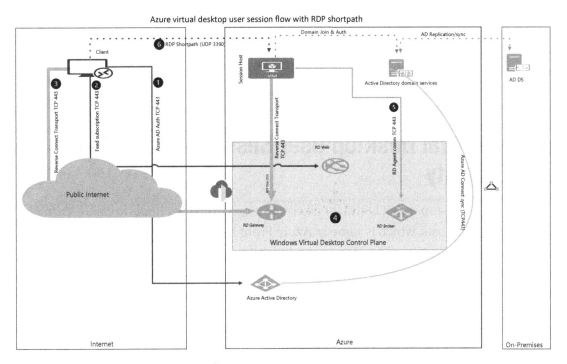

***Figure 2-4.***  *Azure Virtual Desktop user session flow with RDP shortpath*

- Setting up the Azure Virtual Desktop client authentication and selecting authorized resources flow are the same with/without RD shortpath.

- The session host sends IPv4 and IPv6 addresses (private or public, whichever is applicable) to the client after authentication.

- The client starts a parallel UDP-based transport connection directly to one of the host's IP addresses (private or public, whichever is applicable).

- While the client is probing the provided IP addresses, it continues the initial connection establishment over the reverse connect transport to ensure no delay in the user connection (default flow).

- If the client has a direct line of sight and the all-firewall configuration is correct, the client establishes a secure TLS connection with session host (flow 6 in Figure 2-2).

- After establishing the shortpath transport, RDP moves all dynamic virtual channels (DVCs), including remote graphics, input, and device redirection, to the new transport.

- If a firewall or network topology prevents the client from establishing direct UDP connectivity, RDP continues with a reverse connect transport.

# Azure Virtual Desktop User Session Connectivity and Security

Azure Virtual Desktop uses TLS 1.2 for all connections from the clients to Azure Virtual Desktop session hosts, which is same as Azure Front Door. The client and session host connect to the Azure Virtual Desktop gateway with the reverse connect transport and establishe the TCP connection. The client or session host validates the Azure Virtual Desktop gateway's certificate after the TCP connection. Finally, RDP establishes a nested TLS connection between the client and session host using the session host's certificates. By default, the certificate used for RDP encryption is self-generated by the operating system, but you can use an enterprise certification authority certificate as well.

# Azure Virtual Desktop Design Considerations for Cost Savings

Most enterprises are choosing the cloud platform as their first preference because of the cost benefits. The cloud offers organizations unlimited scalability and lower IT costs by charging only for the resources you use. But unfortunately, cloud customers are paying for the resources they ordered earlier but are not using anymore, and that's where cost optimization is important. Cloud cost optimization is the process of reducing your overall cloud spend by identifying mismanaged resources, eliminating waste, reserving capacity for higher discounts, and right-sizing computing services to scale. Additionally, you should consider all cost-saving options at the time of design and implementation instead of waiting to clean it up later. The following are a few different options to save costs for the enterprise. Architect your Azure Virtual Desktop solution while considering these options to reduce costs:

- *Windows 10 multisession*: A Windows 10 multisession desktop can be used for users who have identical compute/application requirements. You can let multiple users log onto a single VM at once and share the compute resources, resulting in considerable cost savings. Windows 10 multisession can be used in a pooled host pool.

- *Azure Hybrid Benefit (Windows Server)*: You can use Azure Hybrid Benefit for Windows Server and SQL if you already have the licenses. See Figure 2-5.

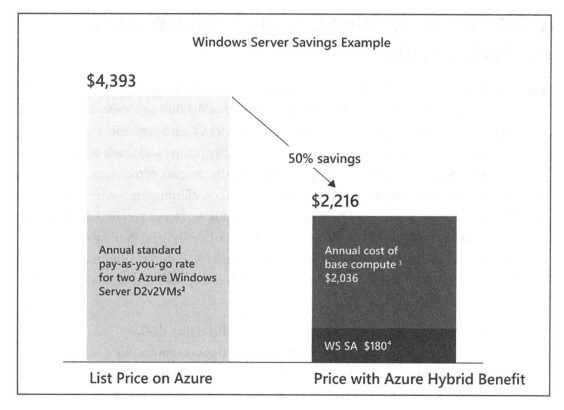

*Figure 2-5. Azure Hybrid Benefit for Windows Server*

- *Azure Reserved Instances*: If you need a specific number of VMs running for a specific number of years, then you can prepay for your VM usage and save money. Combine Azure Reserved Instances with Azure Hybrid Benefit for up to an 80 percent savings over list prices.

- *Autoscaling and session host load-balancing (pooled)*: When setting up pooled session hosts, *breadth-first* is the standard default mode, which spreads users randomly across session hosts. *Depth-first* mode fills up a session host with the maximum number of users before it moves on to the next session host, which allows autoscaling to stop/ shut down unused session hosts to save costs. You can adjust this setting for maximum cost benefits.

- *Autostart VM on connect (personal)*: You can set up the "Start VM on Connect" setting when setting up personal session hosts, which will allow you to stop/shut down session hosts during nonbusiness hours. The VM will get started whenever the user tries to connect to the session host. This can help you to save money on personal session hosts as well.

# Azure Virtual Desktop Limitations

The Azure platform and Azure Virtual Desktop control plane have some limitations that need to be considered during the design phase to avoid changes in the scaling phase. The Azure Virtual Desktop service can scale more than 10,000 session hosts per workspace, but it is recommended to deploy 5,000 or fewer VMs per Azure subscription per region. This recommendation applies to both personal and pooled host pools based on Windows 10 Enterprise single and multisession. Most customers use Windows 10 Enterprise multisession, which allows multiple users to log on to each VM. You can increase the resources of individual session host VMs to accommodate more user sessions. To manage enterprise environments with more than 5,000 VMs per Azure subscription in the same region, you can create multiple Azure subscriptions in a hub-and-spoke architecture and connect them via virtual network peering, as in the preceding example architecture. You could also deploy VMs in a different region in the same subscription to increase the number of VMs.

Other limitations are related to automation and APIs. Azure Resource Manager (ARM) subscription API throttling limits don't allow more than 600 Azure VM reboots per hour via the Azure portal. You can reboot all your machines at once via the operating system using PowerShell remoting, which doesn't consume any Azure Resource Manager subscription API calls. Additionally, for automated session host scaling tools, the limits are around 2,500 VMs per Azure subscription per region, because VM status interaction consumes more resources.

If you are planning to automate session host creation, then you should know that you can currently deploy up to 399 VMs per Azure Virtual Desktop ARM template deployment without availability sets, or 200 VMs per availability set. Also, the Azure VM session host name prefixes support only 11 characters, due to auto-assigning of instance names and the NetBIOS limit of 15 characters per computer account. By default, you can deploy up to 800 instances of most resource types in a resource group, so you have to place resource group structure accordingly. Azure compute doesn't have this limit.

There are some prerequisites and considerations that need to be checked before admins start deploying AVD. The following are some high-level prerequisites that are explained in subsequent chapters.

# Assess Existing Physical and Virtual Desktop Environments

It is important to choose the correct user profile size for the Azure Virtual Desktop to avoid performance issues. The Azure Virtual Desktop user profile size can be determined from the existing environment in case a user is already using any other VDI platform or physical devices. There are a few assessment tools available (i.e., Lakeside, EG innovations) that provide insight into your current IT environment by giving a thorough analysis of end-user activity and resource usage on the current VDI solution.

You can generate a VDI assessment report for the last few months to find out the resource usage on the existing VDI platform including CPU and RAM and accordingly finalize the Azure Virtual Desktop profile size for users. There might be different usages for each user, so group the users with different usage and finalized VM sizes for each group of users.

# Assess Network Capacity and Speed Requirements for Azure Virtual Desktop

Azure Virtual Desktop performance is mainly dependent on network capacity as the session host will be running on the cloud platform. Azure Virtual Desktop uses Remote Desktop Protocol to provide remote display and input capabilities over network connections. RDP dynamically adjusts various parameters to deliver the best user experience based on the availability of computing resources and network bandwidth.

Two different network connections need to be considered while designing Azure Virtual Desktop architecture for better Azure Virtual Desktop performance:

- *Azure Virtual Desktop client to Azure Virtual Desktop session host*: It is recommended to place the Azure Virtual Desktop session host near the user location to get better performance. The user location and Azure Virtual Desktop region can affect the user experience as much as the network conditions. Check out the Azure Virtual Desktop experience estimator (`https://azure.microsoft.com/services/virtual-desktop/assessment/`) to find out the correct Azure region for specific users and the estimated round-trip time (RTT) from the user location to the Azure region. Additionally, the Azure Virtual Desktop user session always goes via Azure Virtual Desktop gateway, so you have to make sure that the Azure Virtual Desktop control planes (gateway, broker) are in the same region or a nearby region.

- *On-premises to Azure bandwidth*: This is important when there are applications hosted on an on-premises datacenter that need to be accessed via Azure Virtual Desktop. In this case, Azure to op-prem bandwidth (S2S/ER) is important, and the application bandwidth requirement needs to be considered to calculate the required bandwidth. See Figure 2-6.

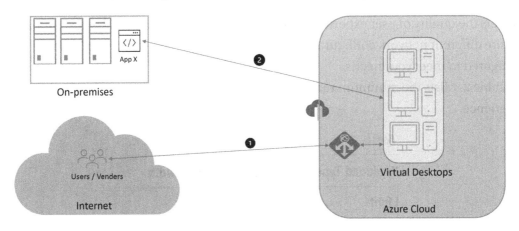

***Figure 2-6.*** *Azure Virtual Desktop network connections*

It is difficult to predict bandwidth usage for Azure Virtual Desktop's Remote Desktop Protocol because user activities generate most of the remote desktop traffic. Every user is unique, and differences in their work patterns may significantly change network use. The amount of data sent over the network via RDP depends on the user activity. For example, a user may work with Visual Studio Code to write code for a full day and consume minimal bandwidth, but then another user may use more bandwidth in less time by sending a 200-page print to the local printer.

The best way to identify network bandwidth requirements is to monitor real user connections by the built-in performance counters in Perfmon or by the network equipment. However, in many cases, you may be able to estimate network utilization by understanding how Remote Desktop Protocol works and by analyzing your users' work patterns.

The Remote Desktop Protocol delivers the graphics generated by the remote server to display it on a local monitor. Sending a desktop bitmap is not simple task and requires a significant number of resources. For example, a 1080p desktop image in its uncompressed form is around 8 MB in size, and displaying this image on the locally connected monitor with the refresh rate of 30 Hz requires a bandwidth of about 237 MB/s. To reduce the amount of data transferred over the network, RDP uses the combination of multiple techniques like frame rate optimizations, screen content classification, content-specific codecs, progressive image encoding, and client-side caching.

When using a remote Windows session, your network's available bandwidth greatly impacts the quality of user experience. Different applications and display resolutions require different network configurations, so it's important to make sure your network is configured to meet your needs.

Table 2-1 lists the minimum recommended bandwidths for a smooth user experience.

***Table 2-1.*** *Bandwidth Recommendations*

| Workload Type | Recommended Bandwidth |
| --- | --- |
| Light | 1.5 Mbps |
| Medium | 3 Mbps |
| Heavy | 5 Mbps |
| Power | 15 Mbps |

The bandwidth requirements may change depending on application workloads and your display resolution, voice or video conferencing, real-time communication, or streaming 4K video.

# Recommended Operating Systems for an Azure Virtual Desktop

Azure Virtual Desktop supports different operating systems for different purposes. Table 2-2 covers operating system and required licenses for AVD.

***Table 2-2.*** *Azure Virtual Desktop License Requirement*

| OS | Required License |
|---|---|
| **Windows 10 Enterprise multisession or Windows 10 Enterprise** | Microsoft 365 E3, E5, A3, A5, F3, Business Premium Windows E3, E5, A3, A5 |
| **Windows 7 Enterprise** | Microsoft 365 E3, E5, A3, A5, F3, Business Premium Windows E3, E5, A3, A5 |
| **Windows Server 2012 R2, 2016, 2019** | RDS Client Access License (CAL) with Software Assurance |

As you know, each operating system has different features that the user can use. The following are the high-level scenarios based on which you can select based on your requirements:

- *Windows 10 Enterprise multisession*: Windows 10 multisession is recommended for pooled host pools when we have users with the same application/software requirements and they don't rely on any system-specific setting/configuration. Multiple users can log in (different session) on a Windows 10 multisession operating system, which helps to optimize costs. You have a pooled desktop support application with user-centric installation so that any user log in to the session host can access the application and the application configuration gets stored in user profile.

- *Windows 7 Enterprise/10 Enterprise*: Both are recommended for personal Azure Virtual Desktop where users are dependent on a system-specific configuration or need a highly intensive or dedicated system configuration to perform certain tasks. Windows 7 is still supported by Azure Virtual Desktop in case the user wants to use an application supported on a legacy operating system.

- *Windows Server 2012 R2, 2016, 2019*: All server operating system are recommended if the user is going to use an application supported only on a server system or services available on a server for day-to-day work. If your organization already has RDS CALs and want to use them instead by buying other Azure Virtual Desktop supported licenses, then the server operating system can be used in AVD.

---

**Note**    Azure Virtual Desktop doesn't support x86 (32-bit), Windows 10 Enterprise N, Windows 10 LTSB, Windows 10 LTSC, Windows 10 Pro, or Windows 10 Enterprise KN operating system images. Windows 7 also doesn't support any VHD or VHDX-based profile solutions hosted on managed Azure Storage due to a sector size limitation.

---

# Plan and Configure Name Resolution (DNS) for Active Directory (AD) and Azure Active Directory Domain Services (Azure AD DS)

DNS is important for Azure Virtual Desktop to work because the session host is always joined to an ADDS domain, and if the DNS is not working, the session host won't be able to resolve a domain name for authentication or resolve external domain names for Internet access on Azure Virtual Desktop.

The following are different DNS types supported for Azure Virtual Desktop, and you can select the correct DNS type for your Azure Virtual Desktop deployment based on these scenarios:

- *Self-hosted DNS*: Most enterprises are using Microsoft AD DS integrated DNS or third-party DNS on on-premises, and the same can be used for Azure Virtual Desktop as well. This is a recommended option as you can manage all the DNS records in one place.

  Depending on the DNS traffic, the on-premises DNS server can be extended to an Azure hub subscription or point Azure Virtual Desktop resources to use on-premises DNS. DNS server IP address and port 53 need to be opened on the firewall between the DNS server and Azure Virtual Desktop. The virtual network uses on-premises DNS for name resolution. Additionally, change the virtual network's DNS setting to point to the DNS server IP address, as shown in Figure 2-7.

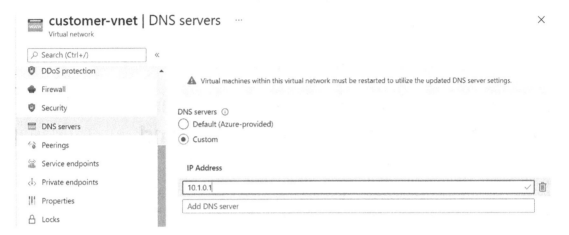

***Figure 2-7.*** *Azure Virtual Desktop DNS setting on Azure Virtual Desktop Virtual Network*

- *Azure private DNS zone*: The Azure private DNS zone can be used to resolve Azure resource names. This provides a reliable and secure DNS service for your virtual network. Azure private DNS zones manage and resolve domain names in the virtual network without the need to configure a custom DNS solution. By using private DNS zones, you can use your own custom domain name instead of the Azure-provided names during deployment. Using a custom domain name helps you tailor your virtual network architecture to best suit your organization's needs. It provides a naming resolution for virtual machines (VMs) within a virtual network and connected virtual networks. Additionally, you can configure zone names with a split-horizon view, which allows a private and a public DNS zone to share the name.

- *Azure-provided name resolution:* Azure-provided name resolution provides only basic authoritative DNS capabilities. If you use this option, the DNS zone names and records will be automatically managed by Azure, and you will not be able to control the DNS zone names or the life cycle of DNS records. If you need a fully featured DNS solution for your virtual networks, you must use Azure DNS private zones or customer-managed DNS servers.

# Plan a Host Pool Architecture and Recommendations for Resource Groups, Subscriptions, and Management Groups

We'll cover several topics in this section.

## What Are Host Pools?

A host pool is a collection of Azure virtual machines with the same configuration. An Azure VM can be registered to Azure Virtual Desktop as session hosts when you run the Azure Virtual Desktop agent on the Azure VM. All session host virtual machines in a host pool should be sourced from the same image for a consistent user experience.

A host pool can be one of two types.

- Personal, where each user gets assigned to an individual session host.

- Pooled, where session hosts can accept connections from any user authorized to an app group within the host pool

You can set additional properties on the host pool to change its load-balancing behavior and the number of sessions each session host can take. You control the resources published to users through app groups. Refer to the "Configure host pool settings" section in Chapter 8 for a detail hostpool configuration.

# What Are App Groups?

An app group is a logical grouping of applications installed on session hosts in the host pool. An app group can be one of two types.

- *RemoteApp*: Users access RemoteApp (a single application like Word or Excel) to individually publish to the app group. To publish to RemoteApp, you must create a RemoteApp app group. You can create multiple RemoteApp app groups to accommodate different worker scenarios. Different RemoteApp app groups can also contain overlapping RemoteApp instances.

- *Desktop*: Users access the full desktop. By default, a desktop app group is automatically created whenever you create a host pool. You can't create another desktop app group in the host pool while a default desktop app group exists, but you can delete the default desktop group and create new one with a different name or use PowerShell/ARM to create a desktop group as per the naming standards you want.

To publish resources to users, you must assign them to app groups. When assigning users to app groups, consider the following:

- A user can be assigned to both a desktop app group and a RemoteApp app group in the same host pool. However, users can't launch both types of app groups at the same time in a single session.

- A user can be assigned to multiple app groups within the same host pool, and their feed will be an accumulation of both app groups.

# What Is a Workspace?

A workspace is a logical grouping of application groups in Azure Virtual Desktop. Each Azure Virtual Desktop application group must be associated with a workspace for users to see the remote apps and desktops published to them.

Figure 2-8 shows the reference architecture for host pool placement.

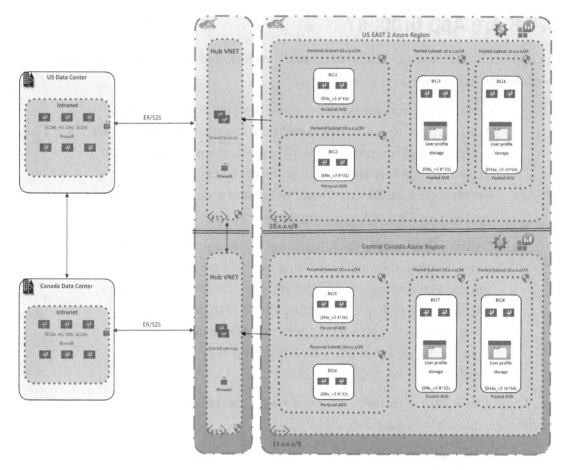

***Figure 2-8.*** *Azure Virtual Desktop host pool, session host, resource group placement*

This diagram shows a typical Azure Virtual Desktop host pool placement recommendations are as follows:

- A dedicated subscription is recommended for Azure Virtual Desktop resources for easy management and scaling on-demand.

- A separate virtual network is recommended with multiple subnets for pooled and personal in each region and peering with a hub virtual network in that region.

- A virtual network scope range needs to be decided on, considering the number of VMs for pooled as well as personal and future growth.

- Multiple host pools of the same type can use the same subnet as far as there is no compliance/InfoSec requirement. Each subnet can be restricted with a set of NSG rules.

- You need a separate host pool for each VM size, each region, and each type (pooled/personal).

- You need a dedicated resource group for each host pool to manage RBAC on the host pool–specific resources.

- RDP properties can be a set of host pool levels, so if we have a set of users that need different RDP properties, then we have to create different host pools. For example, some users need to copy the Azure Virtual Desktop option and some not.

- A separate pooled host pools for users who need a different set of applications.

# Configure a Location for the Azure Virtual Desktop Metadata

Azure Virtual Desktop can be used as a worldwide service depending on your location and the location of the VMs. The control plane is available in the following locations (as of September 2021); however, the host pool can exist in any other Azure region:

- United States (US) (generally available)

- Europe (EU) (generally available)

- United Kingdom (UK) (generally available)

- Canada (CA) (generally available)

Just remember that your performance using a host pool outside of the previous locations might vary until the control plane is added to other regions because all Azure Virtual Desktop client traffic goes through the control plane (if not using shortpath). If you set up a host pool in a non-metadata location with a previous control plane location, you will automatically switch to the local control plane when it's rolled out for your region.

If RDP shortpath is enabled, then RDP shortpath establishes the direct connectivity between the Remote Desktop client and the session host. Direct connectivity reduces the dependency on the Azure Virtual Desktop gateways, improves the connection's reliability, and increases the bandwidth available for each user session

# Calculate a Configuration for Performance Requirements

Azure Virtual Desktop performance is dependent on multiple factors such as the application, user Internet connection, user location and host pool region, Azure Virtual Desktop management service location, network bandwidth to on-premises if the application/AD/ANS is on-premises, and the application. All of these aspects need to be considered while designing the Azure Virtual Desktop architecture.

The following are the recommendations for optimal performance:

- The appropriate VM size needs to be selected (based on assessment) for Azure Virtual Desktop.

- If there are application servers in the on-premises datacenter that need to be accessed from Azure Virtual Desktop, then the application bandwidth recommendation needs to be followed.

- If there are custom/third-party applications that need to be installed on Azure Virtual Desktop, then the application sizing recommendation needs to be followed.

- Round-trip (RTT) latency from the client's laptop to the Azure region (where host pools have been deployed) should be less than 150 ms. Use the Experience Estimator to view your connection health and recommended Azure region.

- To optimize for network performance, Microsoft recommends that the session host's VMs are collocated in the same Azure region as the Azure Virtual Desktop management service.

Make sure to load test these scenarios in your deployment using simulation tools like Login VSI. Vary the load size, run stress tests, and test common user scenarios in remote sessions to better understand your network's requirements before moving into production.

# Calculate a Configuration for Azure Virtual Machine Capacity Requirements

The Azure Virtual Desktop session host size is the main factor that can impact Azure Virtual Desktop performance, so the session host size needs to be calculated based on the existing VDI usage (refer to the assessment) or based on the user application requirement. The following are some of the examples and recommendations for pooled as well as personal desktops:

- *Pooled sizing example*: Consider you have 100 users who want Azure Virtual Desktop and as per the VDI assessment report all users require two CPUs and 4 GB memory. All users are from same region and want to go with a pooled desktop since they are using same set of applications for their day-to-day work. We can go with a D8s_v4 size VM, which comes with eight CPUs and 16 GB memory, and it will allow you to assign four users per VM. Table 2-3 shows the reference size and per user cost calculation.

*Table 2-3.*  *Azure Virtual Desktop Pooled Sizing Example*

| Workload Type | Users per CPU | Assessment Recommendation | Total Users per VM | Total Users | Total VM | Size - vCPU/ RAM/OS Storage Minimum | Profile Storage per User | Total Cost per Month | Cost per User per Month |
|---|---|---|---|---|---|---|---|---|---|
| Power+ | 2/user | 2 CPUs/user | 4 | 100 | 25 | D8s_v4 - 8 vCPUs, 16 GB RAM, 128 GB storage | 30 GB/ user | $3,564.23 | $35.64 |

**Note**    For cost optimization, you can select a higher VM size so that fewer session hosts are required, and operating system disk cost can be saved. Also, the costs shown in all the examples are based on the Azure calculator result as of November 2021 and do not include any discount.

- *Personal sizing example*: Consider you have 100 users who want a new Azure Virtual Desktop, and as per the VDI assessment report, all users require two CPUs and 4 GB memory. All users are from the same region, but they need a different set of application/software for their day-to-day work. In this case, you can create a personal desktop with a D2s_v3 size VM, which comes with two CPUs and 8 GB memory. Table 2-4 is the reference size and per user cost calculation.

***Table 2-4.*** *Azure Virtual Desktop Personal Sizing Example*

| Workload Type | Users per CPU | Assessment Recommendation | Total Users per VM | Total Users | Total VM | Size - vCPU/ RAM/OS Storage Minimum | Profile Storage per User | Total Cost per Month | Cost per User per Month |
|---|---|---|---|---|---|---|---|---|---|
| Power+ | 2/ user | 2 CPUs/user | NA | 100 | 100 | D2s_v3 - 2 vCPUs, 8 GB RAM, 128 GB storage | 30 GB/ user | $ 4,672 | $46.72 |

# General Virtual Machine Recommendations

Here are the general virtual machine recommendations:

- You must follow the VM requirements to run the operating system; see the Windows 10 computer specifications and system requirements article for detailed requirements.

- It is recommended to use premium SSD storage for the OS disk for production workloads.

- Graphics processing units (GPUs) are a good choice for users who regularly use graphics-intensive programs for video rendering, 3D design, and simulations.

- B-series burstable VMs are a good choice for users who don't always need maximum CPU performance. D-series is recommended for general users.

## Azure Virtual Desktop Workload Types

See Table 2-5.

***Table 2-5.*** *Azure Virtual Desktop Workload Types*

| Workload Type | Example Users | Example Apps |
|---|---|---|
| Light | Users doing basic data entry tasks | Database entry applications, command-line interfaces |
| Medium | Consultants and market researchers | Database entry applications, command-line interfaces, Microsoft Word, static web pages |
| Heavy | Software engineers, content creators | Database entry applications, command-line interfaces, Microsoft Word, static web pages, Microsoft Outlook, Microsoft PowerPoint, dynamic web pages |
| Power | Graphic designers, 3D model makers, machine learning researchers | Database entry applications, command-line interfaces, Microsoft Word, static web pages, Microsoft Outlook, Microsoft PowerPoint, dynamic web pages, Adobe Photoshop, Adobe Illustrator, computer-aided design (CAD), computer-aided manufacturing (CAM) |

# Azure Virtual Desktop Multisession (Pooled) Sizing Recommendation

Table 2-6 are the reference usage profiles and VM sizes available for pooled/multisession AVD. The table shows an example of a smaller, proof-of-concept scenario with a user workload of fewer than 20 users.

***Table 2-6.*** *Azure Virtual Desktop Pooled Sizing Recommendation for POC*

| Workload Type | Maximum Users/ vCPU | Example Azure Instances | Profile Storage Minimum |
|---|---|---|---|
| Light | 4 | D4s_v4, F4s_v2, D4as_v4 | 30 GB |
| Medium | 4 | D4s_v4, F4s_v2, D4as_v4 | 30 GB |
| Heavy | 2 | D8s_v4, F8s_v2, D8as_v4, D16s_v4, F16s_v2, D16as_v4 | 30 GB |
| Power | 1 | D4s_v4, F4s_v2, D4as_v4, NV12, NVv4 | 30 GB |

Table 2-7 shows an example of a smaller, proof-of-concept scenario with a user workload of more than 20 users.

***Table 2-7.*** *Azure Virtual Desktop Pooled Sizing Recommendation*

| Workload Type | Maximum Users/ vCPU | Example Azure Instances | Profile Storage Minimum |
|---|---|---|---|
| Light | 6 | D8s_v4, F8s_v2, D8as_v4, D16s_v4, F16s_v2, D16as_v4 | 30 GB |
| Medium | 4 | D8s_v4, F8s_v2, D8as_v4, D16s_v4, F16s_v2, D16as_v4 | 30 GB |
| Heavy | 2 | D8s_v4, F8s_v2, D8as_v4, D16s_v4, F16s_v2, D16as_v4 | 30 GB |
| Power | 1 | D8s_v4, F8s_v2, D8as_v4, D16s_v4, F16s_v2, D16as_v4, NV12, NVv4 | 30 GB |

It is always recommended to consider the application/software recommendations while deciding on the usage profile for pooled instances.

*Multisession (Pooled) sizing example*: Consider you have 100 users who want to use application "xyz" on a pooled host pool, and all users are from the same region. The application xyz recommendation is to have minimum one CPU and 2 GB memory. In this case, you can go with a D8s_v4 size VM, which comes with eight CPUs and 16 GB memory, and it will allow us to assign eight users per VM. D4s_v4 can be used, but it will increase the number of VMs, which results in additional cost for the OS disk. Table 2-8 is the reference size and per user cost calculation.

***Table 2-8.*** *Azure Virtual Desktop Pooled Sizing Example*

| Workload Type | Users per vCPU | App Recommendation | Total Users per VM | Total Users | Total VM | Size - vCPU/RAM/ OS Storage Minimum | Profile storage per User | Total Cost per Month | Cost per User per Month |
|---|---|---|---|---|---|---|---|---|---|
| Power | 1 | 1 CPU/user | 8 | 100 | 13 | D8s_v4 - 8 vCPUs, 16 GB RAM, 128 GB storage | 30 GB | $1,935.23 | $19.35 |

**Note**    It is recommended that you limit the VM size to between 4 vCPUs and 24 vCPUs. Microsoft doesn't recommend using fewer than 2 cores or more than 32 cores for standard and larger environments.

## Azure Virtual Desktop Single-Session (Personal) Sizing Recommendations for Greenfield Deployment

For VM sizing recommendations for single-session scenarios, we recommend at least two physical CPU cores per VM (typically four vCPUs with hyperthreading). If you need more specific VM sizing recommendations for single-session scenarios, ask the software vendors specific to your workload. VM sizing for single-session VMs will likely align with physical device guidelines.

## Test Pooled/Personal Azure Virtual Desktop Workload

Microsoft recommends using simulation tools (such as LoginVSI) to test your Azure Virtual Desktop with both stress tests and real-life usage simulations. Make sure your system is responsive and resilient enough to meet user needs, and remember to vary the load size to avoid surprises after moving into production.

# Summary

In this chapter, you learned about the Azure Virtual Desktop architecture including user session flow, session security, and RDP shortpath. Additionally, you learned about AVD limitations and other cost-saving options that need to be considered during Azure Virtual Desktop design.

Most important, you learned about the host pool, resource group, subscription, management group recommendations for Azure Virtual Desktop, which will definitely help you to design and implement a secure and cost-effective solution for big enterprises.

# CHAPTER 3

# Design for User Identities and Profiles

In this chapter, you will learn about all the identity options available in the Azure cloud, including which identity option is best for Azure Virtual Desktop. You'll also learn about Azure Virtual Desktop licensing model/options, user profile storage plans, and network connectivity recommendations.

Let's begin with the Azure Virtual Desktop licensing options.

## Select an Appropriate Licensing Model for Azure Virtual Desktop Based on the Requirements

Azure Virtual Desktop requires a per-user or per-device license to access the desktop, so you must plan the licensing model before you plan the Azure Virtual Desktop deployment. Azure Virtual Desktop (AVD) supports Windows 7/10 and Windows Server licenses as well, and you can select the appropriate licenses based on the operating system you want to use for AVD. The following are the supported licenses for Azure Virtual Desktop:

- *BYOL Windows 10 and Windows 7*: You are eligible to access Windows 10 and Windows 7 with Azure Virtual Desktop if you have one of the following per-user licenses:

  - Microsoft 365 E3/E5

  - Microsoft 365 A3/A5/Student Use Benefits

  - Microsoft 365 F3

  - Microsoft 365 Business Premium

© Arun Sabale and Balu N Ilag 2022
A. Sabale and B. N. Ilag, *Microsoft Azure Virtual Desktop Guide*,
https://doi.org/10.1007/978-1-4842-8063-8_3

- Windows 10 Enterprise E3/E5

- Windows 10 Education A3/A5

- Windows 10 VDA per user

- *BYOL Windows Server*: You are eligible to access Windows Server with Azure Virtual Desktop if you have a per-user or per-device RDS CAL license with active Software Assurance (SA).

- *Per user access pricing for external users*: You can also pay a monthly per-user fee to access Azure Virtual Desktop for external users.

# Recommended Storage Solution (Including Azure NetApp Files vs. Azure Files)

Azure Virtual Desktop performance is dependent on the storage type you are using, so it is important to select the appropriate storage for the operating system disk as well as the user profile data. Here are two different storages required for Azure Virtual Desktop:

- *Operating system storage*: For optimal performance, it is recommended that you use premium SSD storage for the Azure Virtual Desktop session host's operating system disk for production workloads. The operating system disk size depends on the operating system and applications installed on the C: drive.

- *User data storage*

  - *Storage* for *personal desktop*: A personal desktop is a persistent desktop, meaning the user will get the same desktop every time they log in to Azure Virtual Desktop. The user can store data on the local VM. Additional standard or premium storage can be attached to the personal Azure Virtual Desktop instance to store user data or install applications.

- *Storage for pooled desktop user profile (pooled)*: Since pooled desktops are not persistent desktops, the user will not get the same VM every time they log in to Azure Virtual Desktop. Therefore, the user profile must be stored on remote storage using FSLogix. Pooled Azure Virtual Desktop supports FSLogix, which helps to store user profiles on Azure Files as well as Azure NetApp Files. Both Azure Files and NetApp Files support ADDS authentication as well as secure access over a virtual network, and it is recommended that you restrict the profile storage to a specific virtual network with a private endpoint. You can use a storage domain join so authorized users can access storage and user profiles.

Table 3-1 compares the major differences between Azure Files and NetApp Files to help you make a decision.

***Table 3-1.*** *Differences Between Azure Files and NetApp Files*

| Category | Azure Files | Azure NetApp Files (ANF) |
| --- | --- | --- |
| Description | Azure Files is built on the same Azure storage platform as other services such as Azure Blobs. | ANF is built on NetApp's bare metal with the ONTAP storage OS running inside the Azure datacenter for a consistent Azure experience and on-premises type of performance. |
| Protocols | Premium. | All tiers. |
| | SMB 2.1, 3.0, 3.1.1. | SMB 2.x, 3.x. |
| | NFS 4.1 (preview). | NFS 3.0, 4.1. |
| | REST. | Dual protocol access (NFSv3/SMB). |
| | Standard. | |
| | SMB 2.1, 3.0, 3.1.1. | |
| | REST. | |
| Region availability | Premium, 30+ regions. | All tiers, 28+ regions. |
| | Standard, all regions. | |

(*continued*)

***Table 3-1.*** (*continued*)

| Category | Azure Files | Azure NetApp Files (ANF) |
|---|---|---|
| Redundancy | Premium, LRS, ZRS.<br><br>Standard, LRS, ZRS, GRS, GZRS. | All tiers, built-in local HA. |
| Identity-based authentication and authorization | Active Directory Domain Services (AD DS).<br><br>Azure Active Directory Domain Services (Azure AD DS). | Active Directory Domain Services (AD DS).<br><br>Azure Active Directory Domain Services (Azure AD DS). |
| Encryption | All protocols.<br><br>Encryption at rest (AES 256) with customer or Microsoft-managed keys.<br><br>SMB.<br><br>Kerberos encryption using AES 256 or RC4-HMAC.<br><br>Encryption in transit. | All protocols.<br><br>Encryption at rest (AES 256) with Microsoft-managed keys.<br><br>SMB.<br><br>Encryption in transit using AES-CCM (SMB 3.0) and AES-GCM (SMB 3.1.1). |
| Access options | Internet.<br><br>Secure VNet access.<br><br>VPN Gateway.<br><br>ExpressRoute.<br><br>Azure File Sync. | Secure VNet access.<br><br>VPN Gateway.<br><br>ExpressRoute.<br><br>Global File Cache.<br><br>HPC Cache. |
| Data protection | Incremental snapshots.<br><br>File/directory user self-restore.<br><br>Restore to new location.<br><br>In-place revert.<br><br>Share-level soft delete.<br><br>Azure Backup integration. | Snapshots (255/volume).<br><br>File/directory user self-restore.<br><br>Restore to new volume.<br><br>In-place revert.<br><br>Cross-Region Replication (public preview). |

(*continued*)

*Table 3-1.* (*continued*)

| Category | Azure Files | Azure NetApp Files (ANF) |
|---|---|---|
| Migration tools | Azure Data Box. | Global File Cache. |
| | Azure File Sync. | CloudSync, XCP. |
| | Storage Migration Service. | Storage Migration Service. |
| | AzCopy. | AzCopy. |
| | Robocopy. | Robocopy. |
| | | Application-based (for example, HSR, Data Guard, AOAG). |
| Tiers | Premium. | Ultra. |
| | Transaction Optimized. | Premium. |
| | Hot. | Standard. |
| | Cool. | |
| Minimum share/ volume Size | Premium. | All tiers. |
| | 100 GB. | 100 GB (Minimum capacity pool size: 4 TB). |
| | Standard. | |
| | No minimum. | |
| Maximum share/ volume Size | 100 TB. | All tiers. |
| | | 100 TB (500 TB capacity pool limit). |
| | | Up to 12.5 PB per Azure NetApp account. |
| Maximum share/ volume IOPS | Premium. | Ultra and Premium. |
| | Up to 100k. | Up to 450k. |
| | Standard. | Standard. |
| | Up to 10k. | Up to 320k. |

(*continued*)

***Table 3-1.*** (*continued*)

| Category | Azure Files | Azure NetApp Files (ANF) |
| --- | --- | --- |
| Maximum share/ volume Throughput | Premium. Up to 10 GB/s. | Ultra and Premium. Up to 4.5 GB/s. |
| | Standard. Up to 300 MB/s. | Standard. Up to 3.2GB/s. |
| Maximum file size | 4 TB. | 16 TB. |
| Maximum IOPS per file | Premium. Up to 8,000. | All tiers. Up to volume limit. |
| | Standard. 1,000. | |
| Maximum throughput per file | Premium. 300 MiB/s (Up to 1 GB/s with SMB multichannel). | All tiers. Up to volume limit. |
| | Standard. 60 MiB/s. | |
| SMB multichannel | Yes. | Yes. |
| Latency | Single-millisecond minimum latency (2ms to 3ms for small I/O). | Submillisecond minimum latency (less than 1ms for random I/O). |

# Plan for Azure Virtual Desktop Client Deployment

The Azure Virtual Desktop client helps end users to connect to the Azure Virtual Desktop instance assigned to them over the Internet/intranet. There are different Azure Virtual Desktop clients available based on the end-user device/operating system type. It is recommended to use a desktop client instead of a web client as a desktop client supports audio/video redirection on Azure Virtual Desktop.

The following are the clients available to access Azure Virtual Desktop:

- Windows Desktop clients

- Web clients

- Android clients

- macOS clients

- iOS clients

- Linux or thin clients

There are different ways to install a client on an end-user device.

- *Domain-joined user device (automated deployment)*: SCCM can be used to push the Azure Virtual Desktop client on the end-user device, or the client can be published in the software center so that authorized users can deploy it on their devices/laptops. Alternatively, AD Group Policy can be used to deploy the Azure Virtual Desktop client on an end user's laptop using a logon script, and Group Policy can be assigned to the security group created for each host pool.

- *Nondomain-joined user device (automated deployment)*: An appropriate Azure Virtual Desktop client can be downloaded from a Microsoft site/other app store and installed on the user laptop/device manually.

# Plan for User Profiles

A user profile is an important factor that needs to be considered during pooled Azure Virtual Desktop planning and designing. As we know by now, the pooled version is nonpersistent, and the Azure Virtual Desktop load balancer can send the session to any of the back-end session hosts on the pooled host pool. In this case, the user profile needs to be available on all session hosts so that the user will get the same desktop/settings at every login, and that can be done using FSLogix. FSLogix allows you to store user profiles on the storage account so that FSLogix can attach the user profile to the VM where the user session is redirected by Azure Virtual Desktop.

FSLogix needs to be configured on all session hosts in the host pool, pointing to the same storage account where user profiles are stored. It is recommended to use a premium storage account for each host pool in each region. Storage account support failover so that the user profile data can be fail over to DR region in case of disaster recovery.

Figure 3-1 shows a typical pooled desktop user profile placement. The following are some recommendations:

- You need a separate virtual network with dedicated subnets for each host pool (pooled and personal) in each region, and you need to peer AVD vnet with hub virtual network in that region.

- You need a dedicated user profile storage for each pooled host pool.

- User profile storage access is restricted to a specific virtual network/subnet.

- Enable storage account access over a private endpoint from the virtual network.

- The same type of host pool in the same region (i.e. belongs to the same Business Unit) can use the same storage account for a user profile as far as there is no compliance/information security requirements.

- The storage account needs to join to the domain and allow specific users/groups to access the content.

- Consider GEO replication to a DR region if you are planning to enable disaster recovery for the pooled host pool. Premium file storage does not support GEO replication, so if you want to implement DR, then you must select the standard storage account tier or use an FSLogix cloud cache to store a user profile on multiple storage accounts in different regions.

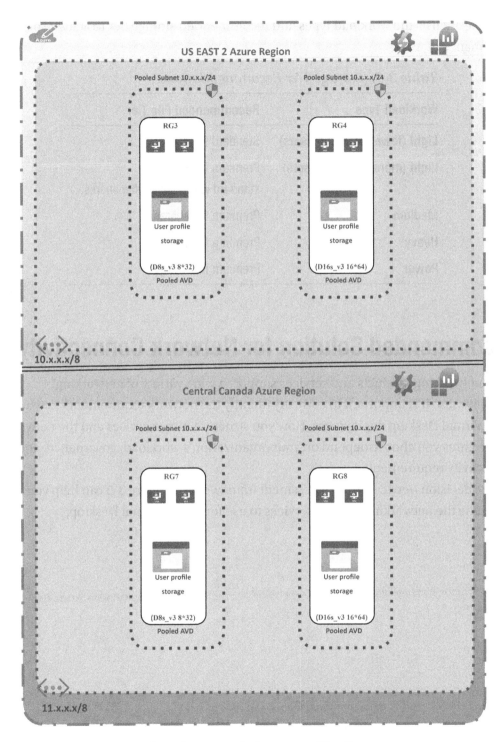

***Figure 3-1.*** *Azure Virtual Desktop pooled user profile placement*

Table 3-2 lists the workload types and recommended storage tier to achieve better performance of AVD.

***Table 3-2.*** *Storage Tier Recommendations*

| Workload Type | Recommended File Tier |
| --- | --- |
| **Light (fewer than 200 users)** | Standard file shares |
| **Light (more than 200 users)** | Premium file shares or standard with multiple file shares |
| **Medium** | Premium file shares |
| **Heavy** | Premium file shares |
| **Power** | Premium file shares |

# Recommended Solution for Network Connectivity

Azure networking products and services support a wide variety of networking capabilities, so it is important to correctly identify the network requirements for your Azure Virtual Desktop deployment. How you structure these services and the networking architectures you choose depend on your organization's workload, governance, and connectivity requirements.

The decision tree (common assessment framework) in Figure 3-2 can help you determine the networking tools or services to use for Azure Virtual Desktop.

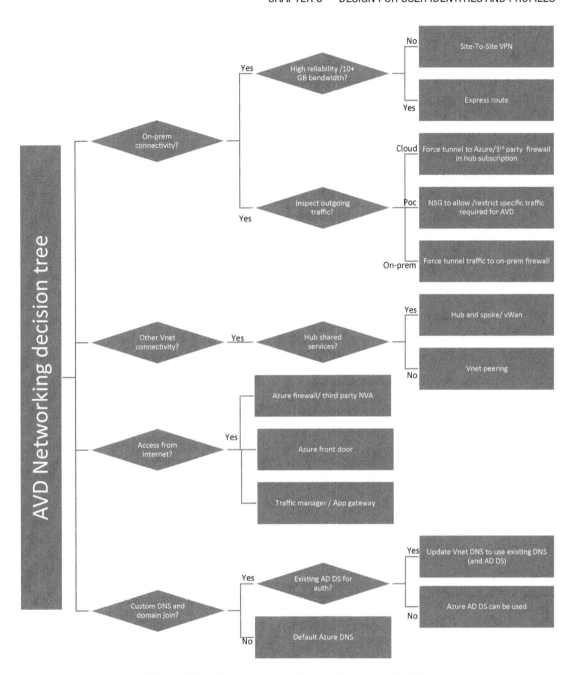

**Figure 3-2.**  *Azure Virtual Desktop network requirement decision tree*

The following questions can help you make decisions based on the Azure networking services:

- How many IP addresses do you need in your virtual network (based on the size of Azure Virtual Desktop virtual network)?

    The number of IP addresses needed in the virtual network will mainly depend on the number of session hosts you want to deploy in the virtual network plus a buffer IP address for future growth. Use appropriate address ranges as defined in your existing networking architecture to be able to scale out your Azure virtual network infrastructure.

- Will your workloads require connectivity between virtual networks and your on-premises datacenter?

    You need on-premises connectivity in case you want to extend your Active Directory on-premises domain in Azure or allow an application that runs on your Azure Virtual Desktop deployment to reach on-premises resources.

- Will you need to inspect and audit outgoing traffic by using on-premises network devices?

    Your security policies might require Internet-bound outgoing traffic to pass through centrally managed devices in the cloud or on-premises environment. This can be achieved by using forced tunneling to direct all traffic to a specific firewall/device.

- Do you need multiple virtual networks?

    The number of virtual networks you will need depends on the number of regions you want to deploy Azure Virtual Desktop session hosts in. If you are planning to deploy Azure Virtual Desktops in multiple regions, then you need a virtual network in that region with all the connectivity and security.

- Do you need to connect multiple virtual networks?

  You can use virtual network peering to connect services in another Azure virtual network. For example, you have all the shared services such as extended ADDS and DNS present in a hub virtual network, and you want Azure Virtual Desktop to use the shared services for name resolution and authentication.

- Will you need custom DNS and a domain join?

  Yes, Azure Virtual Desktop supports domain join for session hosts so that you can apply an organization-specific compliance policy to the session host. AVD virtual network DNS settings can be changed to custom DNS and can point it to organization-specific DNS server so that it can help to resolve Active Directory domain names and join the session host to the domain.

# Plannig Azure AD Connect for User Identities

Azure Virtual Desktop supports desktop authentication with Active Directory Domain Services. The AD DS directory can be synchronized with Azure AD to enable it to authenticate on-premises users.

There are two levels of authentications for Azure Virtual Desktop, one at the Azure Virtual Desktop access level and another at desktop login. The Azure Virtual Desktop session host can join to the AD domain, and domain credentials can be used to log in to the desktop, whereas Azure Virtual Desktop authentication can be done by Azure AD, but AD DS needs to be synced with Azure AD if you want to use same credentials for both logins.

---

**Note**    Azure AD domain services (AAD DS) and Active Directory Domain Services (AD DS) are two different services.

---

There are two different AD DS options available and supported by Azure Virtual Desktop. You can select the appropriate AD DS solution based on your organization requirements.

# Identity Design Considerations

The following are some identity design considerations:

- Azure Virtual Desktop users must be sourced from either the same instance of on-premises Active Directory Domain Services that is synchronized to Azure Active Directory (Azure AD) and the session host needs to be joined to same Active Directory Domain Services (AD DS), or an instance of Azure AD Domain Services (Azure AD DS) synchronized from Azure AD.

---

**Note**   Azure Virtual Desktop does not support business-to-business or Microsoft accounts.

---

- A domain join account can't have multifactor authentication or interactive prompts, and it needs permission on the ADDS OU to add a computer account.

- Azure Virtual Desktop supports AD DS or Azure AD DS, and an appropriate identity provider needs to be selected based on the application requirement.

- When joining to an Azure AD DS domain, the account must be part of the Azure AD DC administrators' group, and the account password must work in Azure AD DS.

- Azure AD DS (AAD DS) is a supported option, but there are limitations:

  - You must have password hash synchronization enabled (uncommon when federating Azure AD).

  - You can project Azure AD DS into only a single virtual network (and single Azure region) that uses a nonpublic IP address range. You can't add domain controllers to an Azure AD DS domain.

  - You cannot use a hybrid join for Azure Virtual Desktop VMs to enable Azure Active Directory seamless single sign-on for Microsoft 365 services.

- Always specify an organizational unit distinguished name (DN) for domain joining without quotation marks.

- The user principal name used to subscribe to Azure Virtual Desktop must exist in the Active Directory domain where the session host virtual machine is joined.

- Smart cards and Windows Hello authentication need a direct connection (line of sight) with an Active Directory domain controller for Kerberos.

- Using Windows Hello for Business requires the hybrid certificate trust model to be compatible with Azure Virtual Desktop.

- Single sign-on can improve user experience, but it requires additional configuration and is supported only using Active Directory Federation Services.

# Identity Design Recommendations

Here are some recommendations for identity design:

- Use Azure AD Connect to synchronize all identities to a single Azure AD tenant.

- Ensure Azure Virtual Desktop session hosts can communicate with Azure AD DS or AD DS.

- Use the least privilege principle to assign the minimum permissions needed for authorized tasks.

- Segregate session host virtual machines into Active Directory organization units for each host pool to manage policies and orphaned objects more easily.

- Use a solution like Local Administrator Password Solution (LAPS) to rotate local administrator passwords on Azure Virtual Desktop session hosts frequently.

- Create conditional access policies for Azure Virtual Desktop. Such policies can enforce multifactor authentication based on conditions such as risky sign-ins to increase an organization's security posture.

- Configure AD FS to enable single sign-on for users on the corporate network.

# Different Directory Options

There are three common ways to use Active Directory–based services in Azure for identity and authentication. This choice of identity solutions is dependent on your organization's needs. For example, if you have cloud-based application and cloud-only users accessing the application, then Azure Active Directory is a suitable solution, but in case you want to assign a policy on cloud-only devices and you don't have on-premises AD DS, then you can select Azure Active Directory domain services (AAD DS). Another use case is if you already have traditional on-premises AD DS and you want to use same domain user to authenticate cloud-based application/devices, then you can sync on-premises AD DS with Azure AD and use the on-premises identity for cloud as well.

Although the three Active Directory–based identity solutions share a common name and technology, they are designed to provide different customer needs.

The following are the three different identity solutions Microsoft provides:

- *Active Directory Domain Services (AD DS)*: This is a traditional Lightweight Directory Access Protocol (LDAP) server that provides key features such as identity and authentication, computer object management, Group Policy, and trusts. AD DS is a service available in Windows Server, and many organizations are already using it as the central component in their on-premises datacenter. Azure Virtual Desktop supports an on-premises ADDS service, and you can either directly sync on-premises AD DS with Azure AD or extend it in Azure and then sync it with Azure AD to avoid authentication and sync traffic going over VPN/ER. Extended AD DS server in Azure can be used for domain joins and AVD desktop authentication as well.

- *Azure Active Directory (Azure AD)*: Azure AD is a cloud-based identity and mobile device management (MDM) provider that gives the ability to create user account and authenticate services for resources such as Microsoft 365, the Azure portal, and software-as-a-service applications. On-premises AD DS can be synchronized with Azure AD to provide a single-user identity across the organization. Azure AD is required for authentication, but it needs to be synced with on-premises AD DS or Azure AD DS.

- *Azure Active Directory Domain Services (Azure AD DS)*: Azure AD DS consists of managed domain services the same as traditional AD DS with features such as domain joins, Group Policy, LDAP, and Kerberos/NTLM authentication with a minimal amount of administrative overhead (but limited admin permission; refer to Azure AD DS). Azure AD DS integrates with Azure AD, which itself can synchronize with an on-premises AD DS. This ability extends central identity use cases. Azure AD DS is one of the best options supported by Azure Virtual Desktop if you don't have any directory solution in place or if you want to set up isolated AVD POC.

# Differences Between Azure AD DS and Self-Managed AD DS

There are two ways to provide AD DS traditional authentication mechanisms (Kerberos or NTLM) in the cloud for cloud-based applications and services:

- *Managed domain (Azure AD DS)*: Microsoft manages the required resources for Azure AD DS, and you can still use all the traditional AD DS features such as domain joins, Group Policy, LDAP, and Kerberos/ NTLM authentication. You don't deploy, manage, patch, and secure the Azure AD DS infrastructure for components such as Windows Server OS or domain controller (DC) VMs. See Figure 3-3.

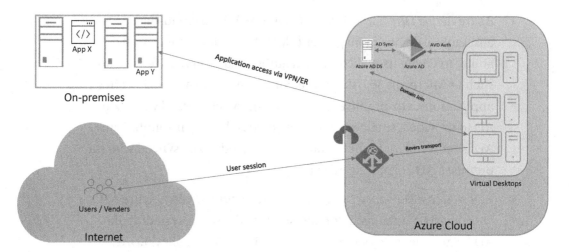

**Figure 3-3.** *Azure Active Directory Domain Services (AAD DS) for Azure Virtual Desktop*

- *A self-managed domain (AD DS service on VM)*: You can create and configure traditional AD DS on Azure virtual machines (VMs) with Windows Server guest OS, and you can use Active Directory Domain Services (AD DS) to extend your on-premises AD DS to the cloud or use on-premises AD DS as is for cloud as well. There's additional maintenance overhead with a self-managed AD DS environment, but you have ability to do additional tasks such as extend the schema or create forest trusts. See Figure 3-4.

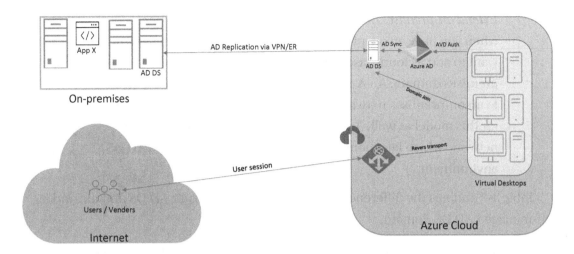

***Figure 3-4.*** *On-premises AD DS for Azure Virtual Desktop*

Common deployment models for a self-managed AD DS in cloud include the following:

- *Stand-alone cloud-only AD DS*: This option is mostly used when you don't have on-premises AD DS and just want to create new self-managed AD DS for the Azure cloud. Azure VMs can be configured as domain controllers to create a cloud-only AD DS environment.

- *Resource forest deployment*: This option is mostly used when you have an on-premises AD DS forest and just want to create a new AD DS domain in an existing on-premises forest for the Azure cloud. Azure VMs can be configured as domain controllers and AD DS domains as part of the existing on-premises forest. A trust relationship is then configured to an on-premises AD DS environment so that other Azure VMs can domain-join to this resource forest in the cloud. User authentication runs over a VPN/ExpressRoute connection to the on-premises AD DS environment.

- *Extend on-premises domain to Azure*: This option is mostly used when you have an on-premises AD DS domain and forest and just want to add a cloud-based domain controller in an existing on-premises domain. An Azure virtual network needs to be connected to an on-premises network using a VPN/ExpressRoute connection for this model as well. Azure VMs connect to this Azure virtual network, which lets them domain-join to the on-premises AD DS environment.

Table 3-3 outlines the differences between a managed Azure AD DS domain and a self-managed AD DS domain.

***Table 3-3.*** *Differences Between a Managed Azure AD DS Domain and a Self-Managed AD DS Domain*

| Feature | Azure AD DS | Self-Managed AD DS |
| --- | --- | --- |
| Managed service | yes | No |
| DNS server | Yes (*managed service*) | Yes |
| Domain or enterprise administrator privileges | ***No*** | Yes |
| Domain join | Yes | Yes |
| Domain authentication using NTLM and Kerberos | Yes | Yes |
| Kerberos constrained delegation | Resource-based | Resource-based and account-based |
| Custom OU structure | Yes | Yes |
| Group Policy | Yes | Yes |
| Schema extensions | No | Yes |
| AD domain/forest trusts | Yes (one-way outbound forest trusts only) | Yes |
| Secure LDAP (LDAPS) | Yes | Yes |
| LDAP read | Yes | Yes |
| LDAP write | Yes (within the managed domain) | Yes |
| Geodistributed deployments | Yes | Yes |

# What Is the Best Identity Solution for Azure Virtual Desktop?

Azure Virtual Desktop uses the AD DS domain join feature for all session hosts, and the user must enter domain credentials to log in to Azure Virtual Desktop. To avoid a dependency on site-to-site VPN/ER for authentication traffic to on-premises AD DS, on-premises AD DS can be extended to the Azure hub subscription by creating a domain controller VM in Azure. Most organizations do not want to store password hashes in the cloud AD and prefer to go with pass-through authentication with on-premises AD. This approach increases traffic and dependency on the site-to-site VPN tunnel by sending all authentication/DNS traffic to the on-prem AD. Extending the AD domain controller to Azure is the recommended option if all application/services are using on-premises AD for authentication or else the Azure AD connect VM can be placed on-premises to sync on-premises AD users directly to Azure AD if you have fewer users using cloud services.

Figure 3-5 shows a reference architecture for on-premises AD sync with Azure AD for Azure Virtual Desktop auth.

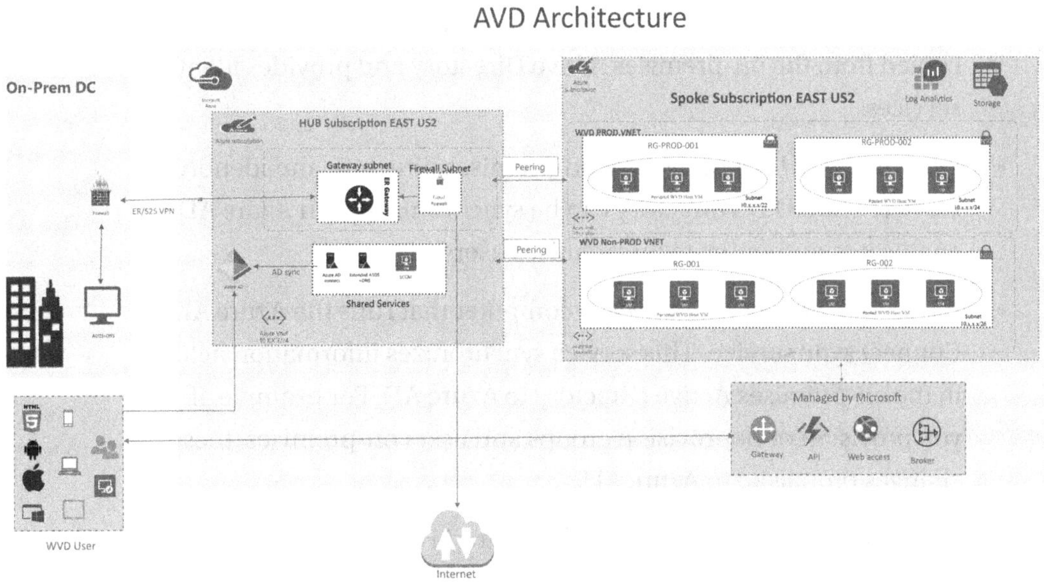

*Figure 3-5.* *Azure Virtual Desktop identity solution*

This diagram shows a typical architectural setup for Azure AD sync.

- All domain controller replication traffic flows over a site-to-site VPN/ER.

- A cloud-extended domain controller can be used for authentication instead of sending traffic on-premises when using pass-through authentication.

- By default, the Azure AD Connect sync server configures password hash synchronization between the on-premises domain and Azure AD, and the Azure AD service assumes that users authenticate by providing the same password that they use on-premises. The security policy of organization may prohibit synchronizing password hashes to the cloud. In this case, your organization should consider pass-through authentication.

The architecture has the following components:

- *Azure AD tenant*: An instance of Azure AD created by organization. It acts as a directory service for cloud applications by storing objects copied from the on-premises Active Directory and provides identity services.

- *On-premises AD DS server*: An on-premises directory and identity service. The AD DS directory can be synchronized with Azure AD to enable it to authenticate on-premises users.

- *Azure AD Connect sync server*: A computer that runs the Azure AD Connect sync service. This service synchronizes information held in the on-premises Active Directory to Azure AD. For example, if you provision or deprovision groups and users on-premises, these changes propagate to Azure AD.

- *User authentication*: By default, the Azure AD Connect sync server configures password hash synchronization between the on-premises domain and Azure AD, and the Azure AD service assumes that users authenticate by providing the same password that they use on-premises. For many organizations, this is appropriate, but if your organization's security policy prohibits synchronizing password hashes to the cloud, then you should consider pass-through authentication. Alternatively, you can configure Azure AD to use Active Directory Federation Services (AD FS) or a third-party federation provider to implement authentication and SSO rather than by using the password information held in the cloud.

# Summary

In this chapter, you learned about Azure Virtual Desktop licensing options, storage options for the session host, and user profile and authentication for AVD.

It is important to know all the options for identity and profiles so that you can design the Azure Virtual Desktop architecture accordingly and select the best options for your enterprise.

# CHAPTER 4

# Implement and Manage Networking for Azure Virtual Desktop

This chapter demonstrates how to plan and implement Azure virtual network connectivity, manage connectivity to the Internet and on-premises networks, implement and manage security aspects for Azure Virtual Desktop, and manage Azure Virtual Desktop (AVD) session hosts by using Azure Bastion. Additionally, this chapter provides detailed information on monitoring and troubleshooting network connectivity and best practices.

Remember, Azure Virtual Desktop on Microsoft Azure is a desktop and application virtualization service that operates on the Microsoft cloud. Azure Virtual Desktop works on multiple devices such as Windows, Mac, iOS, Android, and Linux, with apps that you can use to access remote desktops and apps. You can also use most modern browsers to access Azure Virtual Desktop–hosted experiences.

You will gain experience implementing and managing virtual desktop experiences, connecting to a network, implementing security, and optimizing the desktop to run in virtual environments.

## Implement Azure Virtual Network Connectivity

As you know, Azure Virtual Desktop is a desktop and application virtualization service that runs in the Azure cloud. Azure Virtual Desktop works across devices (Windows, Mac, iOS, Android, and Linux) with apps that you can use to access remote desktops and apps.

© Arun Sabale and Balu N Ilag 2022
A. Sabale and B. N. Ilag, *Microsoft Azure Virtual Desktop Guide*,
https://doi.org/10.1007/978-1-4842-8063-8_4

First you need to understand how this works before digging in more. Azure offers a cloud service that accesses a container for all the virtual machines in your deployment. All the virtual machines in this cloud service are talking to each other and are on the same network.

# What Is Azure Virtual Network?

Azure Virtual Network (VNet) is the foundation for a private network in Azure. VNet allows various kinds of Azure resources, including virtual machines, to firmly communicate with each other, the Internet, and on-premises networks. VNet facilitates Azure resources to securely communicate with each other, the Internet, and on-premises networks.

By linking Azure Virtual Desktop host pools to an Active Directory domain, you can specify the network topology to gain access to virtual desktops and virtual apps from the intranet or Internet, based on company policy. You can connect an Azure Virtual Desktop instance to an on-premises network utilizing a virtual private network (VPN) or, with the help of Azure ExpressRoute, expand the on-premises network into the Azure cloud over a private connection.

There are a number of scenarios that you can achieve by using a virtual network, such as communicating with Azure resources with the Internet, communicating between Azure resources, communicating with on-premises resources, filtering network traffic, routing network traffic, and integrating with Azure services. Let's discuss each scenario in detail starting with communicating with the Internet. The communication between Azure resources is accomplished through a network such as a virtual network, virtual network service endpoint, or virtual network peering. Figure 4-1 shows the access to Azure PaaS and IaaS and on-premises connectivity.

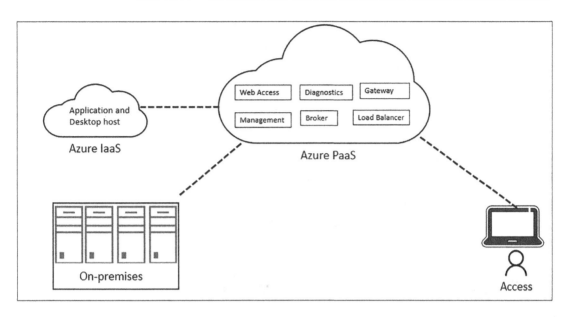

*Figure 4-1.* *Azure VNet*

## Communicate with the Internet

All resources in a virtual network can communicate outbound to the Internet by default. You can communicate inbound to a resource by assigning a public IP address or a public load balancer. You can also use a public IP or public load balancer to manage your outbound connections.

When using only an internal standard load balancer, outbound connectivity is not available until you define how you want outbound connections to work with an instance-level public IP or a public load balancer.

## Connect to Azure Resources

Azure resources communicate securely with each other in one of the following ways:

- *Through a virtual network*: You can deploy VMs and several other types of Azure resources to a virtual network, such as Azure app service environments, Azure Kubernetes Service (AKS), and Azure Virtual Machine Scale Sets.

- *Through a virtual network service endpoint*: Extend your virtual network private address space and the identity of your virtual network to Azure service resources, such as Azure Storage accounts and Azure SQL Database, over a direct connection. Service endpoints allow you to secure your critical Azure service resources to only a virtual network.

- *Through VNet peering*: You can connect virtual networks to each other, enabling resources in either virtual network to communicate with each other, using virtual network peering. The virtual networks you connect can be in the same or different Azure regions.

# Creating a Virtual Network for AVD

VNet and on-premises connectivity are important prerequisites for Azure Virtual Desktop. It is important to set up VNet correctly with the required subnet, DNS settings, and peering with a hub virtual network for on-premises connectivity (or hub shared service connectivity) so that users can use their domain credentials to log in to AVD and access their on-premises applications/services.

Follow these steps to create a VNet instance for AVD:

1. Log in to the Azure portal and select the correct directory and subscription where you want to create the AVD host pool and desktops. Make sure you have correct permissions (contributor or owner) to create network resources. See Figure 4-2.

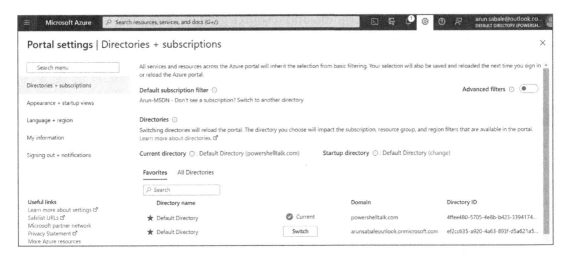

*Figure 4-2.* *Azure subscription selection*

2. Search for *virtual network* in the top search bar. See Figure 4-3.

*Figure 4-3.* *Azure virtual network search*

3. Click Create to create a new virtual network. See Figure 4-4.

*Figure 4-4.* *Azure virtual network creation*

4. Select the correct subscription and resource group names from the drop-down where you want to create the AVD desktops. If the resource group does not exist, then you can create a new resource group by clicking the Create New option. See Figure 4-5.

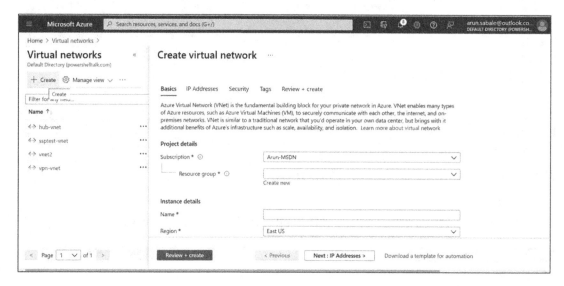

***Figure 4-5.*** *Azure virtual network creation page*

5.  Additionally, provide the virtual network name as per your
    organization's naming standard and select the correct region (the
    same as AVD desktops). Click the Next button once, and enter all
    the information. See Figure 4-6.

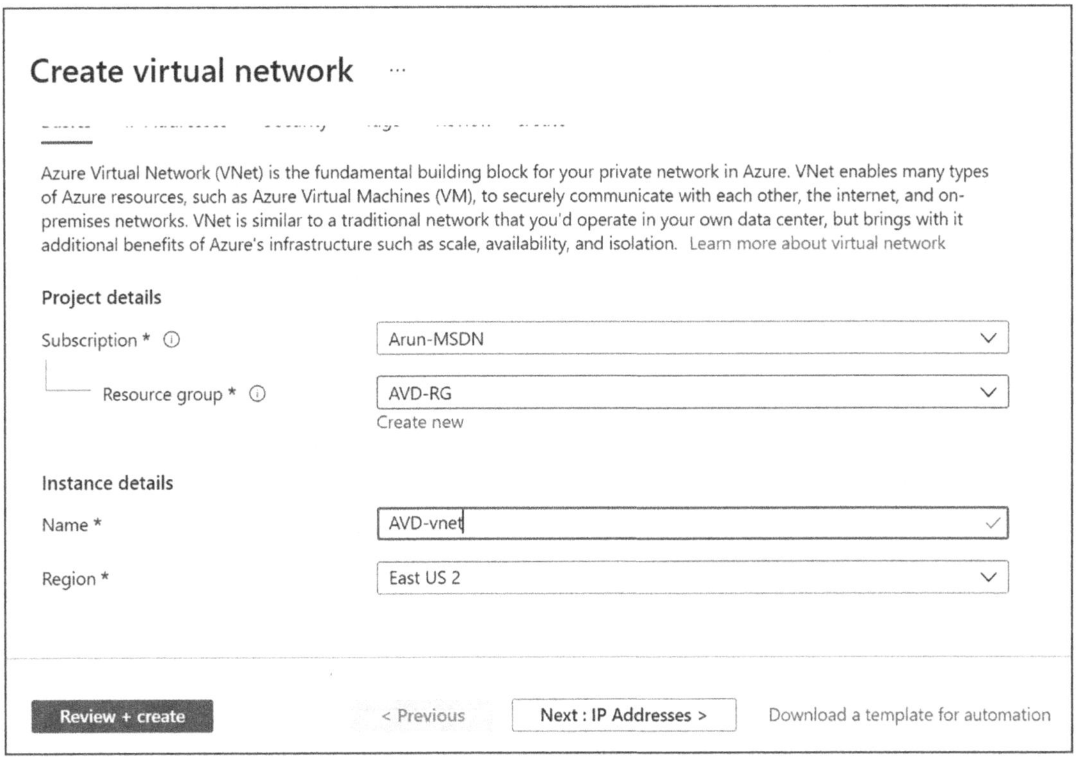

*Figure 4-6.* *Azure virtual network creation, Basic tab*

6.  Provide the IP address space/range for VNet on the IP Addresses tab. You must coordinate with the network team to get the correct IP address range for AVD VNet that does not conflict with an existing VNet or on-premises IP address range. See Figure 4-7.

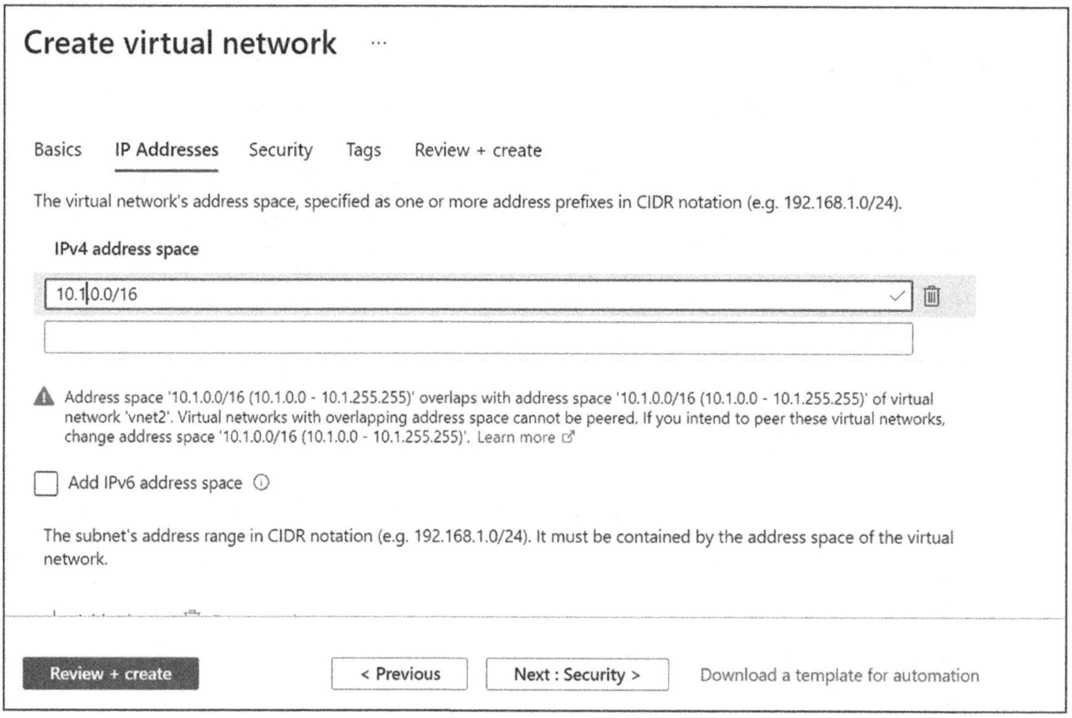

# Create virtual network   ...

Basics    **IP Addresses**    Security    Tags    Review + create

The virtual network's address space, specified as one or more address prefixes in CIDR notation (e.g. 192.168.1.0/24).

**IPv4 address space**

| 10.1.0.0/16 | ✓  🗑 |

⚠ Address space '10.1.0.0/16 (10.1.0.0 - 10.1.255.255)' overlaps with address space '10.1.0.0/16 (10.1.0.0 - 10.1.255.255)' of virtual network 'vnet2'. Virtual networks with overlapping address space cannot be peered. If you intend to peer these virtual networks, change address space '10.1.0.0/16 (10.1.0.0 - 10.1.255.255)'. Learn more ↗

☐ Add IPv6 address space ⓘ

The subnet's address range in CIDR notation (e.g. 192.168.1.0/24). It must be contained by the address space of the virtual network.

Review + create        < Previous        Next : Security >        Download a template for automation

*Figure 4-7.*  *Azure virtual network creation, IP Addresses tab*

7. Additionally, create an appropriate subnet on the same IP
   Addresses tab. You can click the "Add subnet" option to add
   additional subnets. You must consider the number of session
   hosts/VMs you are planning to create under each subnet plus
   some buffer IP addresses for future use and create the subnet
   accordingly. Create the subnet, remembering that each host
   pool needs to be placed in different subnets if they belong to
   different business units and don't want to share any user data. See
   Figure 4-8.

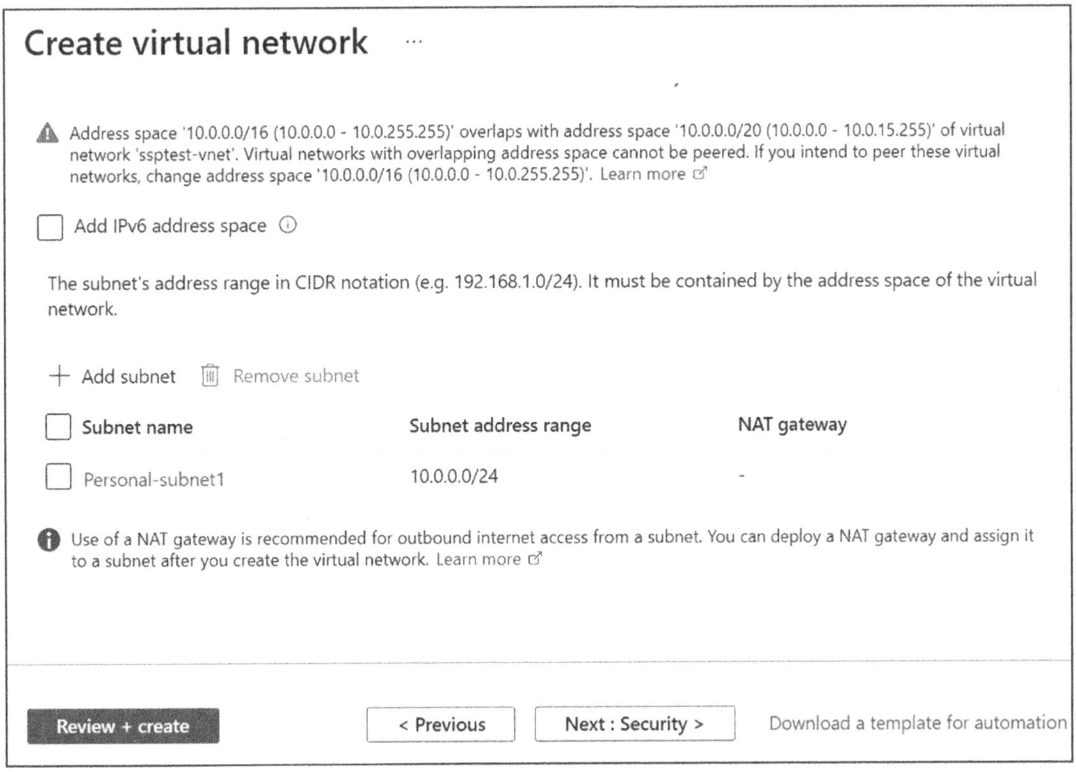

## Create virtual network   ⋯

⚠ Address space '10.0.0.0/16 (10.0.0.0 - 10.0.255.255)' overlaps with address space '10.0.0.0/20 (10.0.0.0 - 10.0.15.255)' of virtual
network 'ssptest-vnet'. Virtual networks with overlapping address space cannot be peered. If you intend to peer these virtual
networks, change address space '10.0.0.0/16 (10.0.0.0 - 10.0.255.255)'. Learn more ☐

☐ Add IPv6 address space  ⓘ

The subnet's address range in CIDR notation (e.g. 192.168.1.0/24). It must be contained by the address space of the virtual
network.

＋ Add subnet    🗑 Remove subnet

| ☐ Subnet name | Subnet address range | NAT gateway |
|---|---|---|
| ☐ Personal-subnet1 | 10.0.0.0/24 | - |

ⓘ Use of a NAT gateway is recommended for outbound internet access from a subnet. You can deploy a NAT gateway and assign it
to a subnet after you create the virtual network. Learn more ☐

| Review + create |   | < Previous | Next : Security > | Download a template for automation |

*Figure 4-8.* *Azure virtual network creation, add subnet*

8. You will get a subnet pop-up to enter additional subnet information like the name and IP address range. Make sure you are entering the subnet name as per your organization's naming standards. Click the Add button to add the subnet. See Figure 4-9.

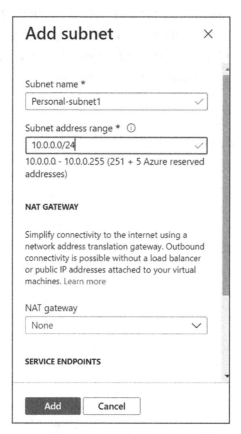

**Figure 4-9.**  *Azure virtual network creation, adding a subnet detail*

9. Once you have entered all the IP address information, then click Next to go to the Security tab and verify whether you want to change anything as per your organization standards, or click Next to go to Tags. Make sure you are adding tags as per your organization's standards and click Next. See Figure 4-10.

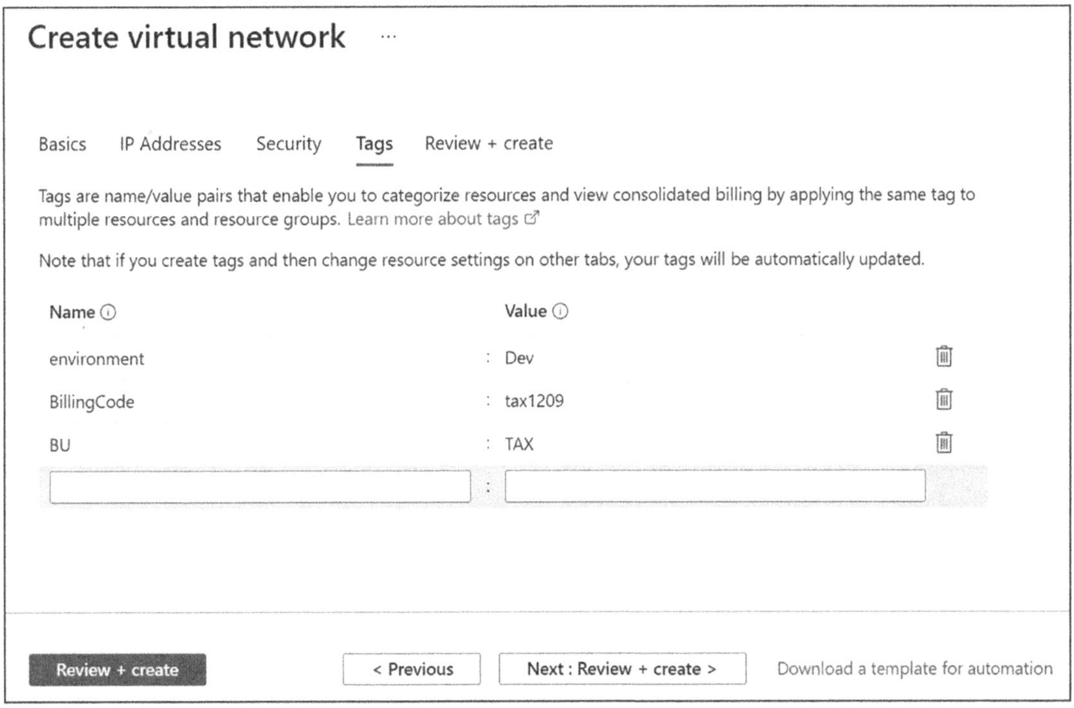

## Create virtual network ⋯

Basics    IP Addresses    Security    **Tags**    Review + create

Tags are name/value pairs that enable you to categorize resources and view consolidated billing by applying the same tag to multiple resources and resource groups. Learn more about tags ☐

Note that if you create tags and then change resource settings on other tabs, your tags will be automatically updated.

| Name ⓘ | | Value ⓘ | |
|---|---|---|---|
| environment | : | Dev | 🗑 |
| BillingCode | : | tax1209 | 🗑 |
| BU | : | TAX | 🗑 |
| | : | | |

Review + create    < Previous    Next : Review + create >    Download a template for automation

***Figure 4-10.*** *Azure virtual network creation, Tags tab*

10. Finally, click "Review + create" and then click Create once the validation is completed. See Figure 4-11.

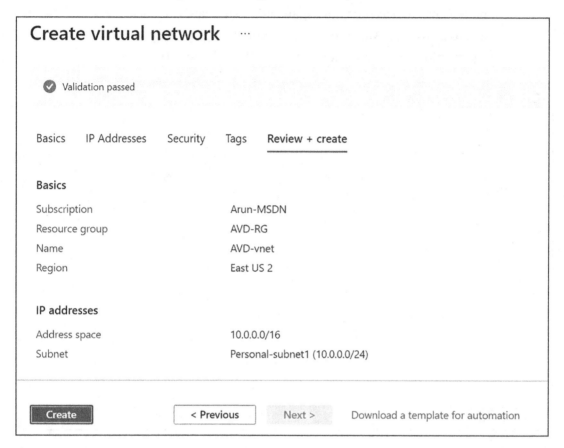

**Figure 4-11.** *Azure virtual network creation, creating and reviewing*

11. You will be able to see deployment progress on the same page, and you can go to the resource once the deployment is completed. See Figure 4-12.

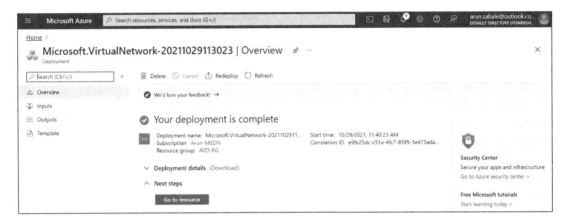

***Figure 4-12.*** *Azure virtual network creation, deployment status*

12. You can verify the VNet details on the Overview page. See Figure 4-13.

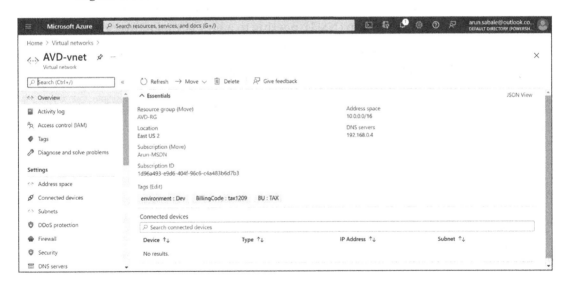

***Figure 4-13.*** *Azure virtual network, AVD VNet details*

13. If you still want to add subnets, then you can go to the Subnet option in the left pane and click to add a subnet. See Figure 4-14.

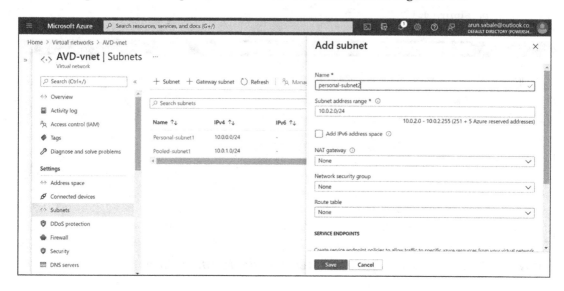

***Figure 4-14.*** *AVD virtual network, adding a subnet*

14. Once the subnet and VNet are ready, then the next step is to create a network security group (NSG), peering to a hub virtual network, and DNS settings. Create the NSG and click the Create option to create a new network security group. See Figure 4-15.

***Figure 4-15.*** *AVD virtual network, creating a NSG*

15. Select the correct subscription and resource group for the network security group (the same as AVD VNet). Add the NSG name and select the correct region the same way as you did for the VNet and AVD desktops. See Figure 4-16.

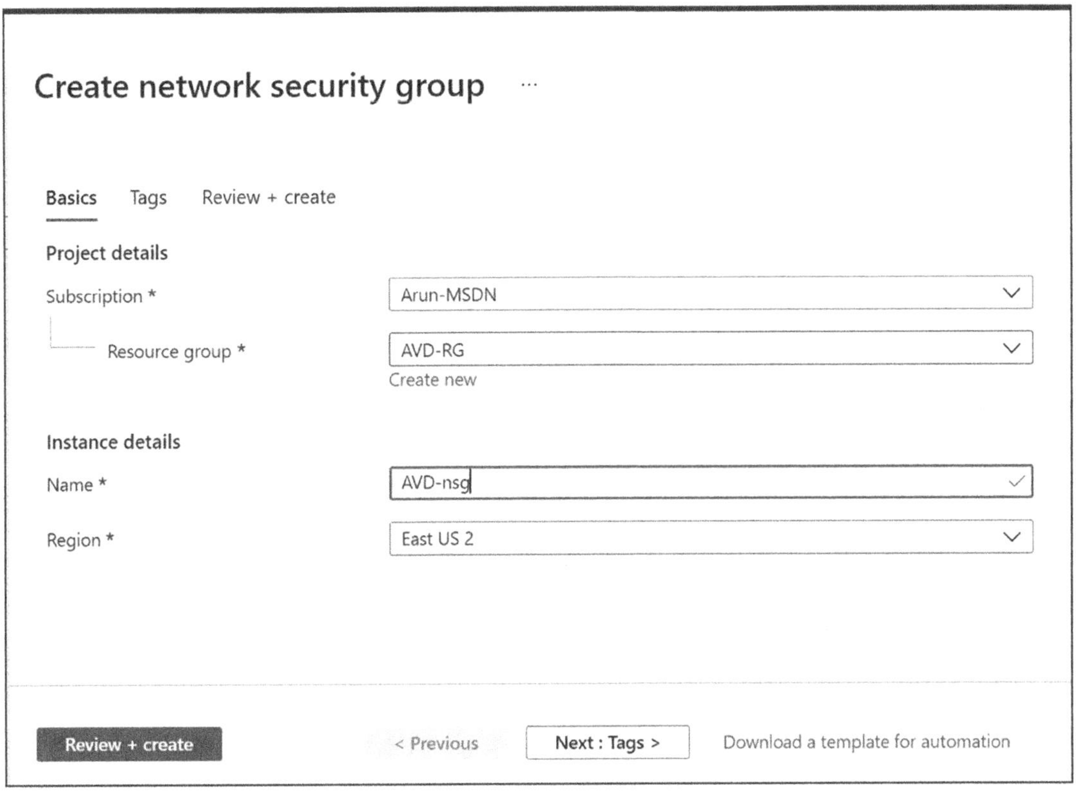

# Create network security group    ...

Basics    Tags    Review + create

**Project details**

Subscription *                    | Arun-MSDN |

Resource group *                  | AVD-RG |
                                    Create new

**Instance details**

Name *                            | AVD-nsg |

Region *                          | East US 2 |

| Review + create |        < Previous    | Next : Tags > |    Download a template for automation

*Figure 4-16.* *AVD NSG creation*

16. You will see the deployment status on the same page. Wait for the deployment to complete and then click "Go to resource." See Figure 4-17.

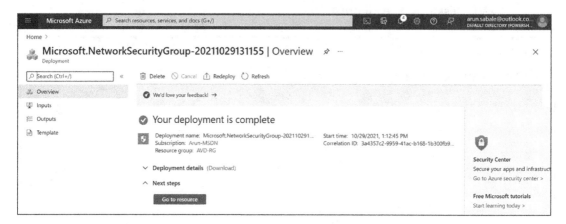

***Figure 4-17.*** *A AVD NSG creation, deployment status*

17. The NSG default rules will be visible on the Overview page. See Figure 4-18.

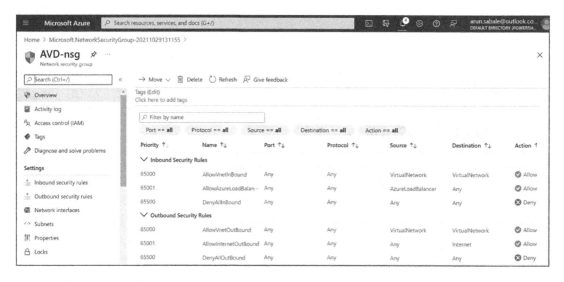

***Figure 4-18.*** *AVD NSG, Overview page*

18.  Make sure to add the AVD-specific IP/port in the outbound rules. The following are the recommended/required IP addresses/ports for AVD. AVD does not require any inbound connection but definitely needs KMS, metadata, health monitoring IP addresses/ports, and a few Azure service tags in case you don't want Internet access on the VM. Refer to Table 4-1 for all AVD-specific port and IP details. See Figure 4-19.

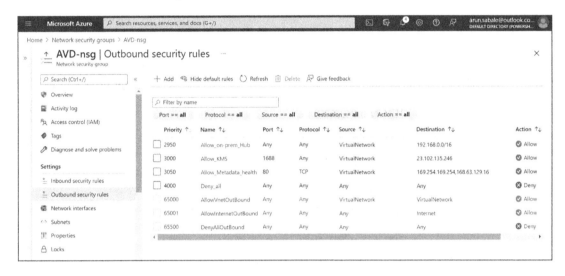

***Figure 4-19.***  *AVD NSG, Outbound security rules*

***Table 4-1.*** *AVD NSG: Outbound Security Rules Requirement*

| Source | Destination | Port | Action | Direction | Remark |
|---|---|---|---|---|---|
| * | * | * | Deny | Outbound | Deny all default NSG rules. |
| Azure AVD VNet | AD DNS IP addresses? | DNS (port 53) | Allow | Outbound | If the DNS is on-premises, we need to open ports from the firewall. |
| Azure AVD VNet | AD domain controllers IP addresses? | TCP 88 (Kerberos Key Distribution Center)<br><br>TCP 135 (Remote Procedure Call)<br><br>TCP 139 (NetBIOS Session Service)<br><br>TCP 389 (LDAP)<br><br>TCP 445 (SMB, Net Logon)<br><br>UDP 53 (DNS)<br><br>UDP 389, 636 (LDAP, LDAPS, DC Locator, Net Logon)<br><br>TCP 49152-65535 (Randomly allocated high TCP ports) | Allow | Outbound | If the target is on-premises, we need to open ports from the firewall. |

*(continued)*

***Table 4-1.*** (*continued*)

| Source | Destination | Port | Action | Direction | Remark |
|---|---|---|---|---|---|
| Azure AVD VNet | Monitoring and patching server IP address range? | ? | Allow | Outbound | If the target is on-prem, we need to open ports from the firewall. |
| Azure AVD VNet | On-Prem application IP address range? | ? | Allow | Outbound | If the target is on-prem, we need to open ports from the firewall. |
| **AVD-specific port** | | | | | |
| Azure AVD VNet | **169.254.169.254 and 168.63.129.16** | **80** | Allow | Outbound | Azure internal: AVD metadata and health monitoring: https://docs. microsoft. com/en-us/ azure/virtual- desktop/safe- url-list |

(*continued*)

***Table 4-1.*** (*continued*)

| Source | Destination | Port | | Action | Direction | Remark |
|---|---|---|---|---|---|---|
| Azure AVD VNet | **kms.core. windows.net** | **1688** | | Allow | Outbound | Internet: KMS port required for AVD: https://docs. microsoft. com/en-us/ azure/virtual- desktop/safe- url-list, KMS (Key Management Service) is one of the methods to activate Microsoft Windows and Microsoft Office. Activation ensures that the software is obtained from and licensed by Microsoft. |
| | **23.102.135.246** | | | | | KMS IP addresses https://docs. microsoft.com/ en-us/azure/ virtual- machines/ troubles hooting/ custom-routes- enable-kms- activation |

(*continued*)

***Table 4-1.*** *(continued)*

| Source | Destination | Port | Action | Direction | Remark |
|---|---|---|---|---|---|
| Azure AVD VNet | **AzureCloud and WindowsVirtual Desktop** OR **Internet service tag** | 443 | Allow | Outbound | 443 to Internet OR 443 to AzureCloud, WindowsVirtual Desktop: https://docs. microsoft. com/en-us/ azure/virtual- desktop/safe- url-list |

19.  Once an NSG is updated with the correct rules, then you have to
     attach it to subnets so that the rules will take effect. Go back to the
     AVD virtual network you created at the start and go to the subnet
     option from the left pane. Now click the subnet name and attach
     the NSG from the right-side pane. See Figure 4-20.

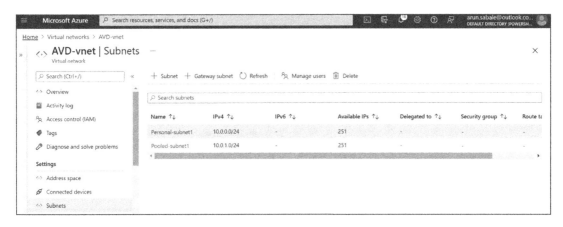

***Figure 4-20.*** *AVD NSG assignment*

20. Select the network security group from the drop-down in the subnet pop-up. See Figure 4-21.

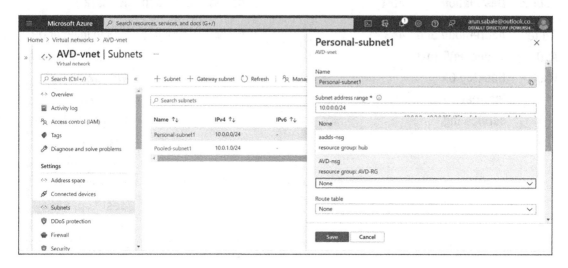

***Figure 4-21.*** *AVD NSG assignment on subnet*

21. Select the correct NSG name and click the Save button. See Figure 4-22.

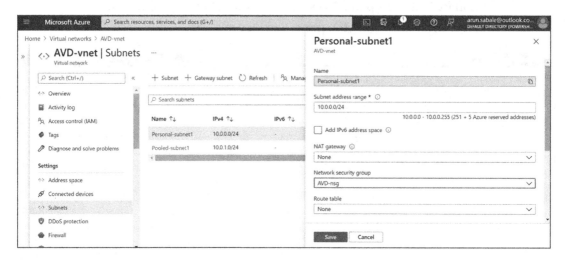

***Figure 4-22.*** *AVD NSG assignment page*

22. You can attach a route table to force-tunnel all traffic to the Azure firewall or third-party firewall in the cloud or on-premises firewall. Select the routing table from the drop-down to attach it to the subnet. See Figure 4-23.

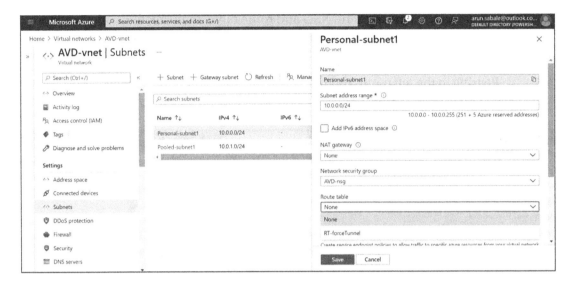

***Figure 4-23.*** *AVD NSG assignment page- route table*

23.  Make sure you have the correct port/IP address open on the
     firewall/NVA when you are force-tunneling all AVD traffic.
     Additionally, the routing table must have the correct route. Refer
     to the route table in Figure 4-24.

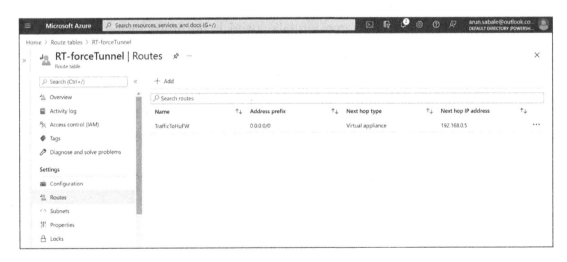

***Figure 4-24.*** *AVD routing table to force-tunnel traffic to the firewall*

24. Once you have updated the NSG and route table, then create
peering with the hub VNet so all traffic to on-premises/the other
VNet can go through the hub VNet. Go to the hub VNet, click
Peering in the left pane, and then click the Add option in the right
pane. See Figure 4-25.

***Figure 4-25.*** *AVD virtual network peering to hub virtual network*

25. Enter the names for peering from the hub to AVD and vice versa.
Additionally, select the target virtual network in the drop-down
to peer with. Most important, allow all traffic as well as gateway
transit so that the gateway will be used for on-premises traffic.
The "Gateway transit" option will be available when you have a
gateway in the hub for a site-to-site VPN or ExpressRoute. Click
the Add button once you select all the options on the peering
page. See Figure 4-26.

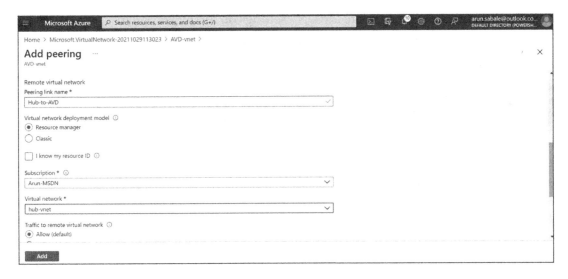

***Figure 4-26.*** *AVD virtual network peering to hub vnet, adding peering*

26.    The peering status will be visible on the same page. Wait until the peering status is connected. See Figure 4-27.

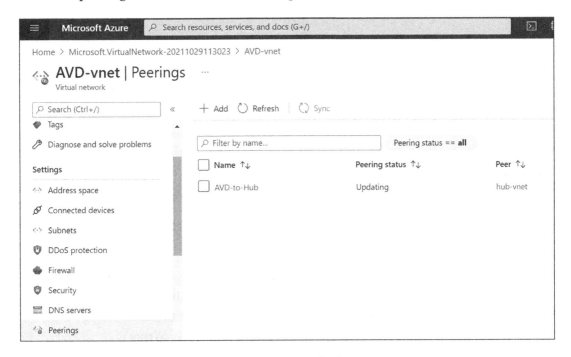

***Figure 4-27.*** *AVD virtual network peering to hub vnet, Overview page*

27. The next step is to update the DNS settings on AVD VNet. Go to AVD VNet and click the DNS Servers option in the left pane. See Figure 4-28.

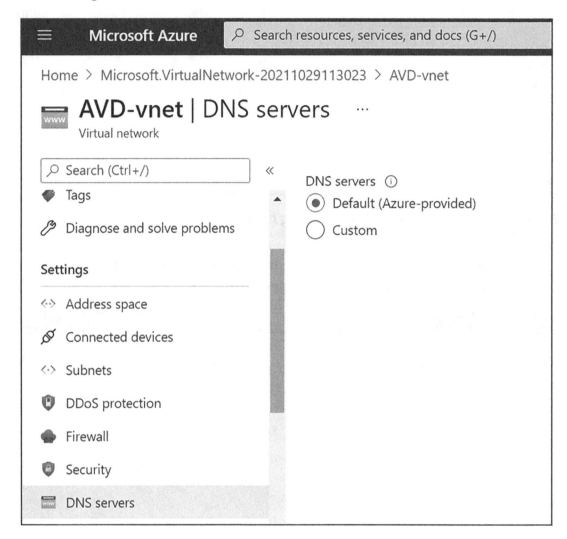

***Figure 4-28.*** *AVD virtual network, DNS server setting*

28. Select the Custom option in the right pane and enter the DNS server's IP address. Additionally, you must make sure the DNS port and IP address are open on all firewalls and NSGs so that the session host can reach the DNS server on port 53. Once the IP address is added, then click the Save button to save the configuration. See Figure 4-29.

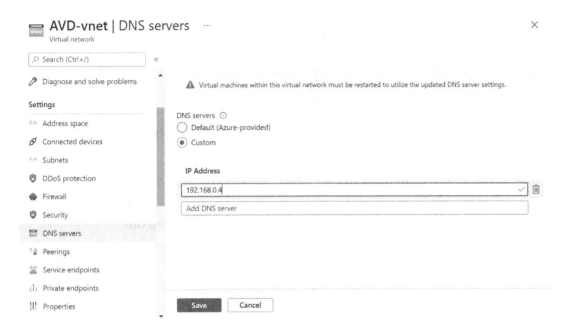

*Figure 4-29.* *AVD virtual network, custom DNS server setting*

# Manage Connectivity to the Internet and On-Premises Networks

How do we manage connectivity between the Internet and on-premises network? This is a commonly asked question because the Internet is an unmanaged network and can be accessed by anyone out there, which raises a lot of security risks. You as an admin can connect your on-premises computers and networks to a virtual network using any combination of the following options (see Figure 4-30):

- *Point-to-site virtual private network*: A point-to-site VPN is established between a virtual network and a single computer in your network. Each computer that wants to establish connectivity with a virtual network must configure its connection. It is ideal for just getting started with Azure, or for developers, because it requires little or no changes to your existing network. Another important point is the communication between your computer and a virtual network is sent through an encrypted tunnel over the Internet, which makes your connectivity protected from unauthorized people.

- *Site-to-site VPN*: A site-to-site VPN is another connectivity
  mechanism. It establishes a connection between your on-premises
  VPN device and an Azure VPN Gateway that is deployed in a virtual
  network. Site-to-site VPN enables any on-premises resource that you
  authorize to access a virtual network. The communication between
  your on-premises VPN device and an Azure VPN gateway is sent
  through an encrypted tunnel over the Internet.

- *Azure ExpressRoute*: By using Azure ExpressRoute partners, you
  can establish communication between your network and Azure.
  This connection is completely private and not shared with other
  customers or the Internet. Also, the Azure traffic does not go over the
  Internet. See Figure 4-30.

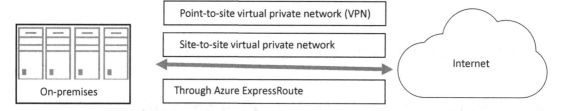

***Figure 4-30.*** *Connectivity options for the Internet and on-premises*

# Understanding Azure Virtual Desktop Network Connectivity

As an Azure Virtual Desktop admin, you must manage virtual desktops and their
connectivity, so understanding virtual desktop network connectivity is important.
Fundamentally, Azure Virtual Desktop utilizes Remote Desktop Protocol (RDP) to offer
remote display and input capabilities over network connections. The connection data
flow for Azure Virtual Desktop starts with a DNS lookup for the closest Azure datacenter.
Figure 4-31 demonstrates the five-step connection process for Azure Virtual Desktop
running in Azure.

1.  When authenticated in the Azure Active Directory, a token is
    returned to the Remote Desktop Services client.

2. The gateway checks the token with the connection broker.

3. The broker queries the Azure SQL database for resources assigned to the user.

4. The gateway and the broker select the session host for the connected client.

5. The session host creates a reverse connection to the client by using the Azure Virtual Desktop gateway. Figure 4-31 shows Azure Virtual Desktop connectivity.

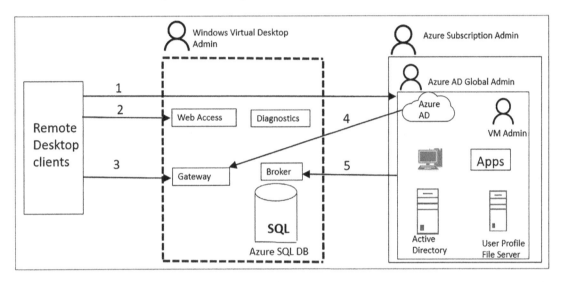

***Figure 4-31.*** *Azure Virtual Desktop connectivity*

When no inbound ports are opened, the gateway acts as an intelligent reverse proxy. The gateway manages all session connectivity, with nothing but pixels reaching the client. Azure Virtual Desktop hosts client sessions on the session hosts running on Azure. Microsoft manages portions of the services on the customer's behalf and provides secure endpoints for connecting clients and session hosts.

# Azure Virtual Desktop Network Connection

Azure Virtual Desktop hosts client sessions on the session hosts operating on Azure. Since Azure is a cloud-based service, Microsoft manages portions of the services on the customer's behalf and offers secure endpoints for connecting clients and session hosts. Figure 4-32 shows a high-level summary of the network connections utilized by Azure Virtual Desktop.

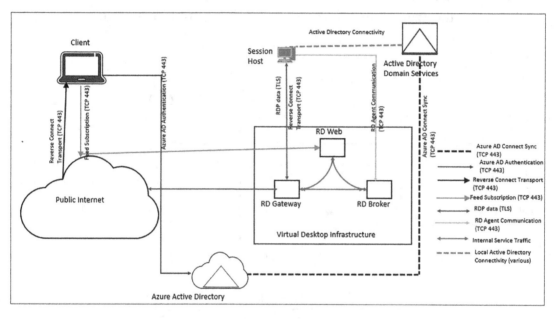

***Figure 4-32.***  *Azure Virtual Desktop Network connections*

- *Session connectivity*: Azure Virtual Desktop uses Remote Desktop Protocol to provide remote display and input capabilities over network connections.

- *Reverse connect transport*: Azure Virtual Desktop is utilizing a reverse connect transport for establishing the remote session and for carrying RDP traffic. Unlike the on-premises Remote Desktop Services deployments, reverse connect transport doesn't use a TCP listener to receive incoming RDP connections. Instead, it is using outbound connectivity to the Azure Virtual Desktop infrastructure over the HTTPS connection.

- *Session host communication channel*: Upon startup of the Azure
  Virtual Desktop session host, the Remote Desktop Agent Loader
  service establishes the Azure Virtual Desktop broker's persistent
  communication channel. This communication channel is layered on
  top of a secure Transport Layer Security (TLS) connection and serves
  as a bus for service message exchange between the session host and
  Azure Virtual Desktop infrastructure.

## How Can You Filter the Network Traffic?

You can filter the network traffic between subnets using either or both of the options
including Network Security Group (NSG), and application security groups. NSG's can
contain multiple inbound and outbound security rules that permit you to filter traffic to
and from resources by source and destination IP address, port, and protocol. Another
option is a network virtual appliance (NVA), which is a VM that performs a network
function, such as a firewall, WAN optimization, or other network function.

## How to Route Network Traffic in Azure?

Azure routes traffic between subnets, connected virtual networks, on-premises networks,
and the Internet, by default. You can implement a route table or Border Gateway
Protocol (BGP) route. Both options override the default routes that Azure creates.

By using *route tables*, you can create custom route tables with routes that control
where traffic is routed to for each subnet. If you connect your virtual network to your
on-premises network using an Azure VPN Gateway or ExpressRoute connection, you can
propagate your on-premises BGP routes to your virtual networks.

## Virtual Network Integration for Azure Services

Integrating Azure services to an Azure virtual network enables private access to the
service from virtual machines or compute resources in the virtual network. You can
integrate Azure services in your virtual network with the following options:

- If deploying dedicated instances of the service into a virtual network,
  the services can then be privately accessed within the virtual network
  and from on-premises networks.

- Using a private link to access a specific instance of the service privately from your virtual network or from on-premises networks.

- You can also access the service using public endpoints by extending a virtual network to the service, through service endpoints. Service endpoints allow service resources to be secured to the virtual network.

No inbound ports are opened. In this version, the gateway acts as an intelligent reverse proxy. The gateway manages all session connectivity, with nothing but pixels reaching the client.

Azure Virtual Desktop hosts client sessions on the session hosts running on Azure. Microsoft manages portions of the services on the customer's behalf and provides secure endpoints for connecting clients and session hosts. The diagram above (Figure 4-32) gives a high-level overview of the network connections used by Azure Virtual Desktop.

# How the AVD Client Connection Sequence Works

It is important to understand the client connection sequence, which will help you to troubleshoot the client connections. Based on the startup of the Azure Virtual Desktop session host, the Remote Desktop Agent Loader service determines the Azure Virtual Desktop broker's persistent communication channel. This communication channel is layered on top of a secure TLS connection and serves as a bus for service message exchange between the session host and Azure Virtual Desktop infrastructure.

1. As the first step, a user utilizing a supported Azure Virtual Desktop client subscribes to the Azure Virtual Desktop workspace.

2. Then Azure Active Directory authenticates the user and returns the token used to enumerate resources available to the user.

3. The client passes the token to the Azure Virtual Desktop feed subscription service.

4. The Azure Virtual Desktop feed subscription service validates the token.

5.  The Azure Virtual Desktop feed subscription service passes the list of available desktops and RemoteApps back to the client in the form of a digitally signed connection configuration.

6.  The client stores the connection configuration for each available resource in a set of .rdp files.

7.  When a user chooses the resource to connect to, the client uses the associated .rdp file, establishes a secure TLS 1.2 connection to the closest Azure Virtual Desktop gateway instance, and passes the connection information.

8.  The Azure Virtual Desktop gateway validates the request and asks the Azure Virtual Desktop broker to orchestrate the connection.

9.  The Azure Virtual Desktop broker identifies the session host and uses the previously established persistent communication channel to initialize the connection.

10. The Remote Desktop stack initiates the TLS 1.2 connection to the same Azure Virtual Desktop gateway instance as used by the client.

11. After both the client and session hosts connect to the gateway, the gateway starts relaying the raw data between both endpoints; this establishes the base reverse connect transport for the RDP.

12. After the base transport is set, the client starts the RDP handshake, and the user can access the Azure Virtual Desktop.

# How Does AVD Secure the Connection?

Azure Virtual Desktop utilizes TLS 1.2 for all connections initiated from the clients and session hosts to the Azure Virtual Desktop infrastructure components. For reverse connect transport, both the client and session hosts connect to the Azure Virtual Desktop gateway. After establishing the TCP connection, the client or session host validates the Azure Virtual Desktop gateway's certificate. After establishing the base transport, RDP establishes a nested TLS connection between the client and session host using the session host's certificates. By default, the certificate used for RDP encryption is self-generated by the OS during the deployment.

# Implement and Manage Network Security

Before understanding how to manage network security in a Azure Virtual desktop, you as an Azure Virtual Desktop admin must remember that when an end user connects to an Azure Virtual Desktop environment, their session is run by a host pool. A host pool is nothing but a collection of Azure virtual machines that register to Azure Virtual Desktop as session hosts.

Since you will connect these virtual desktops remotely in your virtual network, they are subject to the virtual network security controls. They need outbound Internet access to the Azure Virtual Desktop service to operate properly and might also need outbound Internet access for end users. Azure Firewall is an essential part of the network security, and it can assist you in locking down your environment and filtering outbound traffic. The "Filtering outbound traffic" option allows only required connections, and unwanted traffic you can drop at the firewall level. Figure 4-33 shows the Azure Virtual Desktop Security system.

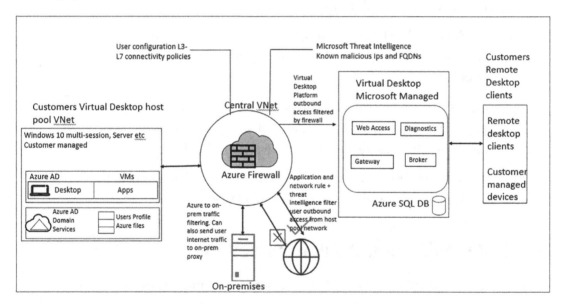

***Figure 4-33.*** *Azure Virtual Desktop Security system*

Additionally, Figure 4-33 provides additional protection for your Azure Virtual Desktop host pool using Azure Firewall.

# Host Pool Outbound Access to Azure Virtual Desktop

The Azure virtual machines you build for Azure Virtual Desktop must have access to several fully qualified domain names (FQDNs) to function properly. Azure Firewall provides an Azure Virtual Desktop FQDN tag to simplify this configuration. Use the following steps to allow outbound Azure Virtual Desktop platform traffic:

1. Deploy an Azure Firewall and configure your Azure Virtual Desktop host pool subnet user-defined route (UDR) to route all traffic via the Azure Firewall. Your default route now points to the firewall.

2. Create an application rule collection and add a rule to enable the WindowsVirtualDesktop FQDN tag. The source IP address range is the host pool virtual network, the protocol is HTTPS, and the destination is WindowsVirtualDesktop.

3. The set of required storage and service bus that accounts for your Azure Virtual Desktop host pool is deployment specific, so it isn't yet captured in the WindowsVirtualDesktop FQDN tag. You can address this in one of the following ways:

   a. Allow HTTPS access from your host pool subnet to *xt.blob.core. windows.net, *eh. servicebus.windows.net, and *xt.table.core. windows.net. These wildcard FQDNs enable the required access but are less restrictive.

   b. You can use the following log analytics query to list the exact required FQDNs and then allow them explicitly in your firewall application rules:

   c. *AzureDiagnostics | where Category == "AzureFirewallApplicationRule" | search "Deny"*
   *| search "gsm*eh.servicebus.windows.net" or "gsm*xt.blob.core. windows.net" or "gsm*xt.table.core.windows.net" | parse msg_s with Protocol "request from "SourceIP ":" SourcePort:int "to "FQDN ":" * | project TimeGenerated,Protocol,FQDN*

   d. Create a network rule collection to add the following rules: for Allow DNS, allow traffic from your ADDS private IP address to * for TCP and UDP ports 53, and for Allow KMS, allow traffic from your Azure Virtual Desktop virtual machines to Windows Activation Service TCP port 1688.

---

**Note**   Certain implementations may not require DNS rules; for instance, Azure Active Directory domain controllers forward DNS queries to Azure DNS at 168.63.129.16.

---

# Important Consideration: Host Pool Outbound Access to the Internet

Based on your organization's requirements, you may need to enable secure outbound Internet access for your end users. In instances where the list of allowed destinations is well-defined (for instance, Microsoft 365 access), you can use Azure Firewall applications and network rules to configure the required access. This routes end-user traffic directly to the Internet for the best performance.

If you want to filter outbound user Internet traffic using an existing on-premises secure web gateway, you can configure web browsers or other applications running on the Azure Virtual Desktop host pool with an explicit proxy configuration. These proxy settings only influence your end-user Internet access, permitting the Azure Virtual Desktop platform outbound traffic directly via Azure Firewall.

# Manage Azure Virtual Desktop Session Hosts by Using Azure Bastion

In this section you'll learn about Azure Bastion.

## Configure AVD Session Hosts Using Azure Bastion

Azure Bastion offers secure connectivity to all VMs in a virtual network in which it is provisioned. Utilizing Azure Bastion protects your virtual machines from exposing RDP/SSH ports to the outside world, while still offering secure access utilizing RDP/SSH.

It is important to verify the criteria that you need to meet. Here is the list:

- You need a VNet with the Bastion host already installed. Make sure that you have set up an Azure Bastion host for the virtual network in which the VM is located. Once the Bastion service is provisioned and deployed in your virtual network, you can make use of it to connect to any VM in the virtual network.

- You need a Windows virtual machine in the virtual network.

- The required roles are as follows: Reader role on the virtual machine, Reader role on the NIC with the private IP address of the virtual machine, and Reader role on the Azure Bastion resource.

- To connect to the Windows VM, you must have the inbound port RDP (3389) open on your Windows VM.

## How to Connect to Bastion?

Here is how you connect to Bastion:

1. Log in to the Azure portal (`https://portal.azure.com`), navigate to the virtual machine that you want to connect to, and select Connect. Select Bastion from the drop-down list. Figure 4-34 shows the Bastion option.

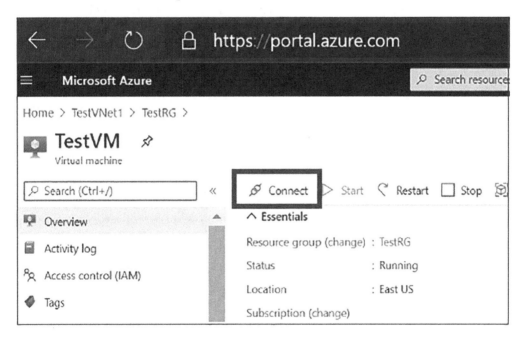

***Figure 4-34.*** *Connecting to Bastion*

2.  After you select Bastion from the drop-down, a sidebar appears that has three tabs: RDP, SSH, and Bastion. Because Bastion was provisioned for the virtual network, the Bastion tab is active by default. Select Use Bastion. For more information, refer to Figure 4-35.

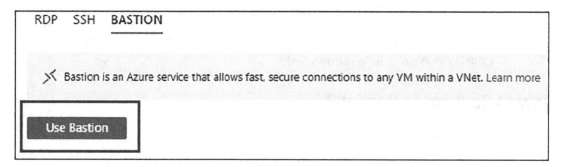

***Figure 4-35.***  *Usong Bastion*

3.  On the "Connect using the Azure Bastion" page, enter the username and password for your virtual machine, and then click Connect. See Figure 4-36.

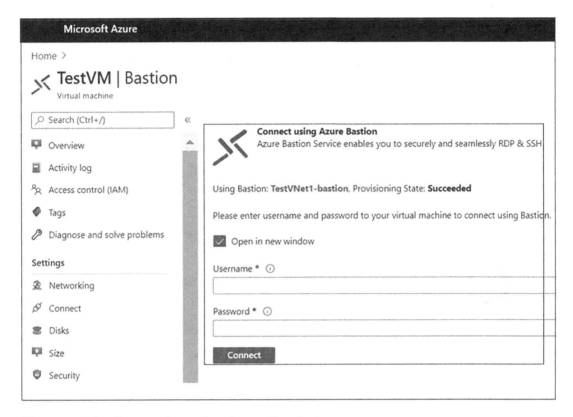

***Figure 4-36.*** *Connecting using Azure Bastion*

4.  The RDP connection to this virtual machine via Bastion will open
    directly in the Azure portal (over HTML5) using port 443 and the
    Bastion service.

# Monitor and Troubleshoot Network Connectivity

After learning about virtual desktop network connectivity and management, you as an
admin must learn about different troubleshooting scenarios for using virtual desktop
connectivity. There are different tools that can you use to troubleshoot the connectivity
issues and diagnosis the problems.

# Azure Virtual Desktop Monitoring

The Azure Network Watcher tool provides helps to monitor, diagnose, view metrics, and enable or disable logs for resources in an Azure virtual network. The Network Watcher is intended to monitor and repair the network health of infrastructure-as-a-service (IaaS) products that include virtual machines, virtual networks, application gateways, and load balancers. Figure 4-37 gives you the general idea about the Azure Network Watcher tool.

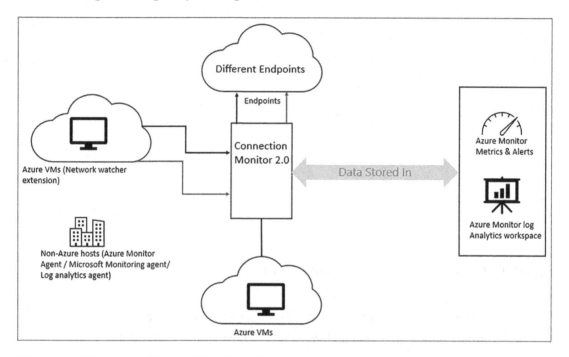

*Figure 4-37.* *Azure Virtual Desktop Connection Monitor 2.0*

## How Do I Monitor Communication Between a Virtual Desktop and an Endpoint?

You as an admin must know how to monitor the communication between an endpoint and the virtual desktops. Endpoints can be another virtual machine (VM), a fully qualified domain name (FQDN), a uniform resource identifier (URI), or an IPv4 address.

Another tool is the Connection Monitor 2.0, which monitors communication at a regular interval and informs you of reachability, latency, and network topology changes between the VM and the endpoint.

If an endpoint becomes unreachable, connection troubleshooting informs you of the reason. Potential reasons are a DNS name resolution problem; the CPU, memory, or firewall within the operating system of a VM; the hop type of a custom route; or a security rule for the VM or subnet of the outbound connection.

Additionally, the Connection Monitor provides the minimum, average, and maximum latency observed over time. After learning the latency for a connection, you may find that you're able to decrease the latency by moving your Azure resources to different Azure regions.

## How Do I View Resources in a Virtual Network and Their Relationships?

As resources are added to a virtual network, it can become difficult to understand what resources are in a virtual network and how they relate to each other. The *topology* capability enables you to generate a visual diagram of the resources in a virtual network and the relationships between the resources. Figure 4-38 shows an example topology diagram for a virtual network that has three subnets, two VMs, network interfaces, public IP addresses, network security groups, route tables, and the relationships between the resources.

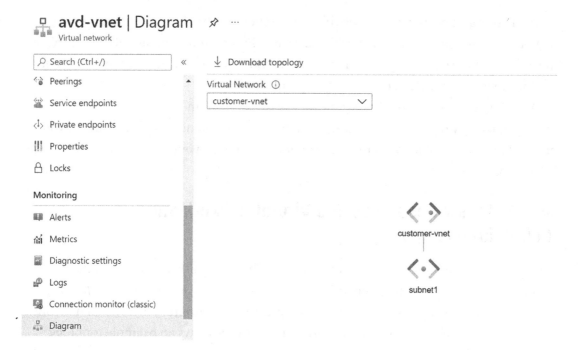

***Figure 4-38.*** *An Azure virtual network, topology diagram*

## How Do I Diagnose Network Traffic Filtering Problems to or from a VM?

After you implement a VM, Azure applies various default security rules to the VM that allow or deny traffic to or from the VM. You as an admin might override Azure's default rules or create additional rules. If you see a VM that may become unable to communicate with other resources, because of a security rule, the *IP flow verify* capability enables you to specify a source and destination IPv4 address, port, protocol (TCP or UDP), and traffic direction (inbound or outbound). IP flow verifies the tests the communication and informs you if the connection succeeds or fails.

---

**Important**    If the connection fails, IP flow checks and tells you which security rule allowed or denied the communication so that you can resolve the problem.

---

## How Do I Diagnose Network Routing Problems from a VM?

While supporting the VM environment as an admin, you may encounter the network routing issue, and you must know how to diagnose the routing problem. Once you create a virtual network, Azure creates several default outbound routes for network traffic. The outbound traffic from all resources, like VMs, deployed in a virtual network, are routed based on Azure's default routes. You might override Azure's default routes or create additional routes. You may find that a VM can no longer communicate with other resources because of a specific route.

To troubleshoot the issue, you may check the *next hop* capability enables you to specify a source and destination IPv4 address. The next hop then tests the communication and informs you what type of next hop is used to route the traffic. You can then remove, change, or add a route to resolve a routing problem.

# Azure Monitor Tool

In this section you'll learn about the tool.

## How Do I Monitor Azure Virtual Desktop Using Azure Monitor?

Azure Monitor is another tool that helps you in monitoring Azure Virtual Desktop. It is important to learn how to set up Azure Monitor for Azure Virtual Desktop to monitor your Azure Virtual Desktop environments. Prior to using Azure Monitor for Azure Virtual Desktop, you'll need to set up the multiple things.

- You must have at least one configured Log Analytics workspace. Make use of a designated Log Analytics workspace for your Azure Virtual Desktop session hosts to ensure that performance counters and events are collected only from session hosts in your Azure Virtual Desktop deployment.

- Allow data collection for the following things in your Log Analytics workspace:

    a.   Diagnostics from your Azure Virtual Desktop environment

    b.   Recommended performance counters from your Azure Virtual Desktop session hosts

    c.   Recommended Windows Event Logs from your Azure Virtual Desktop session hosts

- The data setup process explained in this page is the only one you'll need to monitor Azure Virtual Desktop. You can disable all other items sending data to your Log Analytics workspace to save costs.

- Anyone monitoring Azure Monitor for Azure Virtual Desktop for your environment will also need the read-access permissions that are mentioned here:

    a.   Read-access to the Azure subscriptions that hold your Azure Virtual Desktop resources

    b.   Read-access to the subscription's resource groups that hold your Azure Virtual Desktop session hosts

    c.   Read-access to the Log Analytics workspace or workspaces

---

**Note**    Read-access permissions only let admins view data. However, they will need different permissions to manage resources in the Azure Virtual Desktop portal.

---

# Set Up Azure Monitor for Azure Virtual Desktop

To set up or open the Azure Monitor for Azure Virtual Desktop, follow these steps:

    a.   First you need to log in to the Azure portal. After you are logged in to the Azure portal, search for and select Azure Monitor from the Azure portal.

    b.   Select Insights Hub under Insights, and then select Azure Virtual Desktop. See Figure 4-39.

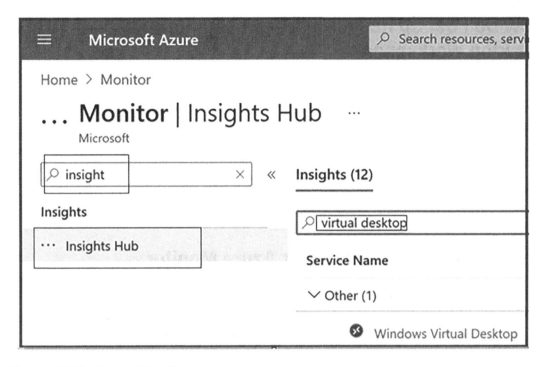

***Figure 4-39.***  *Azure Monitor*

   c.   Once you have the page open, enter the subscription, resource group, host pool, and time range of the environment you want to monitor.

   d.   As an additional step, you will need to set up the log analytics setting, because before you start using the Azure Monitor for Azure Virtual Desktop, you will need at least one Log Analytics workspace. Use a designated Log Analytics workspace for your Azure Virtual Desktop session hosts to ensure that performance counters and events are only collected from session hosts in your Azure Virtual Desktop deployment.

# How Do I Set Up Resource Diagnostic Settings on a Virtual Desktop Workspace?

To gather information on your Azure Virtual Desktop infrastructure, you will need to enable several diagnostic settings on your Azure Virtual Desktop host pools and workspaces (this is your Azure Virtual Desktop workspace, not your Log Analytics workspace). To set your resource diagnostic settings, follow these steps:

1. Select the Diagnostic settings host pool.

2. Under Monitoring, select "Diagnostic settings."

# Log Analytics Workspace for Azure Monitor

It is important to have an analytics workspace, because you will need at least one Log Analytics workspace to start using Azure Monitor for Azure Virtual Desktop. Utilize a designated Log Analytics workspace for your Azure Virtual Desktop session hosts to ensure that performance counters and events are collected only from session hosts in your Azure Virtual Desktop deployment.

If you are new to Azure monitoring and it's the first time you're opening Azure Monitor for Azure Virtual Desktop, you will need set up the Azure Monitor for your Azure Virtual Desktop environment. To configure your resources, follow these steps:

1. Log in and open Azure Monitor for Azure Virtual Desktop in the Azure portal at `https://aka.ms/azmonwvdi`, and then select configuration workbook.

2. Select an environment to configure under Subscription, Resource Group, and Host Pool.

The configuration workbook sets up your monitoring environment and lets you check the configuration after you have finished the setup process. It's important to check your configuration if items in the dashboard aren't displaying correctly or when the product group publishes updates that require new settings. You need to enable the supported diagnostic tables such as Checkpoint, Error, Management, Connection, HostRegistration, and AgentHealthStatus.

# Azure Advisor Tool to Monitor Azure Virtual Desktop

You can use Azure Advisor to monitor Azure Virtual Desktop. Azure Advisor is the go-to tool, and I frequently use it for monitoring issues. Whenever you come across an issue in Azure Virtual Desktop, always check Azure Advisor first. Azure Advisor will give you directions for how to solve the problem, or at least point you toward a resource that can help. This section will tell you how to set up Azure Advisor in your Azure Virtual Desktop deployment to help your users.

## What Is Azure Advisor?

Azure Advisor analyzes your configurations and telemetry to offer personalized recommendations to solve common problems. With these recommendations, you can optimize your Azure resources for reliability, security, operational excellence, performance, and cost.

## How Do I Start Using Azure Advisor?

All you need to get started is an Azure account on the Azure portal. First, open the Azure portal and then select Advisor under Azure Services, as shown in Figure 4-40. You can also enter *Azure Advisor* into the search bar in the Azure portal.

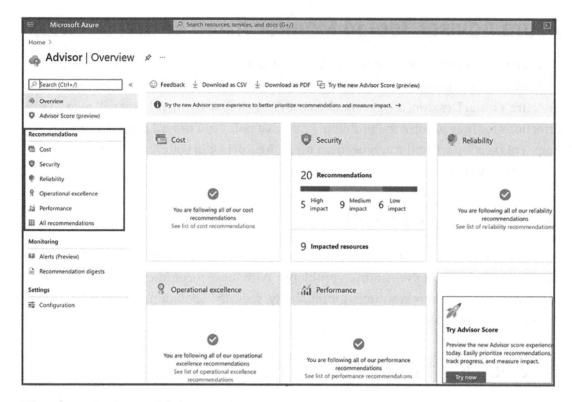

**Figure 4-40.** *Azure Advisor*

When you open Azure Advisor, you will see five different categories: Cost, Security, Reliability, Operational Excellence, and Performance.

---

**Tips**    For Azure Advisor, make sure to check your recommendations regularly. Azure Advisor updates its active recommendations multiple times per day. Reviewing the latest recommendations can help you avoid larger issues by assisting you in spotting and solving smaller ones. Constantly attempt to solve the issues with the highest priority level in Azure Advisor. High-priority issues are marked with red. Leaving high-priority recommendations unresolved can lead to problems down the line.

---

**Best practice:** If a recommendation seems less important, you can dismiss it or postpone it. But do not dismiss recommendations until you know why they are appearing and are sure they won't have a negative impact on you or your users.

# How Do I Resolve Azure Advisor Recommendations?

This section describes how you can resolve recommendations that appear in Azure Advisor for Azure Virtual Desktop. Resolving recommendations involve "No validation environment enabled," "Not enough production (non-validation) environments enabled," and "Not enough links are unblocked to successfully implement your VM." Here are the details for resolving each mentioned recommendation:

## No Validation Environment Enabled

This recommendation is under Operational Excellence. The recommendation should also show you a warning message like this: *You don't have a validation environment enabled in this subscription. When you made your host pools, you selected No for "Validation environment" in the Properties tab. To ensure business continuity through Azure Virtual Desktop service deployments, make sure you have at least one host pool with a validation environment where you can test for potential issues.*

You as an admin can make this warning message disappear by allowing a validation environment in one of your host pools. To enable the validation environment, follow these steps:

1. Log in to your Azure portal home page and choose the host pool you want to change.

2. Choose the host pool you want to change from a production environment to a validation environment.

3. In your host pool, select Properties on the left column. Next, scroll down until you see "Validation environment." Select Yes, and then select Apply.

---

**Note**   These changes won't make the warning disappear immediately. Allow enough time for the recommendations to disappear on their own.

---

As a best practice, you can check the Azure Advisor updates twice a day.

# Not Enough Production (Non-validation) Environments Enabled

Not enough production environment is another recommendation that appears under Operational Excellence. For this recommendation, the warning message appears because you have too many host pools in your validation environment or you don't have any production host pools. Microsoft recommends users have fewer than half of their host pools in a validation environment. To resolve this warning, follow these steps:

1. Log in to the Azure portal home page.

2. Choose the host pools you want to change from validation to production.

3. In your host pool, select the Properties tab in the column on the right side of the screen. Next, scroll down until you see "Validation environment." Select No, and then select Apply. See Figure 4-41.

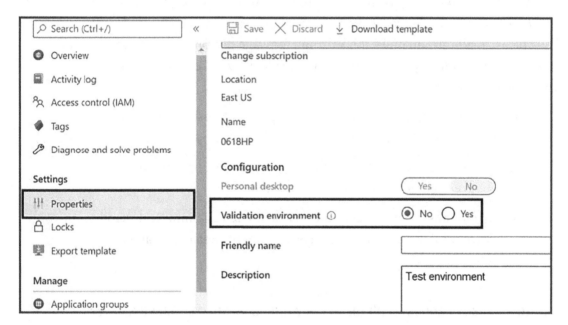

***Figure 4-41.*** *Nonproduction environment recommendation*

## Not Enough Links Are Unblocked to Successfully Implement Your VM

Another recommendation occurs under Operational Excellence. You need to unblock specific URLs to make sure that your virtual machine (VM) functions properly. You can find the list on the Safe URL list. If the URLs aren't unblocked, then your VM won't work properly. To resolve the recommendation, make sure you unblock all the URLs on the Safe URL list and use the Service Tag or FQDN tags to unblock URLs.

# Azure Virtual Desktop Common Issues and Their Troubleshooting

**Problem:** Unable to open remote virtual desktop client or its stops responding for Windows 10.

**Solution:** You as an admin can reset the user data from the About page or use the `msrdcw.exe /reset [/f]` command. Use this command to remove your user data, restore default settings, and unsubscribe from all workspaces.

**Problem:** Unable to open web client.

**Solution:** There are multiple reasons for being unable to open the web client.

   a.  As a first step, test your Internet connection by opening another website in your browser or using different browser.

   b.  Additionally, you can use `nslookup` to confirm DNS can resolve the FQDN or use a command prompt to run the command `nslookup rdweb.AVD.microsoft.com`.

   c.  You can try connecting with another client, for instance, Remote Desktop client for Windows 10 to see if you can open the web client.

**Problem:** The Virtual Desktop web client keeps prompting for credentials.

**Solution:** If the web client keeps prompting for credentials, do the following:

   1.  Check and confirm the web client URL is correct. If there is any typo, then correct the URL and try accessing the correct URL.

   2.  If the issue persists, then check and confirm that the credentials you are entering are for the Azure Virtual Desktop environment tied to the URL.

117

3. If issue persists, then clear the browser cookies and browser cache.

4. You can open your browser in private mode.

Troubleshoot application issues related to AVD using User Input Delay.

The User Input Delay counter can assist in discovering the root cause for bad end-user RDP experiences. Do the following if you see issues:

- First check the counter measures how long any user input remains in the queue before it is picked up by a process.

- The User Input Delay counter measures the max delta between the input being queued and when it's picked up by the app in a message loop. Figure 4-42 shows input relay.

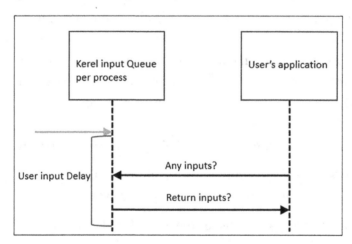

*Figure 4-42.* *AVD using input relay*

# Troubleshoot Graphic Performance and Quality Issues

You as an admin must know how to detect and troubleshoot experience quality issues with your remote desktop sessions. Counters are offered under the "RemoteFX Graphics" section of Performance Monitor. Below question assists you in identifying and resolving graphics-related performance bottlenecks during Remote Desktop Protocol (RDP) sessions using these counters.

- **How Do I Find the Remote Session Name?**

It is important to find the remote session name to find the graphics performance counters. Follow these steps to identify your instance of each counter:

1. First open the Windows command prompt from your remote session and then run the `qwinsta` command and find your session name.

If your session is hosted in a multisession virtual machine (VM), your instance of each counter is suffixed by the same number that suffixes your session name, such as rdp-tcp 37.

If your session is hosted in a VM that supports virtual graphics processing units (vGPUs), your instance of each counter is stored on the server instead of in your VM. Your counter instances include the VM name instead of the number in the session name, such as "Win8 Enterprise VM."

- **How Do I Access Performance Counters?**

Once you have decided your remote session name, then perform these steps to collect the *RemoteFX* Graphics performance counters for your remote session:

1. First click Start ➤ Administrative Tools ➤ Performance Monitor.

2. In the Performance Monitor dialog box, expand Monitoring Tools, select Performance Monitor, and then select Add.

3. In the Add Counters dialog box, from the Available Counters list, expand the section RemoteFX Graphics. Then choose the counters to be monitored.

4. In the "Instances of selected object" list, select the specific instances to be monitored for the selected counters and then select Add. To select all the available counter instances, select All instances, and then after adding the counters, select OK.

Finally, the chosen performance counters will appear on the Performance Monitor screen.

- **How Do I Diagnose the Graphics-Related Performance Issues?**

Remember, the graphics-related performance problem normally fall into four types: low frame rate, random stalls, high input latency, and poor frame quality.

To address low frame rate, random stalls, and high input latency, first check the Output Frames/Second counter. This measures the number of frames made available to the client. If this value is less than the Input Frames/Second counter, frames are being skipped. To identify the bottleneck, use the Frames Skipped/Second counters. There are three types of Frames Skipped/Second counters.

- Frames Skipped/Second (Insufficient Server Resources)

- Frames Skipped/Second (Insufficient Network Resources)

- Frames Skipped/Second (Insufficient Client Resources)

A high value for any of the Frames Skipped/Second counters implies that the problem is related to the resource the counter tracks. If the Output Frames/Second counter matches the Input Frames/Second counter, you will still notice unusual lag or stalling, and Average Encoding Time may be the culprit. Encoding is a synchronous process that occurs on the server in the single-session (vGPU) scenario and on the VM in the multisession scenario. Average Encoding Time should be less than 33 ms.

Since RDP supports an Average Encoding Time value of 33 ms, it supports an input frame rate up to 30 frames/second. Note that 33 ms is the maximum supported frame rate. In many cases, the frame rate experienced by the user will be lower, depending on how often a frame is provided to RDP by the source.

- **How to Check the Poor Frame Quality?**

Make use of the Frame Quality counter to diagnose frame quality issues. This counter expresses the quality of the output frame as a percentage of the quality of the source frame. The quality loss may be due to RemoteFX, or it may be inherent to the graphics source. If RemoteFX caused the quality loss, the issue may be a lack of network or server resources to send higher-fidelity content.

## Best Practices

Here are some best practices:

- It is a best practice to post issues or bugs on a tech community so that other admins in the field and community contributor can help solve the problem.

- Another best practice is to put forward new feature requirements or vote for existing new feature requests.

- When you make a post asking for help or propose a new feature, make sure you describe your topic in as much detail as possible.

# Summary

In this chapter, you learned about Azure Virtual Desktop network requirements, including implementing Azure virtual network connectivity, managing connectivity to the internet and on-premises networks from Azure Virtual Desktop, implementing and managing network security for AVD, and managing Azure Virtual Desktop session hosts by using Azure Bastion.

It is important to learn all about the network requirements for Azure Virtual Desktop so that you can keep the network ready before virtual desktop implementation.

# CHAPTER 5

# Implement and Manage Storage for Azure Virtual Desktop

In this chapter you will learn about the FSLogix tool, which can be used to store user profiles on remote storage so that they can get the same profile every time they log in to a pooled desktop.

Azure Virtual Desktop has pooled desktop offerings where multiple users can log in to the same back-end VM and use it as a virtual desktop. A pooled desktop is possible with Windows 10 multisession, which allows multiple sessions on the same VM. Azure provides multiple load balancing types to send user sessions to the back-end VMs, which means the user session can go to any of the VMs available in the pooled desktop pool. FSLogix allows admins to configure remote user profile storage so that the user can get the same profile and desktop experience on any back-end VM they log in to.

## Configure Storage for FSLogix Components

FSLogix is the tool used to manage user profiles for *pooled* desktops since pooled desktops are not persistent desktops. FSLogix allows you to configure the user profile location on the desktop, and the user profile gets attached to the desktop whenever the user logs in to the desktop. Pooled desktops can have multiple session hosts, so you must make sure the FSLogix configuration is the same on all session hosts under the same host pool.

There are multiple ways to implement the FSLogix configuration on the session host, but the easiest and preferred way is to configure the FSLogix configuration in the image

© Arun Sabale and Balu N Ilag 2022
A. Sabale and B. N. Ilag, *Microsoft Azure Virtual Desktop Guide*,
https://doi.org/10.1007/978-1-4842-8063-8_5

itself and create different images for each host pool so that each image will have host pool-specific FSLogix and application configuration.

You have to provide the user profile storage account details as part of the FSLogix configuration, so you must create a storage account with the required configuration before you can capture an image for each pooled host pool.

The following are a few recommendations for storage accounts for the FSLogix user profile:

- Keep a separate storage account for each pooled host pool's user profile in each region.

- Use a high IOPS/premium storage account for the user profile.

- Join the storage account to an AD DS domain.

- Always create an AD security group for each host pool and assign it to the Storage File Data SMB Share Contributor role so that authorized users can read/write profile data from a storage account.

- Restrict user profile storage access to a specific VNet/subnet.

- Enable storage account access over private endpoints to a specific VNet.

- The same type of host pool in the same region (i.e., belongs to the same BU) can use the same storage account for the user profile as far as there is no compliance/InfoSec requirement.

- Consider GEO replication to a DR region if you're planning to enable DR for the pooled host pool. Premium file storage does not support GEO replication, so if you want to implement DR, then you have to select the standard storage account tier or use the FSLogix cloud cache to store the user profile on multiple storage accounts in different regions.

Follow these steps to create a user profile storage account:

1. Log in to the Azure portal and select the correct directory and subscription where you want to create the AVD host pool and desktops. Make sure you have the correct permission (contributor or owner) to create the storage account. See Figure 5-1.

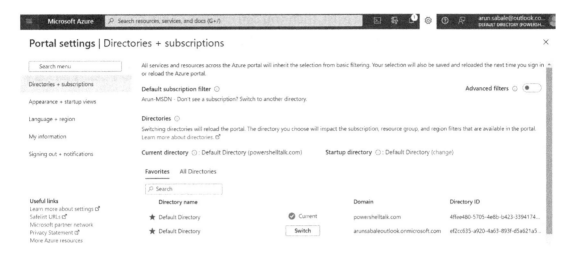

**Figure 5-1.** *Azure Virtual Desktop, selecting a subscription*

2. Search for *storage account* in the top search bar. See Figure 5-2.

**Figure 5-2.** *Azure Virtual Desktop, storage account search*

3. Click the Create option to create a new storage account. See Figure 5-3.

**Figure 5-3.** *Azure Virtual Desktop user profile storage account creation*

4. Select the correct subscription and resource group names from the drop-down where you want to create the AVD desktops. If the

resource group does not exist, then you can create a new resource
group by clicking the Create new option. See Figure 5-4.

***Figure 5-4.*** *AVD user profile storage account creation page*

5. Scroll down and provide the storage account details such as the
name, region, performance (SKU), account type, and redundancy.
The following are the recommended values for each field:

*Name*: As per your organization's standards, but Azure accepts
only 24 lowercase characters and numbers.

*Region*: This is the same as the AVD host pool.

*Performance (SKU)*: Premium (no GEO replication supported).

*Premium account type*: File share.

*Redundancy*: Zone redundant (ZRS).

Click the Next button once you have filled in all the details.
See Figure 5-5.

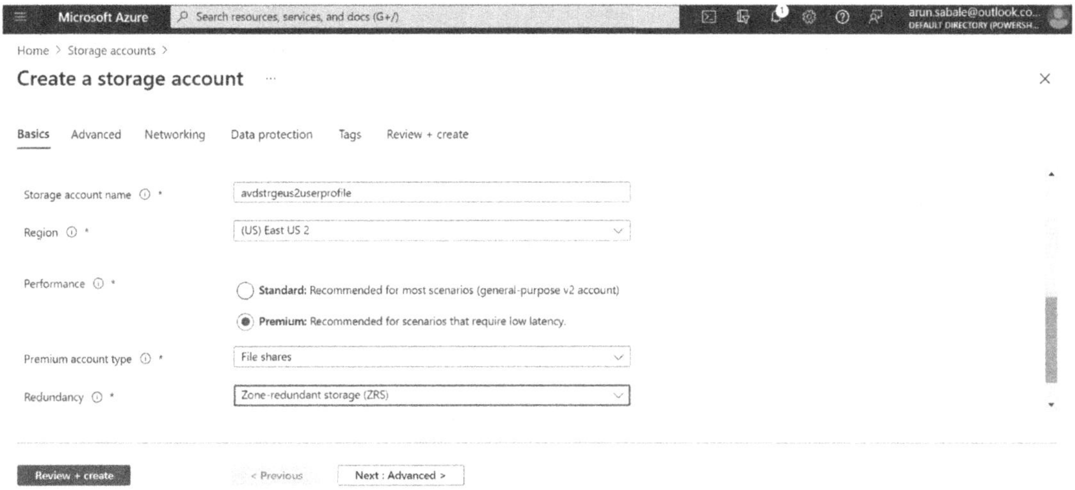

**Figure 5-5.** *AVD user profile storage account creation, Basic tab*

6.  You can verify the options available on the Advanced tab and
    make sure they align with your organization's requirements.
    Click the Next button once you have filled in all the details. See
    Figure 5-6.

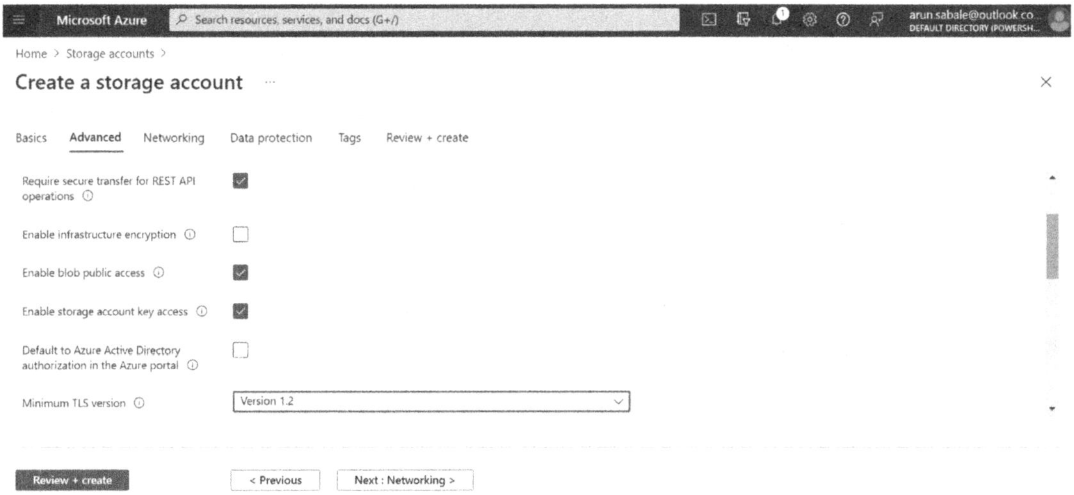

**Figure 5-6.** *AVD user profile storage account creation, Advanced tab*

---

**Note**    By default, Azure encrypts the storage account data at rest. Infrastructure encryption adds a second layer of encryption to your storage account data.

---

7.  Select "Private endpoint" on the Networking tab and click the "Add private endpoint" option. See Figure 5-7.

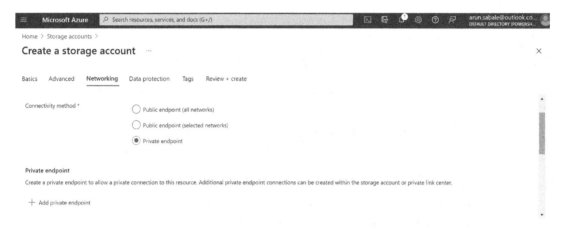

***Figure 5-7.***  *AVD user profile storage account creation, Networking tab*

8.  Select the subscription, resource group, region, endpoint name, storage sub resource (must be a file), and VNet/subnet in the private endpoint pop-up.

    *Endpoint name*: As per your organization's naming standards.

    *Storage subresource*: This must be a file.

    *VNet/subnet*: This is the same VNet where you want to create a pooled host pool.

    Click OK and the Next button once you have filled in all the details. See Figure 5-8.

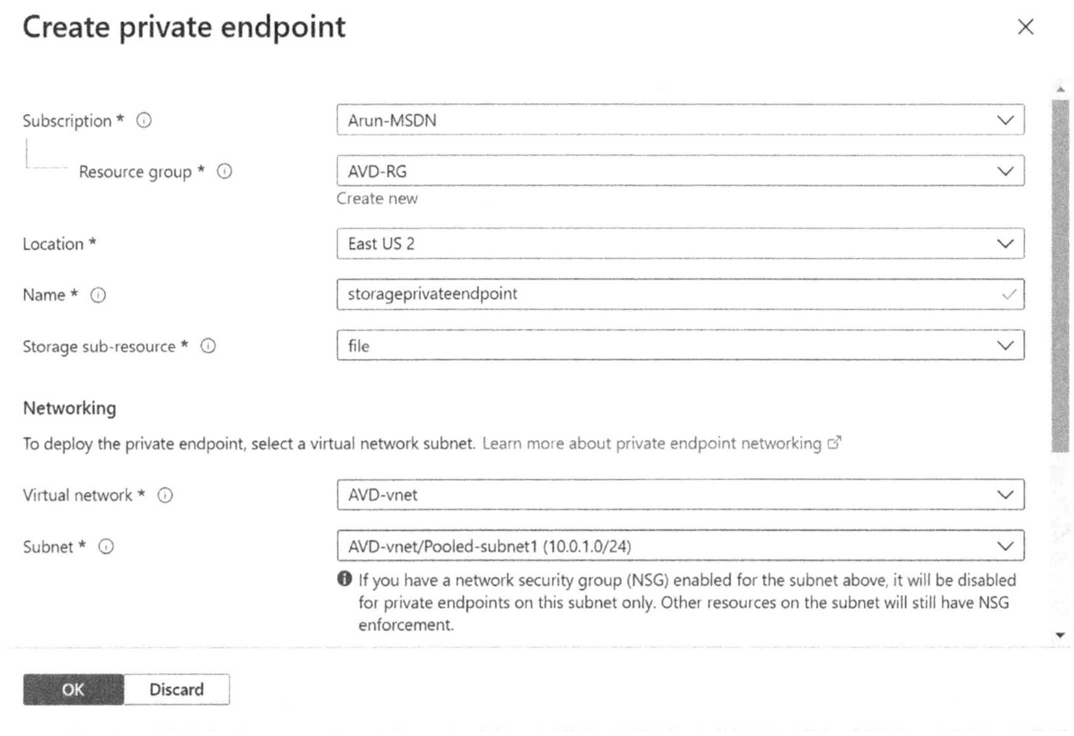

## Create private endpoint                                                    ✕

| | |
|---|---|
| Subscription * ⓘ | Arun-MSDN ⌄ |
| Resource group * ⓘ | AVD-RG ⌄ |
| | Create new |
| Location * | East US 2 ⌄ |
| Name * ⓘ | storageprivateendpoint ✓ |
| Storage sub-resource * ⓘ | file ⌄ |

**Networking**

To deploy the private endpoint, select a virtual network subnet. Learn more about private endpoint networking ☐

| | |
|---|---|
| Virtual network * ⓘ | AVD-vnet ⌄ |
| Subnet * ⓘ | AVD-vnet/Pooled-subnet1 (10.0.1.0/24) ⌄ |

❶ If you have a network security group (NSG) enabled for the subnet above, it will be disabled for private endpoints on this subnet only. Other resources on the subnet will still have NSG enforcement.

| OK | Discard |
|---|---|

**Figure 5-8.**  *AVD user profile storage account creation, Private endpoint creation*

9.  Select "Enable soft delete for file shares" if you want to keep the deleted files for specific days. Click Next and add the tag details as per your organization's standards. Click the "Review + create" button once you have entered all the required information. See Figure 5-9.

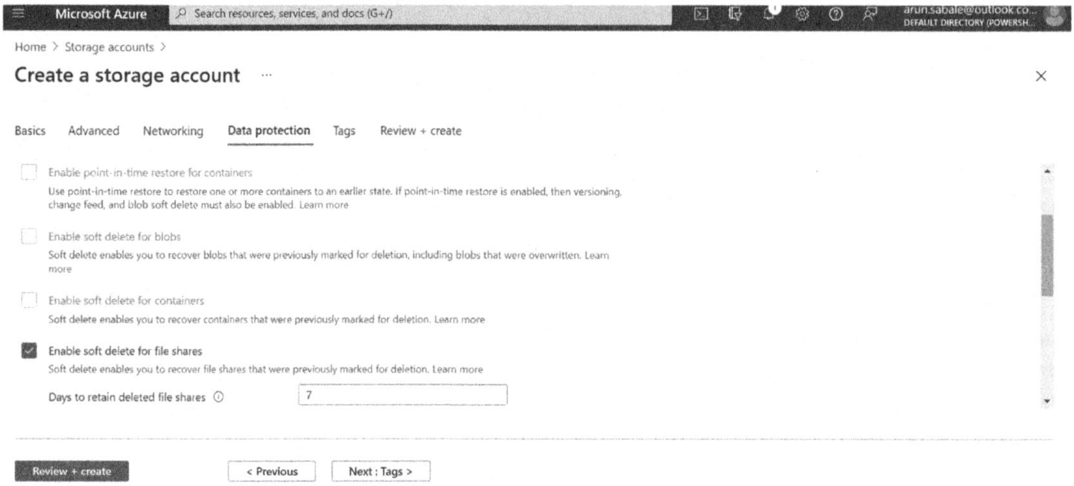

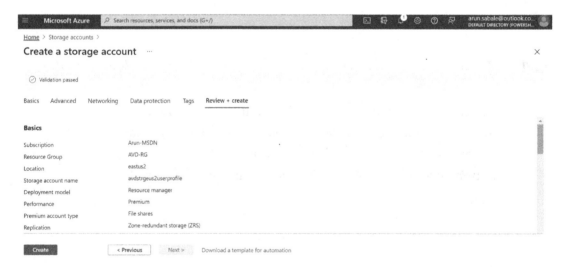

**Figure 5-9.** *AVD user profile storage account creation, Data protection tab*

10.   Click Create once the validation is completed. See Figure 5-10.

**Figure 5-10.** *AVD user profile storage account creation, creating and reviewing*

11.   Click "Go to resource" to open the storage account's Overview page. See Figure 5-11.

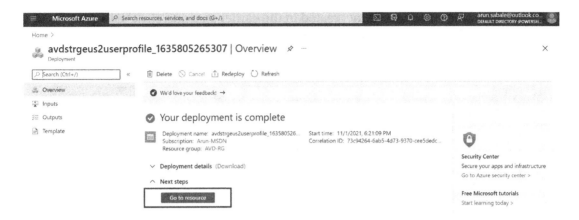

***Figure 5-11.*** *AVD user profile storage account creation, deployment status*

12. Verify all the information on the Overview page such as the name, storage account SKU, and region. See Figure 5-12.

***Figure 5-12.*** *AVD user profile storage account, Overview page*

# Create File Shares

File shares need to be created once the storage account is ready. FSLogix will be using the Azure storage account file share to store user profiles in the storage account.

Follow these steps to create file shares in the storage account created in the earlier step:

1.  Go to the storage account created in the earlier step and click "File share" in the left pane. Click "+ File share" to add an additional share. See Figure 5-13.

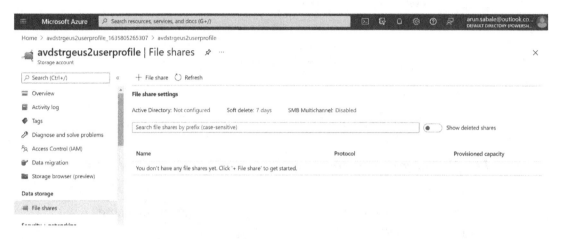

***Figure 5-13.***  *AVD user profile storage file share creation*

2.  Enter the file share name and size, and click the Create button in the file share pop-up. See Figure 5-14.

---

**Note**    File share names can contain only lowercase letters, numbers, and hyphens, and they must begin and end with a letter or a number. The name cannot contain two consecutive hyphens.

The minimum share size is 100 GB, but provision more capacity to get more performance (as of November 2021).

---

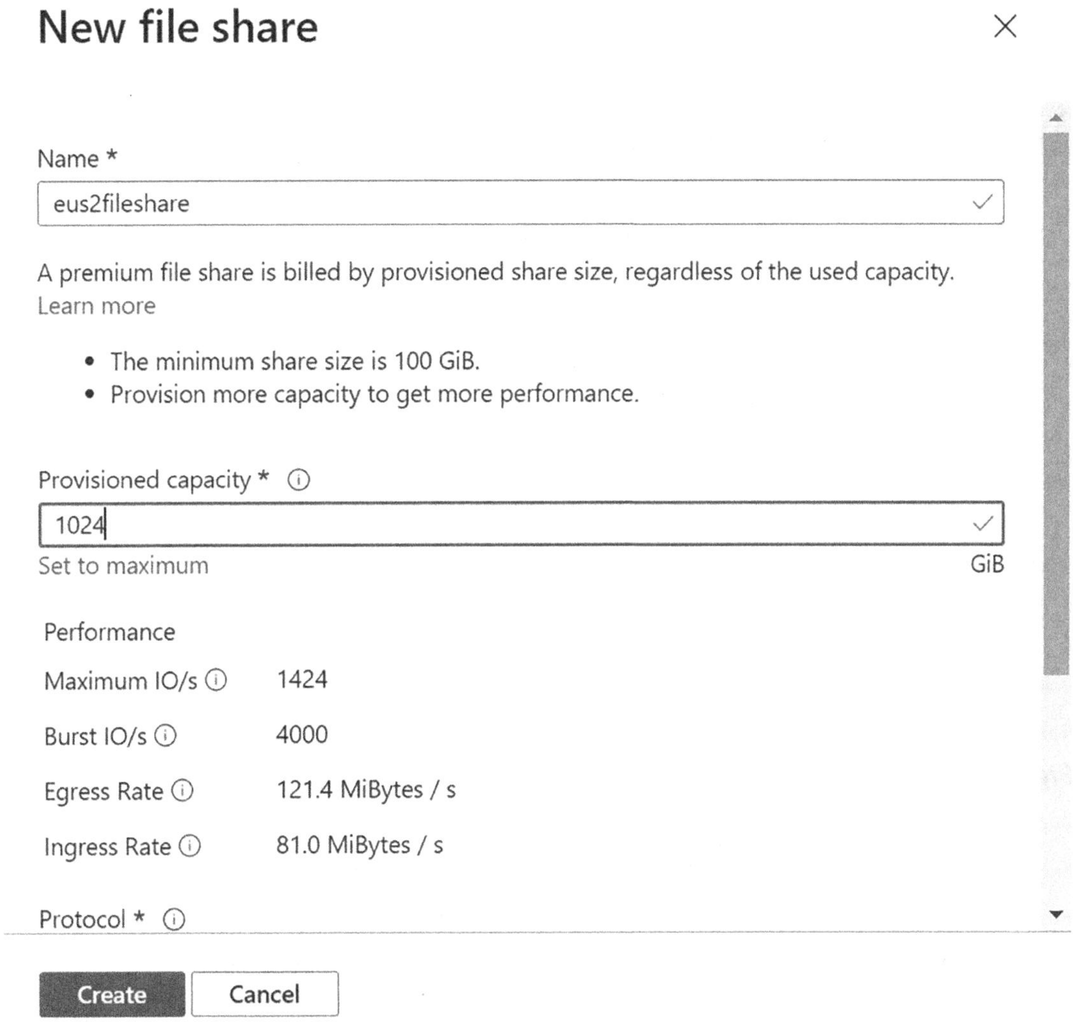

# New file share                                                    ✕

Name *

| eus2fileshare                                                    ✓ |

A premium file share is billed by provisioned share size, regardless of the used capacity.
Learn more

- The minimum share size is 100 GiB.
- Provision more capacity to get more performance.

Provisioned capacity *  ⓘ

| 1024|                                                            ✓ |
Set to maximum                                                       GiB

Performance

Maximum IO/s ⓘ      1424

Burst IO/s ⓘ        4000

Egress Rate ⓘ       121.4 MiBytes / s

Ingress Rate ⓘ      81.0 MiBytes / s

Protocol *  ⓘ

[ Create ]  [ Cancel ]

**Figure 5-14.**  *AVD user profile storage file share creation, new share*

3.  Once the file share is ready, it will be visible under the "File share" option on the storage account. See Figure 5-15.

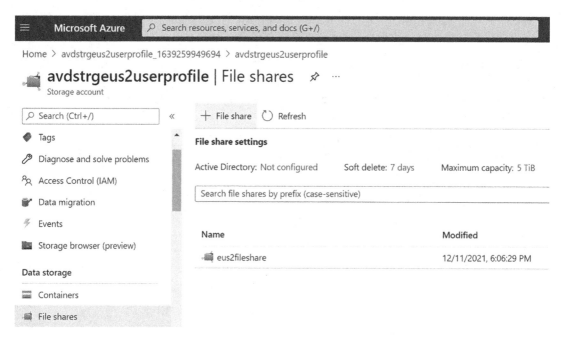

***Figure 5-15.*** *AVD user profile storage file share, new share creation*

4.  Click the file share name, and you will be able to see the permission error in Figure 5-16 as the file share is locked to AVD Azure VNet. Resources/VMs from that VNet instance can access only the file share. It is always recommended to enable the private endpoint for the storage account to the AVD VNet, so the file share will be accessible directly from AVD VM over a private endpoint, and the traffic will not go over the Internet.

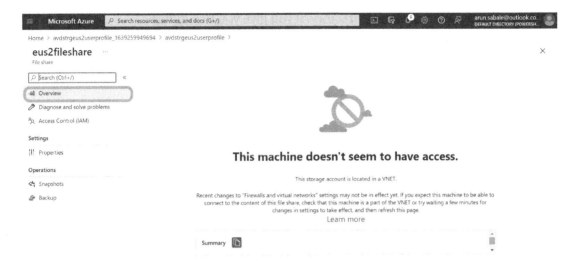

*Figure 5-16.* *AVD user profile storage file share, Overview page*

5.  Now you can go back to the "File share" option under the storage
    account to configure Active Directory for the file share. Click
    Active Directory on the right side, as shown in Figure 5-17.

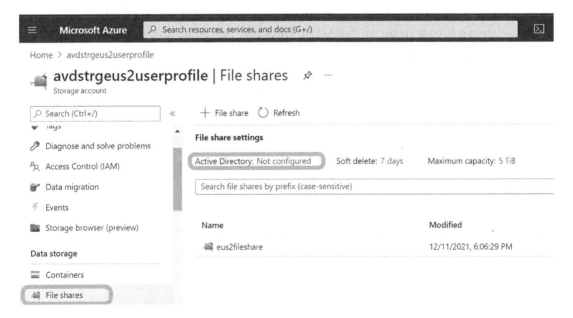

*Figure 5-17.* *AVD user profile storage file share, domain join*

6. Once you click Active Directory, it will give you two different Active Directory options, as shown in Figure 5-18.

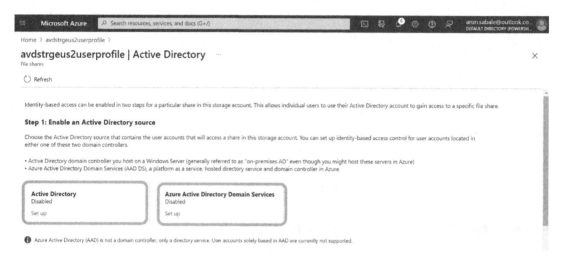

***Figure 5-18.*** *AVD user profile storage file share, domain join options*

7. Select the appropriate Active Directory that you are using and click the Setup button. If you are using Azure AD domain services, then it is easy to set up the Active Directory option for the storage account file share, as shown in Figure 5-19.

***Figure 5-19.*** *AVD user profile storage file share, domain join to Azure ADDS*

8.  Once you enable Azure ADDS, then you will be able to see the
    screen in Figure 5-20. Note that you can use/configure only one
    AD (Azure ADDS or on-premises AD).

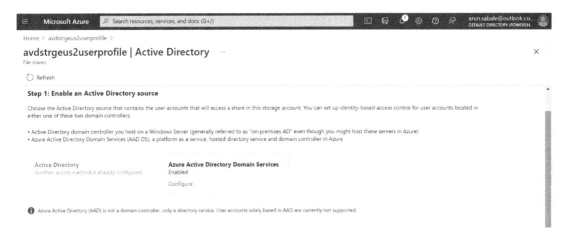

***Figure 5-20.***  *AVD user profile storage file share, domain join status*

9.  Additionally, if you have an Active Directory user and a computer
    console connected to your Azure AD domain, then you can
    check the Azure storage file share account/object under the
    AzureFilesConfig OU. See Figure 5-21.

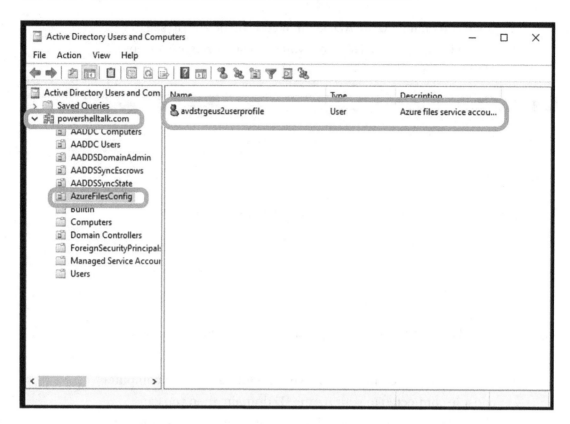

***Figure 5-21.***   *AVD user profile storage file share, domain join object*

10.  If you are using an on-premises Active Directory Service
     (ADDS), then you need the AzFilesHybrid module (`https://`
     `github.com/Ar-Sa/azure-files-samples/tree/master/`
     `AzFilesHybrid` ) on the domain join so that you can run the `Join-`
     `AzStorageAccountForAuth` command to domain-join the file
     share. The following is the script you can run from any domain-
     joined VM (or download the PowerShell code from `https://`
     `github.com/Ar-Sa/Arun/blob/master/Powershell/Azure%20`
     `storage%20account%20file%20share%20domain%20join/set-`
     `AzStorageDomainJoin.ps1`):

```
# Change the execution policy to unblock importing AzFilesHybrid.
psm1 module

Set-ExecutionPolicy -ExecutionPolicy Unrestricted -Scope CurrentUser

# Navigate to where AzFilesHybrid is unzipped and stored and run to copy
the files into your path
.\CopyToPSPath.ps1

# Import AzFilesHybrid module

Import-Module -Name AzFilesHybrid

# Login with an Azure AD credential that has either storage account owner
or contributer Azure role assignment
# If you are logging into an Azure environment other than Public
(ex. AzureUSGovernment) you will need to specify that.
# See https://docs.microsoft.com/azure/azure-government/documentation-
government-get-started-connect-with-ps
# for more information.

Connect-AzAccount

# Define parameters, $StorageAccountName currently has a maximum limit of
15 characters

$SubscriptionId = "<Subscription id of storage account>"
$ResourceGroupName = "<Storage account resource group name>"
$StorageAccountName = "<Storage account name>"
$DomainAccountType = "ComputerAccount"

# Default is set as ComputerAccount
# If you don't provide the OU name as an input parameter, the AD identity
that represents the storage account is created under the root directory.

$OuDistinguishedName = "<OU path in format -  ou=workstations,Dc=abc,
dc=org>"
```

```
# Specify the encryption agorithm used for Kerberos authentication. Default
is configured as "'RC4','AES256'" which supports both 'RC4' and 'AES256'
encryption.

$EncryptionType = "<AES256|RC4|AES256,RC4>"

# Select the target subscription for the current session

Select-AzSubscription -SubscriptionId $SubscriptionId

# Register the target storage accountc with your active directory
environment under the target OU (for example: specify the OU with Name
as "UserAccounts" or DistinguishedName as "OU=UserAccounts,DC=CONTOSO,
DC=COM").
# You can use to this PowerShell cmdlet: Get-ADOrganizationalUnit to
find the Name and DistinguishedName of your target OU. If you are
using the OU Name, specify it with -OrganizationalUnitName as shown
below. If you are using the OU DistinguishedName, you can set it with
-OrganizationalUnitDistinguishedName. You can choose to provide one of the
two names to specify the target OU.
# You can choose to create the identity that represents the storage account
as either a Service Logon Account or Computer Account (default parameter
value), depends on the AD permission you have and preference.
# Run Get-Help Join-AzStorageAccountForAuth for more details on
this cmdlet.

Join-AzStorageAccountForAuth `
        -ResourceGroupName $ResourceGroupName `
        -StorageAccountName $StorageAccountName `
        -DomainAccountType $DomainAccountType `
        -OrganizationalUnitDistinguishedName $OuDistinguishedName `
        -EncryptionType $EncryptionType

#Run the command below if you want to enable AES 256 authentication. If you
plan to use RC4, you can skip this step.
```

```
Update-AzStorageAccountAuthForAES256 -ResourceGroupName $ResourceGroupName
-StorageAccountName $StorageAccountName

#You can run the Debug-AzStorageAccountAuth cmdlet to conduct a set
of basic checks on your AD configuration with the logged on AD user.
This cmdlet is supported on AzFilesHybrid v0.1.2+ version. For more
details on the checks performed in this cmdlet, see Azure Files Windows
troubleshooting guide.
```

11.  The next step is to create the ADDS group for AVD users and
     assign permissions on the file share.

12.  If you are using the Azure AD domain service, then you can create
     a security group in Azure AD itself, and it will sync with Azure
     ADDS. Go to Azure AD and click Groups. On the All Groups plane
     click "New group." See Figure 5-22.

***Figure 5-22.***  *AVD user profile permission, user group creation*

13.  Enter the group name and select the correct members to whom
     you want to give access to the AVD desktop. See Figure 5-23.

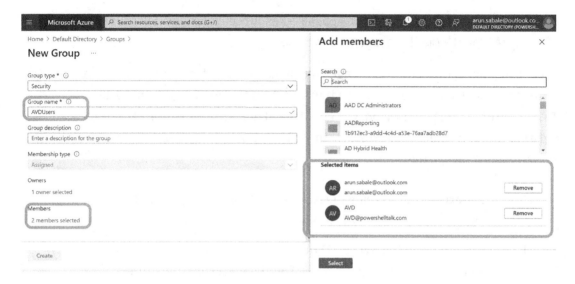

***Figure 5-23.*** *AVD user profile, group creation*

14. The group will be also available in the Azure ADDS Active Directory User and Computer (ADUC) console. See Figure 5-24.

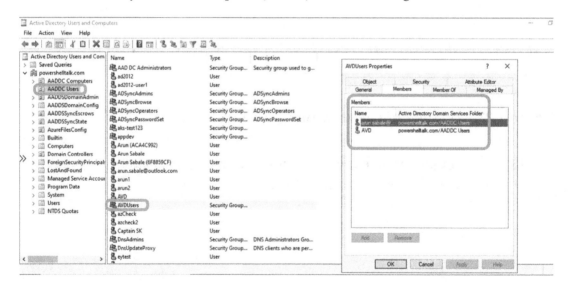

***Figure 5-24.*** *AVD user profile, verify group creation*

15. If you are using on-premises ADDS, then simply go to the ADDS ADUC console and create new group, and it will sync with Azure AD.

16. Go to the file share, select Access control (IAM), click Add, and select "Add role assignment." See Figure 5-25.

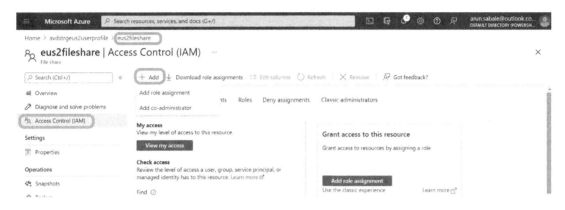

***Figure 5-25.*** *AVD user profile permission on file share*

17. Select the Storage File Data SMB Share Contributor role, and click Next. See Figure 5-26.

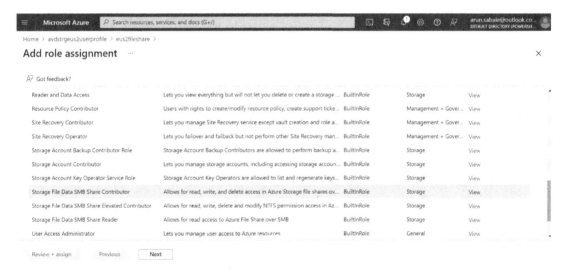

***Figure 5-26.*** *AVD user profile permission on file share, SMB contributor*

18. Select the AVD group we created in an earlier step, and click Select. See Figure 5-27.

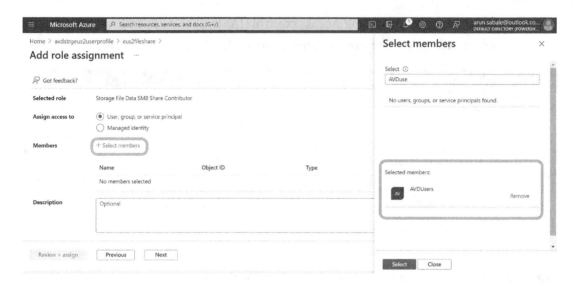

***Figure 5-27.*** *AVD user profile permission on file share, select a group*

19.   Click "Review + assign." See Figure 5-28 and Figure 5-29.

***Figure 5-28.*** *AVD user profile permission on file share, review and assign final page*

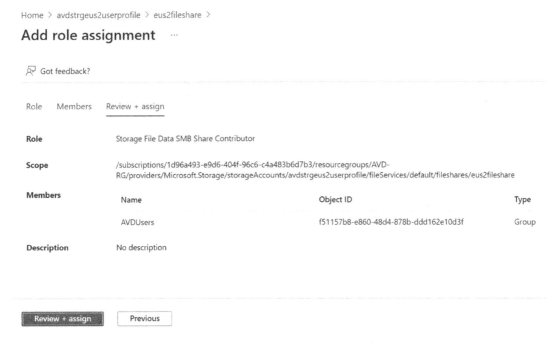

***Figure 5-29.*** *AVD user profile permission on file share, review and assign*

# Summary

In this chapter, you learned about creating an Azure storage account and configuring the Azure file share for a user profile. Additionally, you can use the Azure NetApp for your user profile instead of the Azure file share, but you have to make sure you are adding share permissions for the AVD group we created.

# CHAPTER 6

# Implement and Manage FSLogix

In this chapter, you will learn about FSLogix, which is used to store user profiles on remote storage. It is important to understand the FSLogix options so that you can select an appropriate option for your requirements. In this chapter, you will be planning, installing, and configuring FSLogix for pooled desktops and all the profile options such as containers and cloud caches to store the user profile on remote storage.

User profile storage is important in a pooled desktop, because user sessions can go to any back-end session host (Azure VM) based on the load balancing set on a pooled desktop; therefore, user profiles need to be stored on remote storage so that the user can get the same profile/desktop experience on any session host.

Let's get started with planning FSLogix for Azure Virtual Desktop (AVD).

## Plan for FSLogix

FSLogix enhances and simplifies nonpersistent Windows computing environments. AVD recommends FSLogix profile containers as a user profile solution. FSLogix is designed to roam user profiles in Azure Virtual Desktop by storing a complete user profile in a single container on remote storage. A user profile contains data elements about an individual, including configuration information such as desktop settings, persistent network connections, and application settings. At the time of user sign-in, this container dynamically gets attached to the Azure Virtual Desktop session host using a natively supported virtual hard disk (VHD) and Hyper-V virtual hard disk (VHDX). The user profile is immediately available and appears in the system exactly like a native user profile at the time of sign-in.

© Arun Sabale and Balu N Ilag 2022
A. Sabale and B. N. Ilag, *Microsoft Azure Virtual Desktop Guide*,
https://doi.org/10.1007/978-1-4842-8063-8_6

By default, the Windows operating system creates a local user profile that is tightly integrated with the OS, but FSLogix allows you to use a user profile on a remote file share/storage. See Figure 6-1.

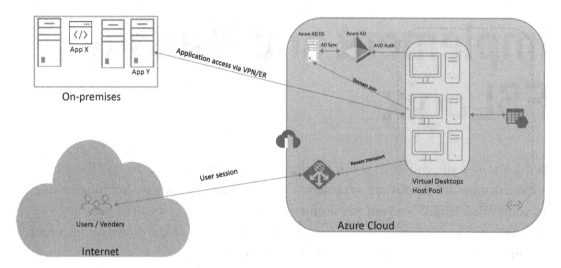

*Figure 6-1.*  *FSLogix remote user profile on Azure storage*

User profiles can be copied to and from the network when a user signs in and out of AVD, but user profiles can often be large, and sign-in and sign-out times often became unacceptable due to coping profiles to network storage. That's where FSLogix helps to redirect a profile instead of copying it from the network. FSLogix containers redirect user profiles to a network location, and user profiles are placed in VHDx files so that they can easily be mounted at runtime/sign-in time. Mounting and using a profile on the network eliminates the delays often associated with solutions that copy files.

# Are Multiple User Profile Connections Possible?

Having concurrent or multiple connections to user profiles means the user is connected to multiple hosts/sessions and using the same user profile stored on remote storage. Concurrent or multiple connections are not recommended in Azure Virtual Desktop, because they may result in temp profiles on a concurrent session and lead to data loss. The best practice is to create a different user profile storage for each host pool. Users cannot have concurrent sessions on the same host pool, so you can use only one profile storage per host pool.

# Profile Storage Performance Requirements

FSLogix depends on the storage type used for the user profile VHDx files, as well as on the host pool location and storage location.

Profile storage IOPS needs to be considered and calculated properly for all users while selecting profile storage. For example, you may need around 1,000 input/output operations per second (IOPS) for 100 users, and around 5,000 IOPS during sign-in and sign-out. If you increase the number of users or if many users log in during a short period of time creating a log-in storm, then it will impact the Azure Virtual Desktop performance.

# Storage Options for FSLogix Profile Containers

Azure offers multiple storage solutions that you can use to store your FSLogix user profile container. Azure recommends storing FSLogix profile containers on Azure Files or Azure NetApp Files for most customer scenarios. Check Chapter 3 for the difference between Azure Files and Azure NetApp Files before you select the profile storage solution for your organization.

Azure NetApp Files has been proven to be a great managed storage solution for FSLogix user profiles and Azure Virtual Desktop. The low latency and high amount of IOPS is a great combination for enterprises at scale.

# Azure File Share Best Practices for Pooled User Profile Storage

Azure Virtual Desktop offers full control over the size, type, and count of VMs so that the customer can configure Azure Virtual Desktop based on their requirements, but at the same time the customer has to follow all the best practices for a better user experience. See Figure 6-2. The following are the best practices for using an Azure file share for pooled user profile storage.

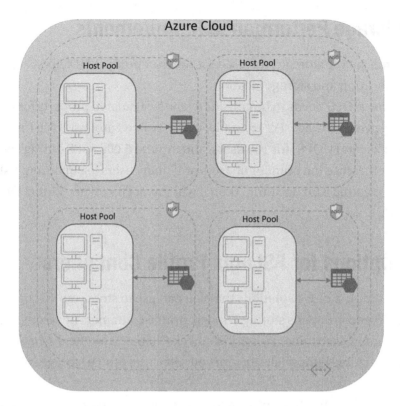

***Figure 6-2.*** *FSLogix user profile storage best practices (profile storage per host pool)*

- The Azure Files storage account must be in the same region (and data center) as the session host VMs.

- Azure Virtual Desktop users must have the minimum Storage File Data SMB Share Contributor permissions on Azure Files (refer to Chapter 5 for details).

- Each session host from the same host pool must be built of the same type, size, and master image.

- Exclude the VHD(x) files for profile containers from antivirus scanning to avoid performance bottlenecks.

- Separate the user profile storage per host pool, while having two active sessions.

# Install and Configure FSLogix

FSLogix is mandatory for a pooled host pool with the Windows 10 multisession operating system. You can install FSLogix in the existing Windows 10 multisession golden image, and you can also use a marketplace multisession image, create a VM, and proceed with the FSLogix installation before you start creating a pooled host pool. You will learn how to install FSLogix and capture the image in this and the next chapter. You have to create a VM using Windows 10 multisession image (marketplace or existing) before we can get started with the FSLogix installation. These are the steps to create a VM and install FSLogix:

1. Log in to the Azure portal and click "Create a resource" to create a new VM. See Figure 6-3.

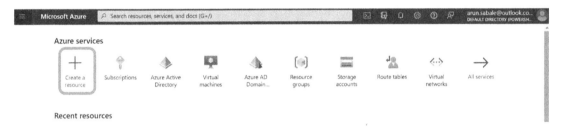

***Figure 6-3.*** *FSLogix installation, image VM creation*

2. Click Compute and then select "Virtual machine." See Figure 6-4.

***Figure 6-4.*** *FSLogix installation, image VM creation- select resource type*

3.  Select a subscription and resource group where you create
    an image and enter all the information such as the VM name
    and region. Select an image for the Windows 10 enterprise
    multisession. See Figure 6-5.

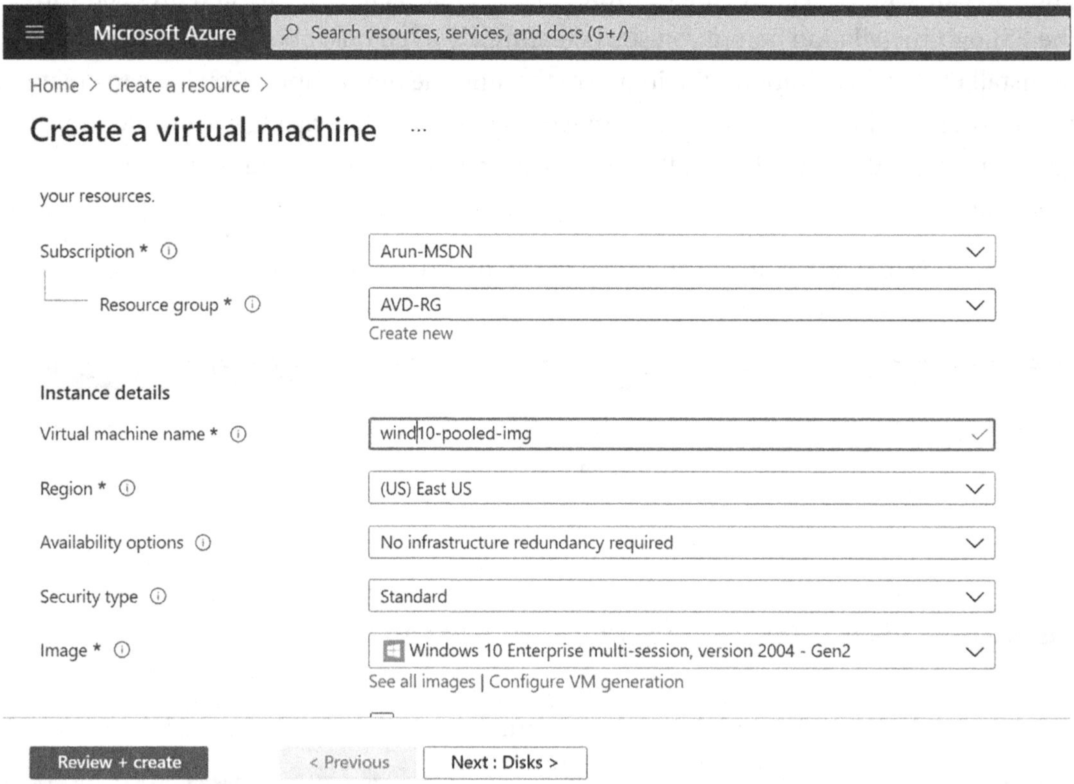

*Figure 6-5.* *FSLogix installation, image VM creation page- virtual machine*
*information*

4.  On the same page, select the size and enter a username and
    password for the VM. See Figure 6-6.

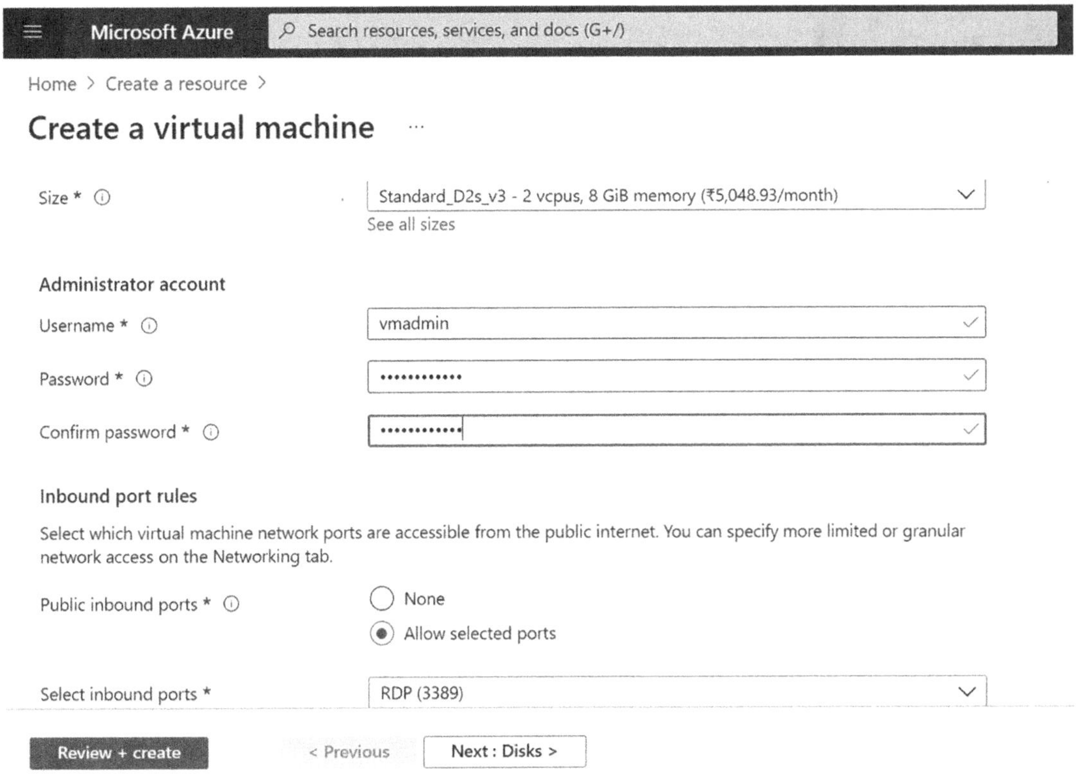

**Figure 6-6.**  *FSLogix installation, image VM creation page 2*

5.  Select the inbound port to 3389, which is required for you to
    connect to the VM and install FSLogix. Select the Licensing
    checkbox and click the Next button. See Figure 6-7.

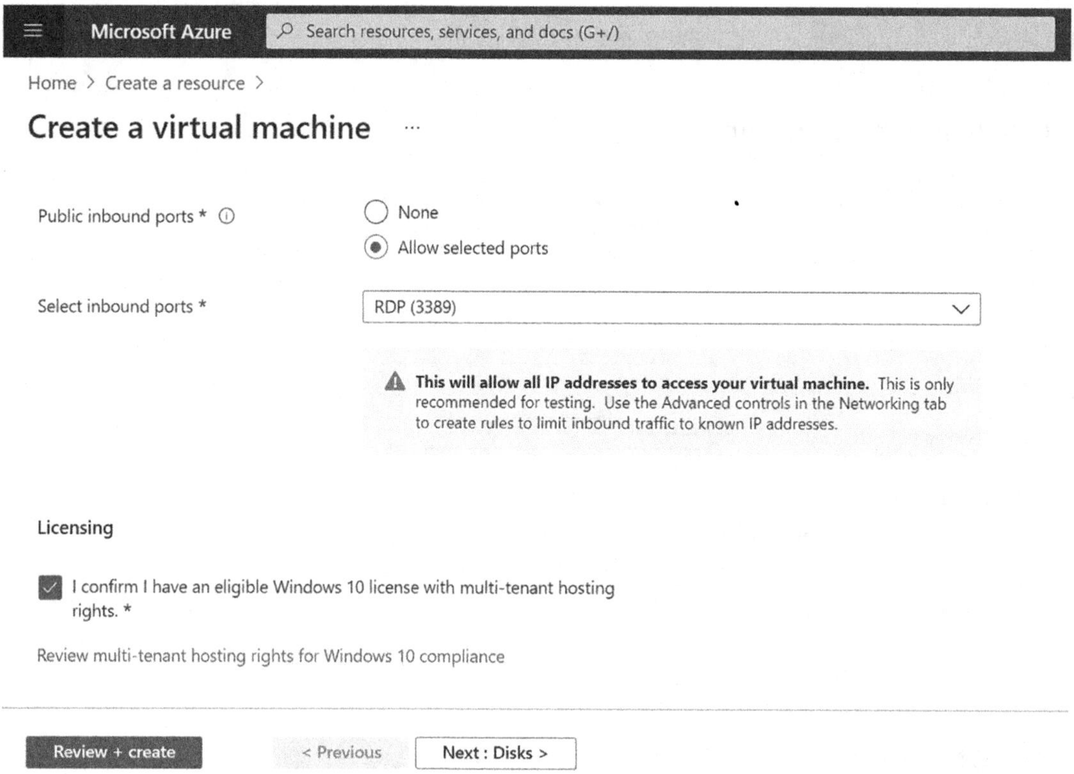

**Figure 6-7.** *FSLogix installation, image VM creation, NSG tab*

6.   On the Disks page, select the HDD type and click Next. See
     Figure 6-8.

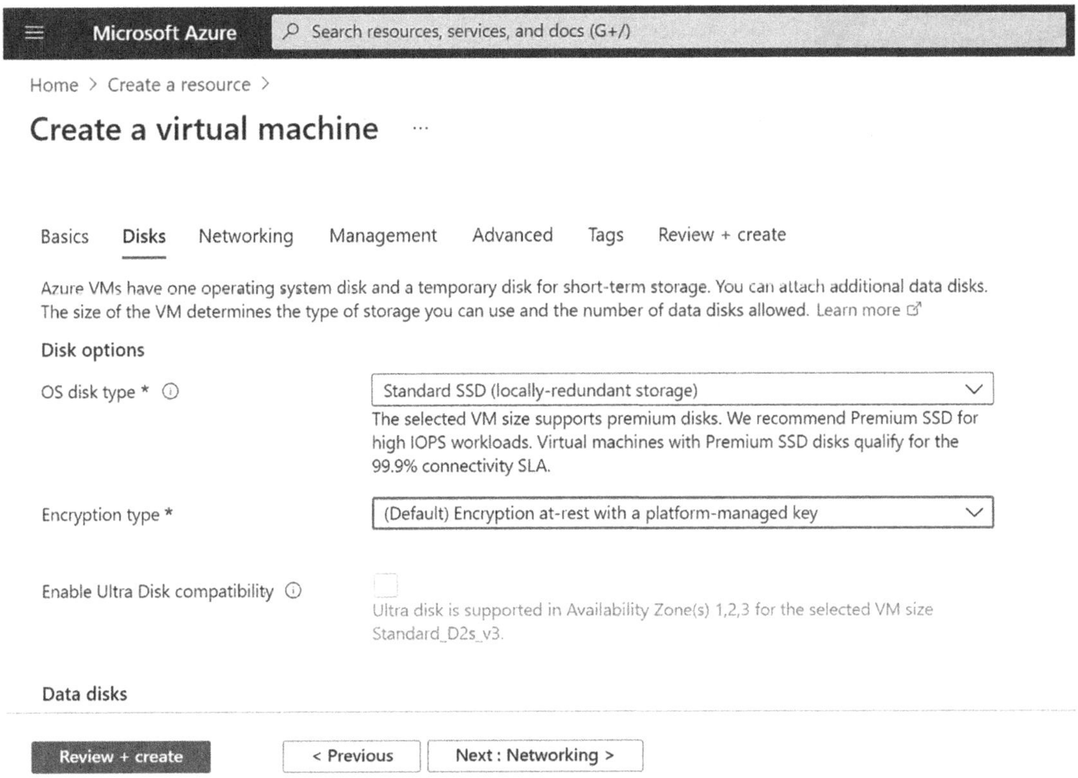

**Figure 6-8.** *FSLogix installation, image VM creation, Disks tab*

7.  On the Networking tab, select the existing VNet or subnet or create a new VNet in case you want to keep the image in an isolated environment. Click the Next button. See Figure 6-9.

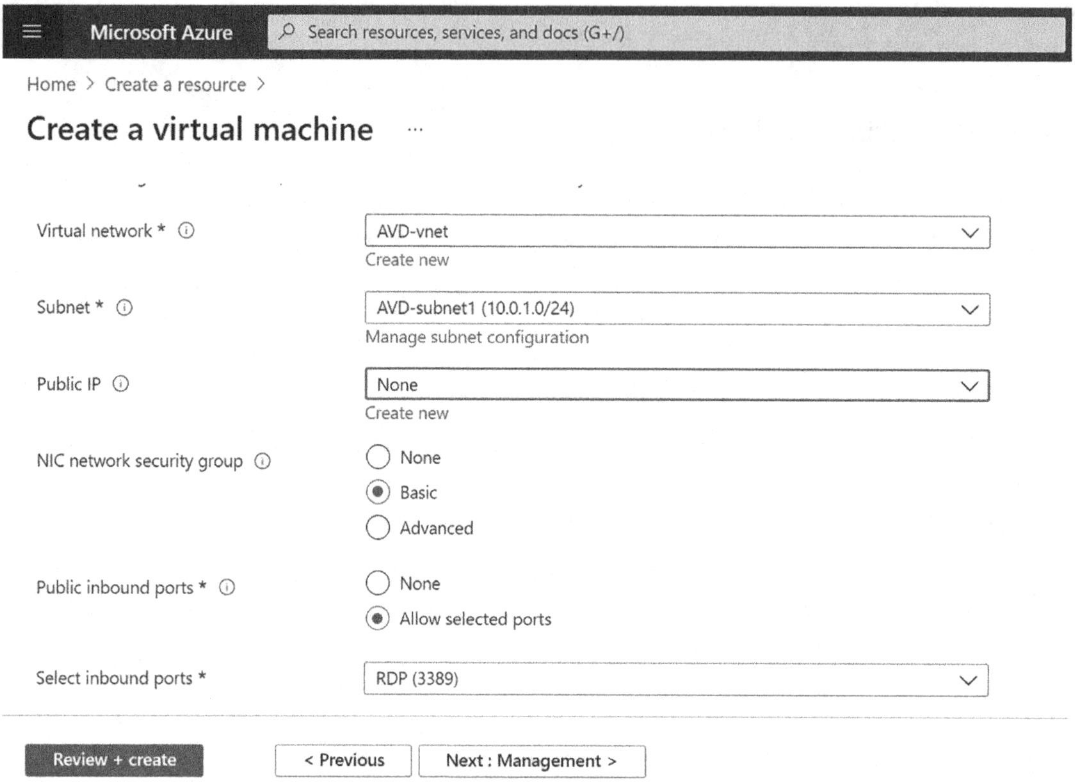

**Figure 6-9.** *FSLogix installation, image VM creation, Networking tab*

8. On the Management tab, deselect "Enable auto-shutdown" so that the VM will not shut down during the image creation process. Keep the auto updates enabled so that the image will have all the updates installed. Click Next once you're done with all the changes. See Figure 6-10.

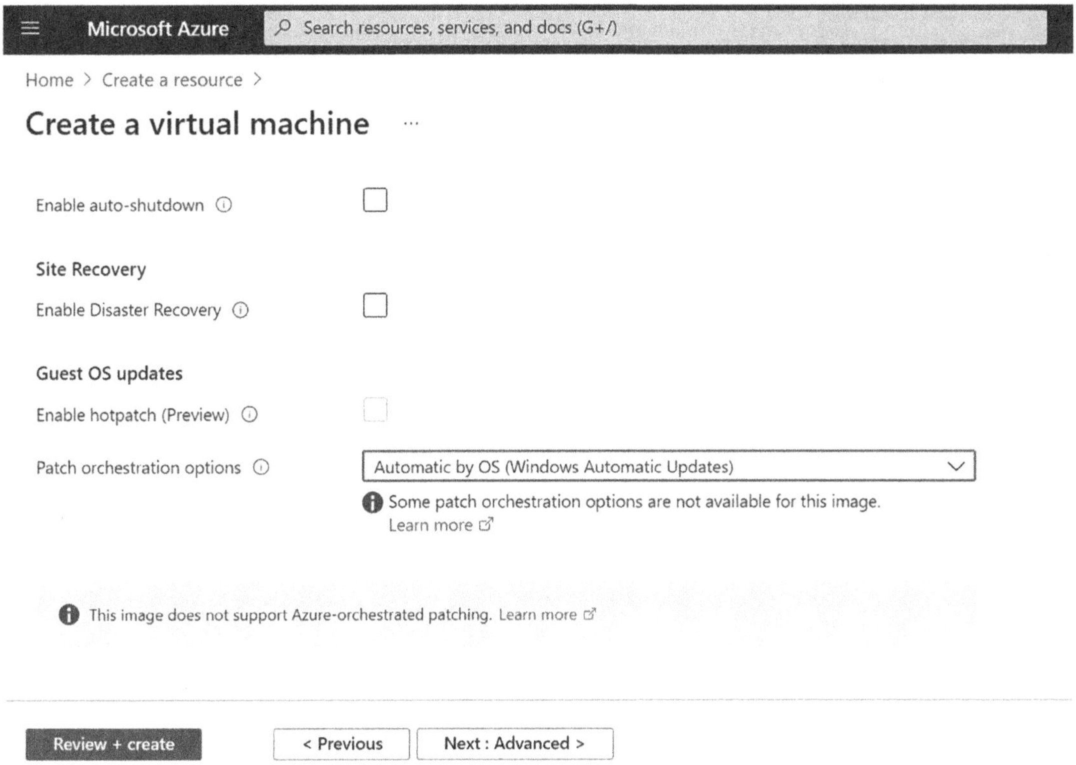

**Figure 6-10.** *FSLogix installation, image VM creation, Management tab*

9. You can keep the default values on the Advanced tab and click the Next button. See Figure 6-11.

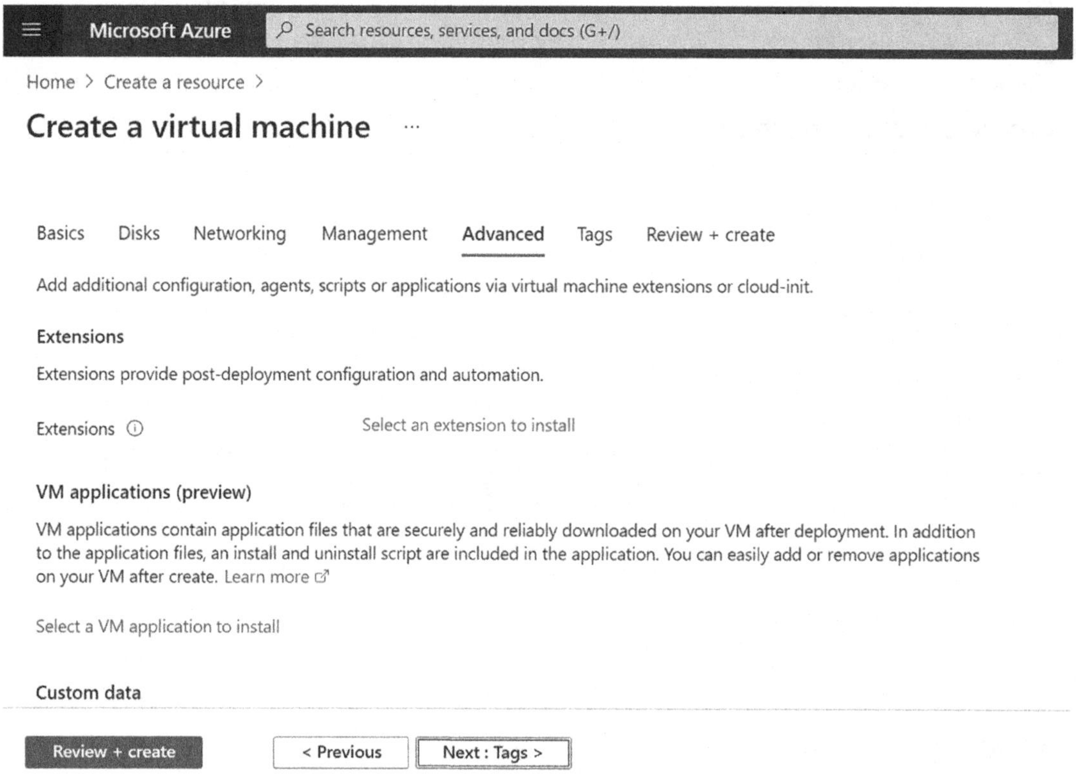

**Figure 6-11.** *FSLogix installation, image VM creation, Advanced tab*

10. Add tags on the Tags tab and click the Next button. See Figure 6-12.

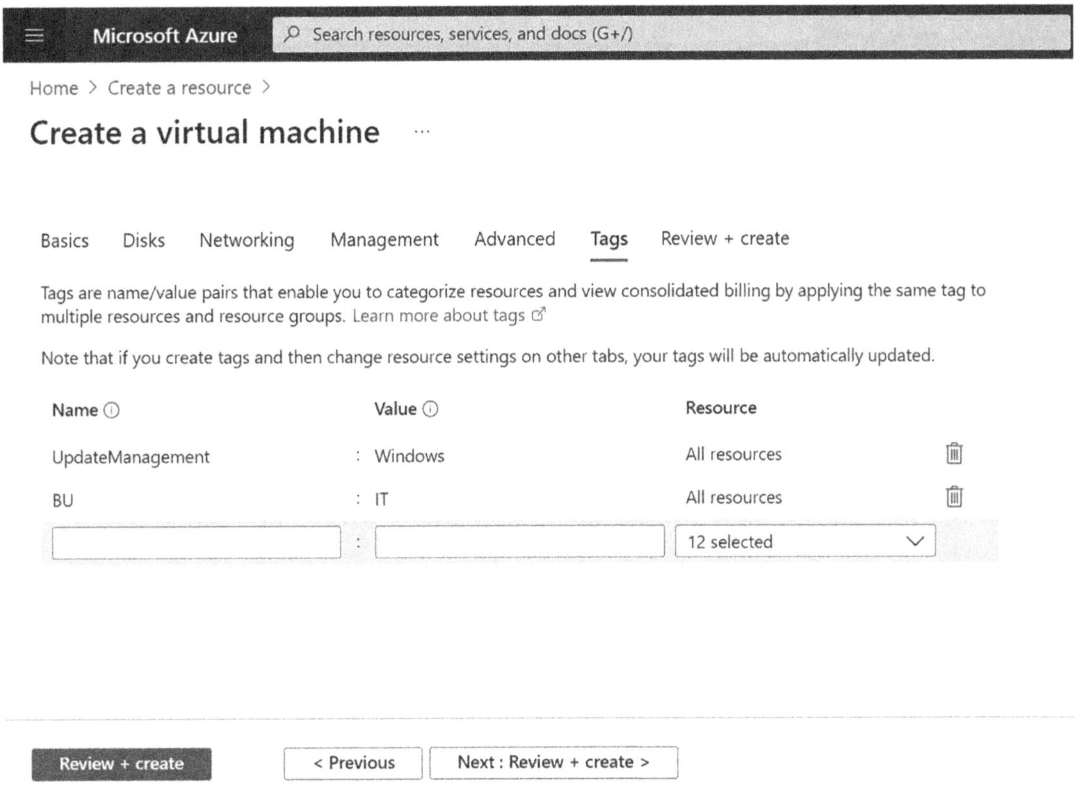

**Figure 6-12.** *FSLogix installation, image VM creation, Tags tab*

11.   Click "Review + create" and then after validation click the Create
button. See Figure 6-13.

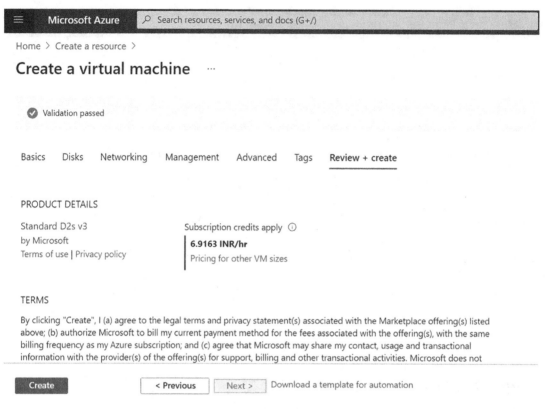

Figure 6-13. *FSLogix installation, image VM creation, Review + create tab*

12.  Once the VM is ready, then go to the Overview page and click the Connect button at the top. See Figure 6-14.

Figure 6-14. *FSLogix installation, image VM, Overview page*

13.  Since we have not created a public IP for the image VM, you must use Bastion to connect to the VM. Once you click Bastion, it will ask for the VM credentials and connect to the VM. If Bastion is not enabled on the VM/VNet, then it will prompt you to create a Bastion subnet and enable it. See Figure 6-15.

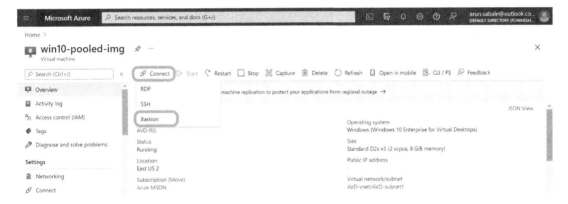

**Figure 6-15.**  *FSLogix installation, image VM, Connect menu*

14.  Enter the Bastion credentials and click the Connect button. See Figure 6-16.

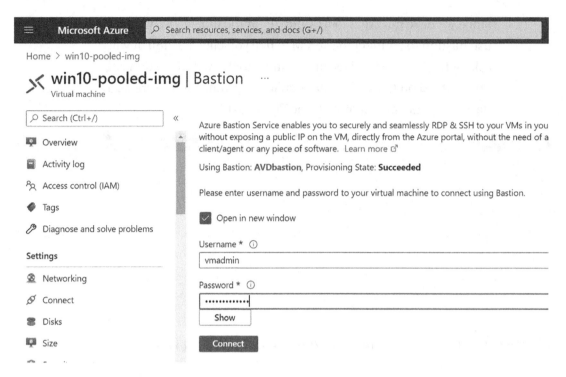

***Figure 6-16.*** *FSLogix installation, image VM connect, credentials*

15.    You will be able to see the Windows 10 multisession login screen.
See Figure 6-17.

***Figure 6-17.*** *FSLogix installation, image VM login screen*

16. Windows 10 multisession comes with FSLogix pre-installed, so please verify if FSLogix is already there in the VM, before you proceed further with download and installation of FSLogix. Now open your favorite browser and download FSLogix from https:// aka.ms/fslogix/download.

17. Extract the downloaded ZIP file and open the connect setup file from the subfolders. If you are using a 64-bit system, then go to the x64 folder and run the FSLogixAppSetup.exe file. See Figure 6-18.

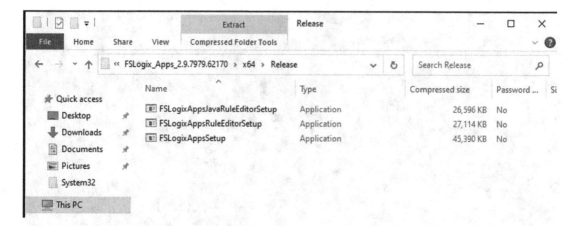

***Figure 6-18.*** *FSLogix installation, FSLogix download*

18. Once you run the FSLogix EXE file, you will be able to see the setup screen, select the license and condition checkbox, and click the Install button. See Figure 6-19.

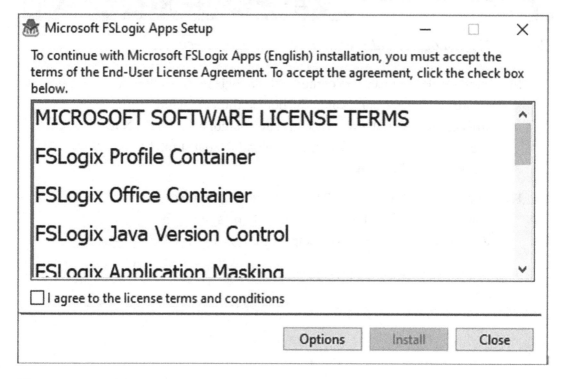

***Figure 6-19.*** *FSLogix setup*

19.    Wait for setup to complete. See Figure 6-20.

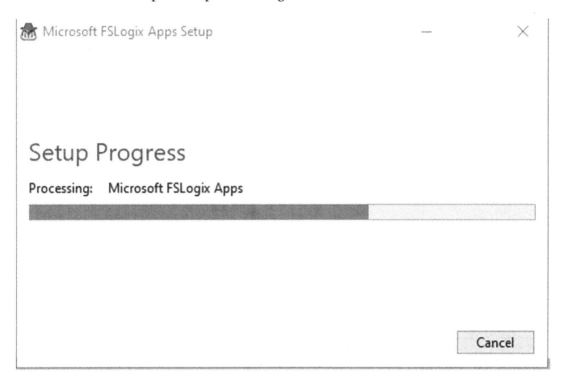

*Figure 6-20.* *FSLogix setup status*

20.    Restart the VM after setup. See Figure 6-21.

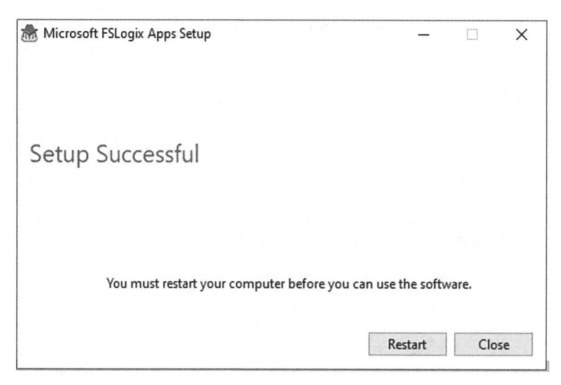

***Figure 6-21.*** *FSLogix restart*

21. The next step would be to configure the FSLogix profile container registry once you are done with the setup and VM reboot.

# Configure Profile Containers

First let's understand what the FSLogix profile container is, and then we will see the steps to configure it. The profile container is a fully remote profile solution for nonpersistent environments like pooled virtual desktops; it allows you to store the user profile on remote storage. The profile container redirects the entire user profile to a remote location like an Azure file share or NetApp. The profile container configuration defines how and where the profile is redirected.

It's recommended that you use dedicated storage for each host pool, so you must decide if you want to set up this FSLogix container setting in the image or use GPO for it. If you set up the FSLogix profile container setting inside the image, then you need different images for each host pool as the image will have the storage information in the container registry. You can always also use GPO to deploy the settings after creating the host pool and the session host and use a single image for all host pools.

Additionally, you also must decide if you want to store the user profile to single storage or want multiple copies of the user profile in the case of DR. If you want a user profile copy in a DR region, then you can go with the cloud cache instead of the profile container.

The following are the major differences between the FSLogix VHDLocation and the cloud cache.

## VHDLocation vs. the Cloud Cache

There are two ways to define the profile locations in FSLogix for Azure Virtual Desktop. The first is the traditional SMB share path, which allows you to write to effectively any represented SMB share including a Windows file share and Azure storage file share. If you use the VHDLocation setting for the Azure Virtual Desktop pooled user profile, then there will be only one active profile location. FSLogix does not limit you to defining one location in the VHDLocation registry; however, only one location based on the order defined in registry and the location which is reachable and readable will be considered as active.

The second option is the FSLogix cloud cache, which provides the active profile locations. The cloud cache allows you to define multiple profile storage locations including an SMB share and an Azure blob at the same time. All the locations mentioned in the registry will be updated if there are changes in the profile data, and it's a better option if you want to consider DR for the primary region.

If the profile container is the option you want to go with, then follow the next steps to configure the profile container settings in the image or go to the "Configure the Cloud Cache" section.

## Configure the Profile Container Registry Settings

The profile container can be enabled through the registry settings and FSLogix user groups. As you have learned, the registry settings may be managed manually inside the image or manually on each session host or with GPOs, and you can make the decision based on your requirements. It is always recommended to automate the profile registry by GPO or image creation to avoid typing mistakes. The configuration settings for the profile container are set in `HKLM\SOFTWARE\FSLogix\Profiles` on each VM inside the same host pool.

The settings in Table 6-1 are required to enable the profile container and to specify the location for the profile VHD to be stored.

***Table 6-1.*** *FSLogix User Profile Container Registry Setting*

| Value | Type | Configured Value | Description |
|---|---|---|---|
| `Enabled` (required setting) | `DWORD` | 1 | 0: Profile containers disabled. 1: Profile containers enabled. |
| `VHDLocations` (required setting) | `MULTI_SZ` or `REG_SZ` | | A list of file system locations to search for the user's profile VHD(X) file. If one isn't found, one will be created in the first listed location. |

# Adding a Profile Container Registry Key

Follow these steps:

1.  You have to get the Azure file share path from the storage account we created for the user profile before you add the registry key. Let's go to the user profile storage account and click "+File share." See Figure 6-22.

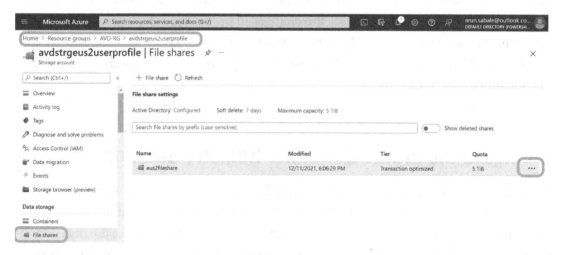

***Figure 6-22.*** *FSLogix container registry, getting the storage file share*

2.  Click the three dots in front of the file share and click Connect. See Figure 6-23.

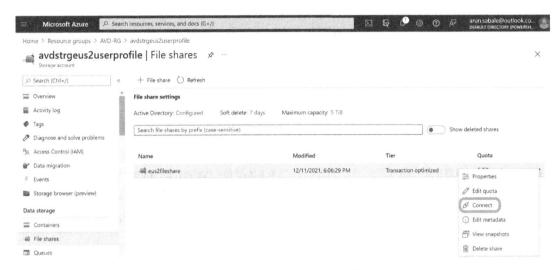

**Figure 6-23.** *FSLogix container registry, getting the storage file share, step 2*

3.  Copy the storage account path from the Connect pop-up, as shown in Figure 6-24.

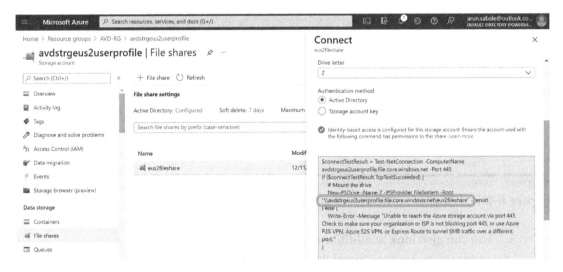

**Figure 6-24.** *FSLogix container registry, getting the storage file share, step 3*

4. Now log in to the image VM using Bastion and open the registry
   with the Administrator context (Run as Administrator). Browse
   the registry path HKLM\SOFTWARE\Fslogix\Profiles and create
   both registry keys mentioned in Table 6-2. See Figure 6-25.

**Table 6-2.** *VHDLocation Registry Key*

| Value | Type | Configured Value | Description |
|---|---|---|---|
| Enabled (required setting) | DWORD | 1 | 0: Profile containers disabled. 1: Profile containers enabled. |
| VHDLocations (required setting) | MULTI_SZ or REG_SZ | | A list of file system locations to search for the user's profile VHD(x) file. If one isn't found, one will be created in the first listed location. |

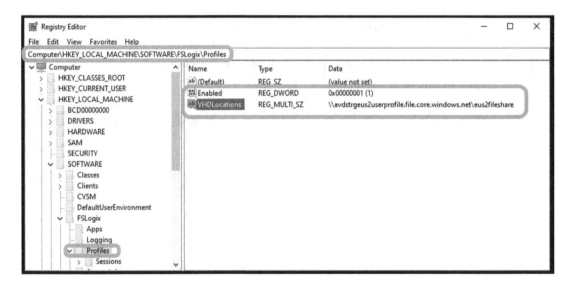

**Figure 6-25.** *FSLogix container registry, VHDlocation registry key*

5. You can also look at additional registry keys in Table 6-3 and
   add them in case you want them based on the organization
   requirements.

# Optional Registry Settings for Profile Container

Table 6-3 shows the addition registry keys.

***Table 6-3.*** *VHDLocation All Extra Registry Keys*

| Value | Type | Configured Value | Description |
|---|---|---|---|
| DeleteLocalProfile WhenVHDShouldApply | DWORD | 0 | 0: No deletion. 1: Delete local profile if it exists and matches the profile being loaded from the VHD. |
| FlipFlopProfileDirectoryName | DWORD | 0 | When set to 1, the SID folder is created as "%username%%sid%" *instead of the default* "%sid%%username%". This setting has the same effect as the setting SIDDirNamePattern = "%username%%sid%" and SIDDirNameMatch = "%username%%sid%". |
| PreventLoginWithFailure | DWORD | 0 | If set to 1, the profile container will load FRXShell if there's a failure attaching to or using an existing profile VHD(x). The user will receive the FRXShell prompt (default prompt to call support), and the users' only option will be to sign out. |
| PreventLoginWithTempProfile | DWORD | 0 | If set to 1, the profile container will load FRXShell if it's determined a temp profile has been created. The user will receive the FRXShell prompt (default prompt to call support), and the users' only option will be to sign out. |

# Can User Groups Be Included and Excluded in FSLogix?

Yes, you can include and exclude user groups in an FSLogix profile. There are often users whom you want to keep local profiles for such as local administrators. During installation, four user groups are created to manage users whose profiles are included and excluded from the profile container and office container redirection. See Figure 6-26.

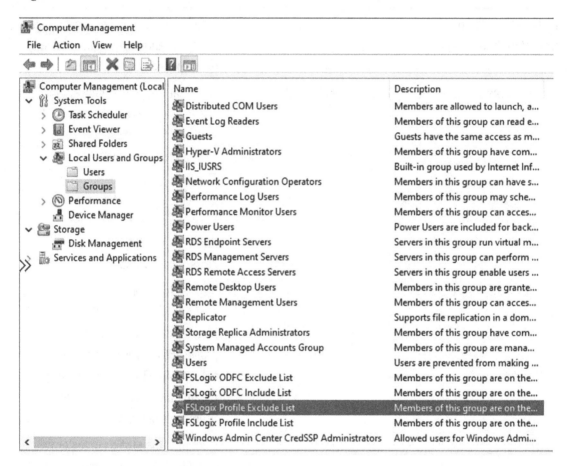

***Figure 6-26.*** *FSLogix container registry, profile exclude list*

By default, everyone is added to the FSLogix Profile Include List group, which means all users who log in to the VM/system will have an FSLogix remote profile. See Figure 6-27.

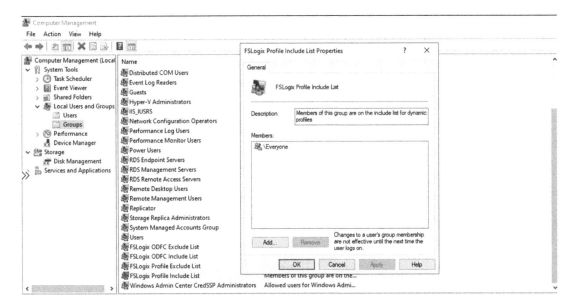

***Figure 6-27.*** *FSLogix container registry, default profile include list*

It always recommends using a dedicated group for the Azure Virtual Desktop permission such as Azure file share permissions, FSLogix include group, and Azure Virtual Desktop app group so that it will be easy to add/remove permissions by simply adding/removing members in the group. You can remove everyone from the include group and add the group you created for AVD users, as shown in Figure 6-28.

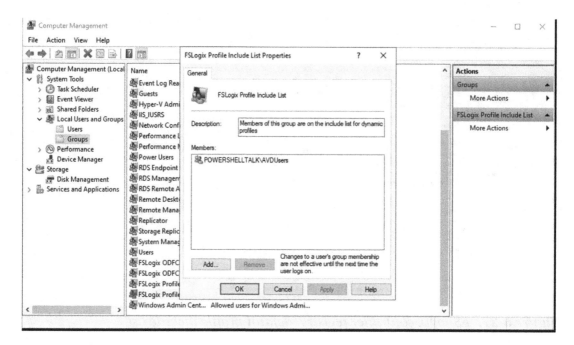

**Figure 6-28.**    *FSLogix container registry, modifying profile include list*

Adding a user to the FSLogix Profile Exclude List group means that the FSLogix agent will *not* create FSLogix remote user profile (profile container) for the user and the user profile remains locally. Exclude takes priority in case the user is a member of both the exclude and include groups.

In Figure 6-29, VMadmin is member of the Everyone group, meaning part of include as well as exclude, so the exclude will take priority, and the profile will remain locally.

***Figure 6-29.*** *FSLogix container registry, modifying the profile exclude list*

Once both the mandatory registry keys are added to all the VMs in the pool, then users can log in with the user ID that is part of the include group and also have permission on the file share and verify whether the profile is on the Azure storage file share.

# What Are the Possible Scenarios with the Profile Container?

These are the options:

> *Single SMB file share with FSLogix*: You can have a single file share (any file or Azure file sharc) to store a user profile using FSLogix as shown in Figure 6-30. If you use Azure file share, then it can be connected over a private endpoint from the AVD virtual network.

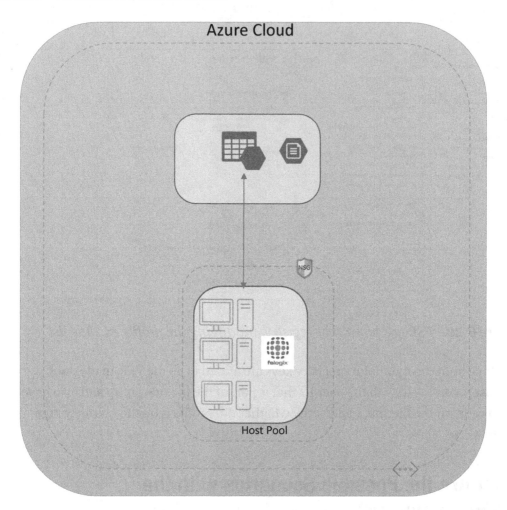

***Figure 6-30.*** *FSLogix, single SMB share with FSLogix*

There is one more option distributed file system (DFS file share) that
comes with file shares in different locations and syncing with each
other, and you will get a single namespace that you can use in the
VHDLocation registry key. You can set up DFS on Windows Server
inside the AVD virtual network and set up a replica in a DR location,
and DFS will take care of replicating data to another region share.
See Figure 6-31.

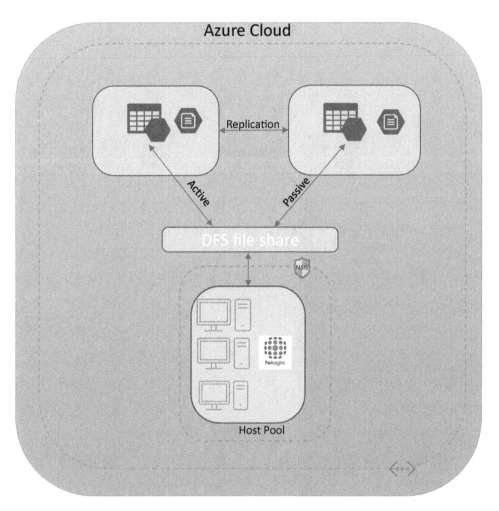

***Figure 6-31.*** *FSLogix, DFS SMB share with FSLogix*

*Multiple SMB shares with FSLogix*: You can have multiple file shares
(any file or Azure file share) to store the user profile using FSLogix, as
shown in Figure 6-32. Only one file share at a time will be active and
available based on the order the shares are added in the FSLogix config.
The replication between two shares needs to be managed by you using
different tools like robocopy/AZ copy/CLI/PowerShell.

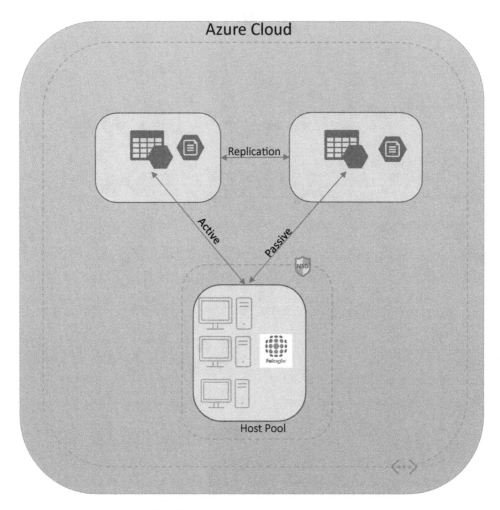

***Figure 6-32.*** *FSLogix, multiple SMB share with FSLogix*

# Configure the Cloud Cache

In this section, you'll learn how to configure the cloud cache.

## What Is the Cloud Cache?

The cloud cache is an alternative to the profile container, and it also provides some additional functionality to the profile container. The cloud cache uses a local profile to service all reads from a redirected profile or office container, after the first read. The cloud cache also allows the use of multiple remote locations, which are all continually updated during the user session. Using the cloud cache can insulate users from short-term loss of connectivity to remote profile containers. The cloud cache can also provide a real-time, "active-active" redundancy for the profile container and office container.

It's important to understand that, even with cloud cache, all initial reads are accomplished from the redirected location. Likewise, all writes occur to all remote storage locations, although writes go to the local cache file first.

The cloud cache doesn't improve the users' sign-on and sign-out experience when using poorly performing storage. It's common for environments using cloud cache to have slightly slower sign-on and sign-out times, relative to using traditional VHDLocations, using the same storage. After initial sign-on, the cloud cache can improve the user experience for subsequent reads of data from the profile container or office container, as these reads are serviced from the local cache file.

## Cloud Cache Design and Functionality

The cloud cache uses one or more remote profile containers, along with metadata. The combination of a profile container and metadata is referred to as a *cloud cache provider*. The cloud cache uses a local cache file that contains part of the dataset stored in the cloud cache providers. The data gets stored and accessed from the local cache file after any read from a cloud cache provider. Additionally, the local cache file will service any writes from the system and then send those writes to all cloud cache providers in the cloud cache configuration registry. This is a synchronous process that depends on the performance of the various components such as client, network, and storage.

If a provider is not available, then the system will continue to operate with the remaining provider. If a provider that was unavailable becomes available before the user signs out, then it will be brought up-to-date from the local cache. When a provider isn't available when the user signs out, it will be brought up-to-date in subsequent sessions by having all its data replaced from an existing and up-to-date provider. If all remote providers are stale, the provider with the latest metadata is considered the source of truth.

## Configure Registry Settings for the Cloud Cache with SMB

The cloud cache can be configured using the registry as a profile container. All the settings are applied here under the registry: HKLM\SOFTWARE\Fslogix\Profiles. Make sure you remove VHDLocation and replace it with the CCDLocation key with the format shown in Table 6-4.

The following are two different examples of using the cloud cache with a file share or blob.

## Cloud Cache with File Share

Table 6-4 shows the registry key for a file share.

***Table 6-4.*** *CCDLocation Registry Key for File Share*

| Registry Value | Type | Value |
|---|---|---|
| CCDLocations | REG_SZ / MULTI_SZ | type=smb,connectionString=<\Location1\Folder1>; type=smb,connectionString=<\Location2\folder2> |
| Enabled | DWORD | 1 |

## Cloud Cache with Blob

Table 6-5 shows the registry key for a file share.

***Table 6-5.*** *CCDLocation Registry Key for Blob*

| Registry Value | Type | Value |
|---|---|---|
| CCDLocations | REG_SZ / MULTI_SZ | type=azure,connectionString="DefaultEndpointsProtocol= https;AccountName=|FSLogix/account|;AccountKey= |FSLogix/key|;EndpointSuffix="; type=azure,connectionString="DefaultEndpointsProtocol= https;AccountName=|FSLogix/account|;AccountKey= |FSLogix/key|;EndpointSuffix=" |
| Enabled | DWORD | 1 |

## Combing a File Share and Blob for a Single Host Pool

Table 6-6 shows the registry key for a file share.

***Table 6-6.*** *CCDLocation Registry Key for Blob and File Share*

| Registry Value | Type | Value |
|---|---|---|
| CCDLocations | REG_SZ / MULTI_SZ | type=smb,connectionString=<\FILESERVER\SharedFolder>; type=azure,connectionString="DefaultEndpointsProtocol= https;AccountName=\|FSLogix/account\|;AccountKey= \|FSLogix/key\|;EndpointSuffix=" |
| Enabled | DWORD | 1 |

# Adding a Cloud Cache Registry Key with a File Share

Here are the steps to add a cloud cache registry key with a file share:

1. You have to get the Azure file share path from the storage account we created for the user profile before you add the registry key. You can follow the same instructions mentioned in the profile container to get the file share name.

2. Now log in to the image VM using Bastion and the open registry with an Administrator context (Run as Administrator). Browse the registry path HKLM\SOFTWARE\Fslogix\Profiles and create both registry keys mentioned in Table 6-7. Note: If there is a VHDLocation key present, you have to delete it before adding the cloud cache key. See Figure 6-33.

***Table 6-7.*** *CCDLocation Registry Key for File Share*

| Registry Value | Type | Value |
|---|---|---|
| CCDLocations | REG_SZ / MULTI_SZ | type=smb,connectionString=<\Location1\Folder1>; type=smb,connectionString=<\Location2\folder2> |
| Enabled | DWORD | 1 |

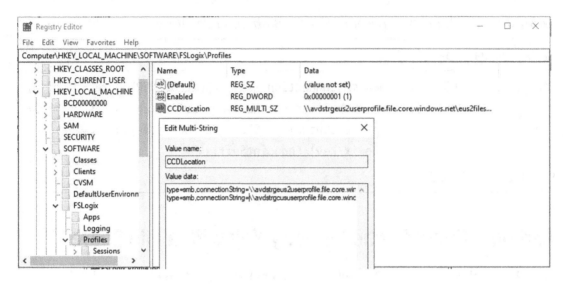

***Figure 6-33.*** *FSLogix: CCDLocation registry key*

3.  Make sure that the correct user group is added in the FSLogix include group. See Figure 6-34.

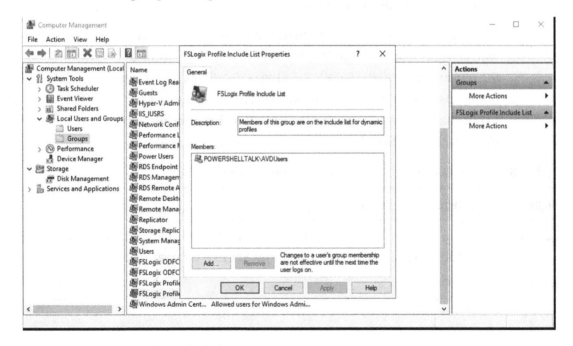

***Figure 6-34.*** *FSLogix include list*

4.  Restart the VM and try to log in with the user ID, which is a member of the group added in the FSLogix include list group.

# Adding a Cloud Cache Registry Key with a Blob

Here are the steps to add the cloud cache registry key with a blob:

1.  You have to get the Azure blob connection string from the storage account we created earlier for the user profile, before you add the registry key. See Figure 6-35.

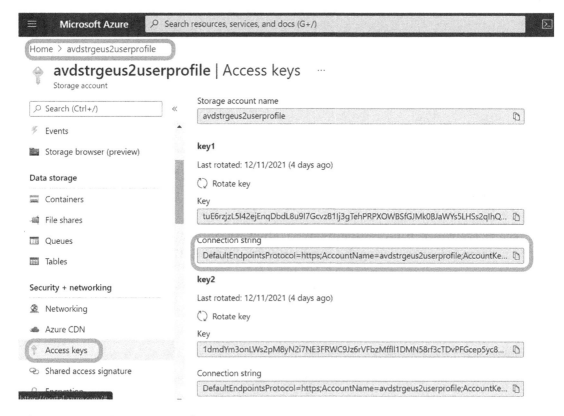

***Figure 6-35.*** *FSLogix config, storage account connection string*

183

2. Since we have the storage name and key in the connection string, we should not store it directly in the registry, because users can read the registry with read permission. So, the best way to protect the storage account name and key is to store them in a credential manager on a VM. To do that, you must log in to the image VM using Bastion, open the command prompt as an administrator (CMD), and go to the `C:\Program Files\Fslogix\Apps` folder. See Figure 6-36.

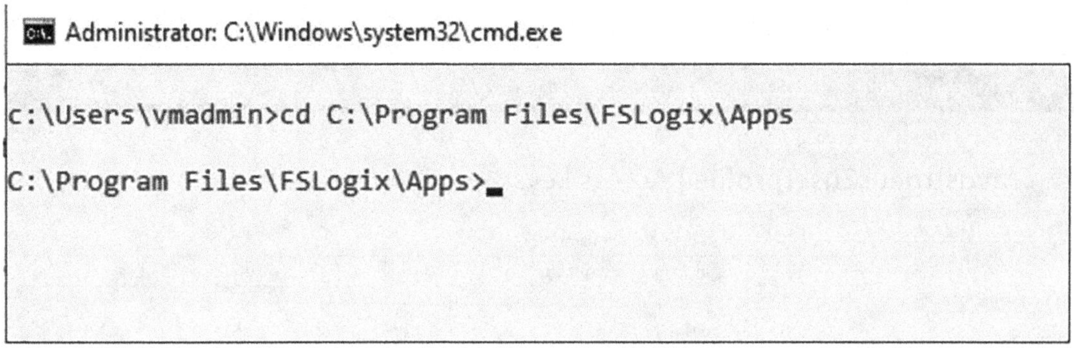

```
Administrator: C:\Windows\system32\cmd.exe

c:\Users\vmadmin>cd C:\Program Files\FSLogix\Apps

C:\Program Files\FSLogix\Apps>_
```

***Figure 6-36.*** *FSLogix configuration, adding the password in to the credential manager, step 1*

3. Type the following command and change the storage account name before executing the command. See Figure 6-37.

   ```
   frx.exe add-secure-key -key account -value <storage-account-name-here>
   ```

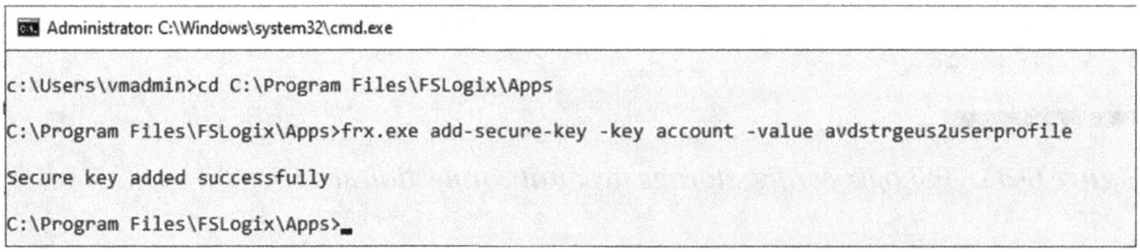

```
Administrator: C:\Windows\system32\cmd.exe

c:\Users\vmadmin>cd C:\Program Files\FSLogix\Apps
C:\Program Files\FSLogix\Apps>frx.exe add-secure-key -key account -value avdstrgeus2userprofile
Secure key added successfully
C:\Program Files\FSLogix\Apps>_
```

***Figure 6-37.*** *FSLogix config- add password in credential manager step 2*

4.   Add the storage account key using the following command. See Figure 6-38.

```
frx.exe add-secure-key -key key -value <storage-account-
key-here>
```

```
Administrator: C:\Windows\system32\cmd.exe

c:\Users\vmadmin>cd C:\Program Files\FSLogix\Apps

C:\Program Files\FSLogix\Apps>frx.exe add-secure-key -key account -value avdstrgeus2userprofile

Secure key added successfully

C:\Program Files\FSLogix\Apps>frx.exe add-secure-key -key key -value tuE6rzjzL5I42ejEnqDbdL8u9I7G
Mk0BJaWYs5LHSs2qIhQVQGsZ7EWcqPylUEQ==

Secure key added successfully

C:\Program Files\FSLogix\Apps>_
```

***Figure 6-38.*** *FSLogix config, add password in credential manager step 3*

5.   Repeat the steps for an additional storage blob in case you want to use multiple blobs, but make sure you are changing the key name and value and not overwriting the same key and value. The following are example commands to add an additional storage blob:

```
frx.exe add-secure-key -key account1 -value <storage-
account1-name-here>
frx.exe add-secure-key -key key1 -value <storage-account1-
key-here>
```

6.   Open the registry with the Administrator context (Run as Administrator). Browse the registry path HKLM\SOFTWARE\ Fslogix\Profiles and create both the registry keys mentioned in Table 6-8. Note: if there is a VHDLocation key present, then you have to delete it before adding the cloud cache key.

***Table 6-8.*** *CCDlocation with Credential Manager*

| Registry Value | Type | Value |
|---|---|---|
| CCDLocations | REG_SZ / MULTI_SZ | type=azure,connectionString="DefaultEndpoints Protocol=https;AccountName=\|FSLogix/account\|; AccountKey=\|FSLogix/key\|;EndpointSuffix=";type=azure, connectionString="DefaultEndpointsProtocol=https; AccountName=\|FSLogix/account1\|;AccountKey=\| FSLogix/key1\|;EndpointSuffix=" |
| Enabled | DWORD | 1 |

Table 6-9 shows the registry key syntax without the credential manager. See Figure 6-39.

***Table 6-9.*** *CCDLocation Without Credential Manager*

| Registry Value | Type | Value |
|---|---|---|
| CCDLocations | REG_SZ / MULTI_SZ | type=azure,connectionString="DefaultEndpoints Protocol=https;AccountName=;AccountKey=; EndpointSuffix="; type=azure,connectionString= "DefaultEndpointsProtocol=https;AccountName=; AccountKey=;EndpointSuffix="; |
| Enabled | DWORD | 1 |

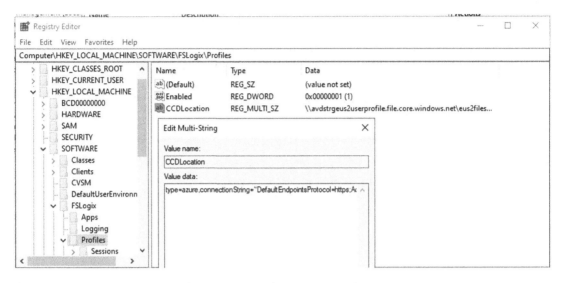

***Figure 6-39.***  *FSLogix config, CCDLocation registry key*

7.  Make sure that the correct user group is added in the FSLogix
    include list group. See Figure 6-40.

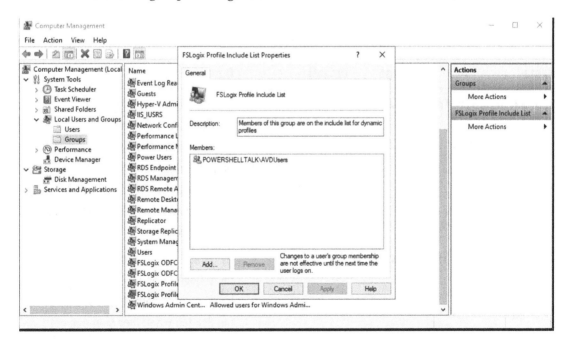

***Figure 6-40.***  *FSLogix config, FSLogix include list group*

8. Restart the VM and try to log in with a user ID that is a member of the group added in the FSLogix include list group and verify if the user profile gets created on the file share. See Figure 6-41.

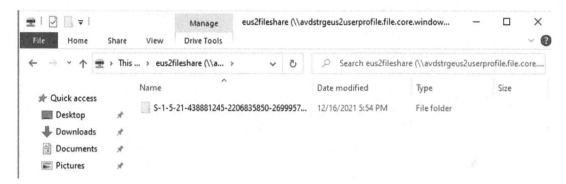

***Figure 6-41.*** *FSLogix, user profile on remote storage*

9. You can also look at an additional registry key for the cloud cache in Table 6-10 and add it if you want it based on the organization requirements.

***Table 6-10.*** *CCDLocation Extra Registry Key*

| Name | Type | Default | Detail |
|---|---|---|---|
| CcdMaxCacheSizeInMBs | DWORD | 0 | CcdMaxCacheSizeinMBs specifies the maximum local cache size in megabytes, per user, during normal operation. Setting CcdMaxCacheSizeinMBs to 0 (default value) means there is no limit of the local cache size. |
| ClearCacheOnLogoff | DWORD | 0 | By default, the local cache file won't be removed when the user signs out. If you want to have the local cache file deleted when they sign out, set ClearCacheOnLogoff to 1. |

(*continued*)

*Table 6-10.*  (*continued*)

| Name | Type | Default | Detail |
|------|------|---------|--------|
| CacheDirectory | REG_SZ | C:\ProgramData\ Fslogix\Cache | CacheDirectory specifies the location of the local cache file. By default, the local cache file will be placed in C:\ProgramData\ Fslogix\Cache. The local cache file may be placed on another mapped drive or a UNC. CacheDirectory and ProxyDirectory must not be in the same location as the proxy file and the cache file are the same name and will conflict. |
| ProxyDirectory | REG_SZ | N/A | ProxyDirectory specifies the location of the local proxy stub file. By default, the local cache file will be placed in C:\ProgramData\ Fslogix\Proxy. |
| SilenceACLWarning | DWORD | N/A | Set SilenceACLWarning to 1 to disable the event log warning the proxy or cache that the ACLs do not match the default values. |

# What Are the Possible Scenarios with the Profile Container?

Here are the scenarios:

- Single SMB file share to store the user profiles in a single region

- Multiple SMB shares to store the user profiles in multiple regions with auto sync

- Multiple Azure blobs to store the user profiles in multiple regions with auto sync

- SMB file share + Azure Blob to store the user profiles in multiple regions with auto sync

# Migrate User Profiles to FSLogix

If you already have some other VDI platform or other desktop solution and you want to migrate user profiles to FSLogix so that you can use an Azure Virtual Desktop pooled host pool, then there are different options available to do that.

If you already have a user profile VHD file, then you just have to create a folder in the file share with the correct naming such as username_SID and copy the VHD file inside the folder. You can get the SID from the registry or from Active Directory. Additionally, you can use the following PowerShell commands to get the user SID (Figure 6-42):

```
$sam = <User-name>
$sid = (New-Object System.Security.Principal.NTAccount($sam)).
translate([System.Security.Principal.SecurityIdentifier]).Value
```

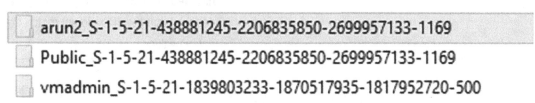

```
Name
```

```
arun2_S-1-5-21-438881245-2206835850-2699957133-1169
Public_S-1-5-21-438881245-2206835850-2699957133-1169
vmadmin_S-1-5-21-1839803233-1870517935-1817952720-500
```

***Figure 6-42.*** *FSLogix, user profile on remote storage*

If you have a user profile on any VM or RDS server, then you can use PowerShell to convert user profiles in the VHD and the folder structure on the target share. The PowerShell file is available on PowerShell to convert the user profile to a VHD and migrate to FSLogix/Migrate-UserProfileToFslogix.ps1. The file can be executed on any Windows VM/server where you have the profile.

Once all user profiles are migrated to the FSLogix file share, the user can simply log in to the Azure Virtual Desktop and FSLogix will check if the profile is there on the file share and use the profile for user login.

Here are the requirements for the migrator script:

1. Change the source and target path in the script.

2. Run the script as an administrator.

3. Install the FSLogix app on the VM you want to execute the script.

4. Copy all the profiles to a single folder, pass it as the source, and run the script so all profiles will get migrated together.

5. The target path can be the FSLogix profile container file share.

```
<#
.SYNOPSIS
This script convert Local Profile to VHD and migrate to FSLogix Profile
Container file share
.NOTES
  Version:        1.0
  Author:         Arun Sabale
#>

#######################################################################
# Requires -RunAsAdministrator
# Requires FSLogix Agent with comes with FSLogix app(frx.exe)
# Modify below parameter
#######################################################################
# fslogix target file share profile path
$FilesharePath = "<\\domain.com\share\path>"
# User profile source path - you can copy all user profiles to single
folder and then run the script
$userProfilePath = "c:\users"
#######################################################################
# Main code
#######################################################################
```

```
$ENV:PATH="$ENV:PATH;C:\Program Files\fslogix\apps\"

$oldprofiles = gci $userProfilePath | ?{$_.psiscontainer -eq $true} |
select -Expand fullname | sort | out-gridview -OutputMode Multiple -title
"Select profile(s) to convert"

# foreach old profile
foreach ($old in $oldprofiles) {

$sam = ($old | split-path -leaf)
$sid = (New-Object System.Security.Principal.NTAccount($sam)).
translate([System.Security.Principal.SecurityIdentifier]).Value

$nfolder = join-path $FilesharePath ($sam+"_"+$sid)

if (!(test-path $nfolder)) {New-Item -Path $nfolder -ItemType directory |
Out-Null}

& icacls $nfolder /setowner "$env:userdomain\$sam" /T /C
& icacls $nfolder /grant $env:userdomain\$sam`:`(OI`)`(CI`)F /T

$vhd = Join-Path $nfolder ("Profile_"+$sam+".vhdx")

frx.exe copy-profile -filename $vhd -sid $sid
}
```

# Summary

In this chapter, you learned how to create an Azure Virtual Desktop host and host pools using the Azure portal, PowerShell, command-line interface (CLI), and Azure Resource Manager templates. Additionally, you learned how to configure host pool settings, assign users to host pools, apply OS and application updates to a running Azure Virtual Desktop host, and apply security and compliance settings to session hosts.

# CHAPTER 7

# Create and Manage Session Host Images

In this chapter, you will learn about golden images and how to create a golden image for Azure Virtual Desktop. You will also learn about the benefits of using a shared image gallery and how to update the images stored in it.

Let's get started with creating a golden image for Azure Virtual Desktop.

## Creating a Golden Image

A golden image is a custom operating system image with all the applications and software installed and configured so that you can create a VM with the image. A golden image is like a preconfigured template for a VM; it saves you time installing and configuring applications on all the VMs after their creation, and it reduces errors and adds consistency across all the VMs.

Let's see how to create a golden image and what other automation options we have that can automate the image creation. See Figure 7-1.

© Arun Sabale and Balu N Ilag 2022
A. Sabale and B. N. Ilag, *Microsoft Azure Virtual Desktop Guide*,
https://doi.org/10.1007/978-1-4842-8063-8_7

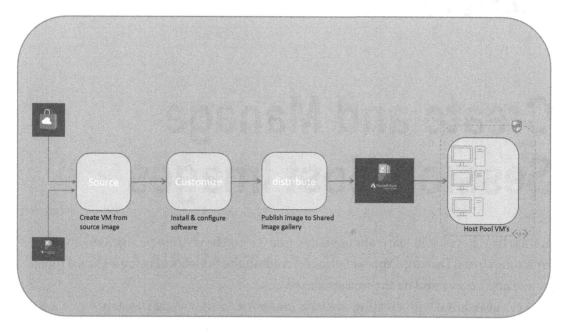

**Figure 7-1.** *Golden image creation steps/process*

The golden image creation process is simple: you can pick an image from the Azure marketplace or use an existing golden image from a shared image gallery and create the VM. You can connect the image VM with Bastion so that you can do all the customization including installing and configuring the applications. Also, you can configure all the compliance policies and settings on the image VM. Once you are done with all the customizations, then the next step is to generalize the VM and capture the image.

## Generalizing and Capturing a VM Image

Generalizing a VM is nothing more than running the sysprep command to remove all personal account information and prepare the machine to be used as an image. The following are the steps to generalize the VM:

1. Connect to the image virtual machine.

2. Open the Command Prompt window as Administrator. Change the directory to %windir%\system32\sysprep, and then run sysprep.exe.

3. In the System Preparation Tool dialog box, select Enter System Out-of-Box Experience (OOBE), and make sure that

the Generalize checkbox is selected. In Shutdown Options, select Shutdown and then click OK.

4. When Sysprep completes, it will shut down the virtual machine. Do not start/restart the VM. See Figure 7-2.

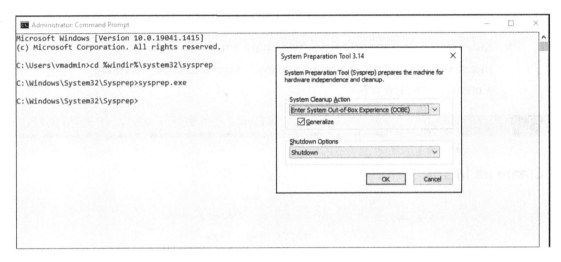

*Figure 7-2.* *Sysprep to generalize image*

5. The VM needs to be deallocated and marked as generalized in Azure. Use the Stop-AzVM PowerShell command to deallocate the VM.

6. Start PowerShell, log in to the Azure subscription, and make sure the correct subscription is selected. Here is the code:

```
###################################################################
# Modify below parameter
$resourceGroup = <myResourceGroup>
$VMName= <myVM-name>
$subscriptionID= <subscription-ID>
###################################################################

Connect-AzAccount
Select-AzSubscription $subscriptionID
Stop-AzVM -ResourceGroupName $resourceGroup -Name $VMName -Force
Set-AzVM -ResourceGroupName $resourceGroup -Name $VMName -Generalized
```

7.  Now you can go back to the Azure portal and select the image from the virtual machines listed.

8.  Check the virtual machine status.

9.  On the "Virtual machine" page for the VM, on the upper menu, select Capture.

10. Enter all the details and select "Yes, share it to a gallery as a VM image version" on the "Create an image" page, and click "Review + create." See Figure 7-3.

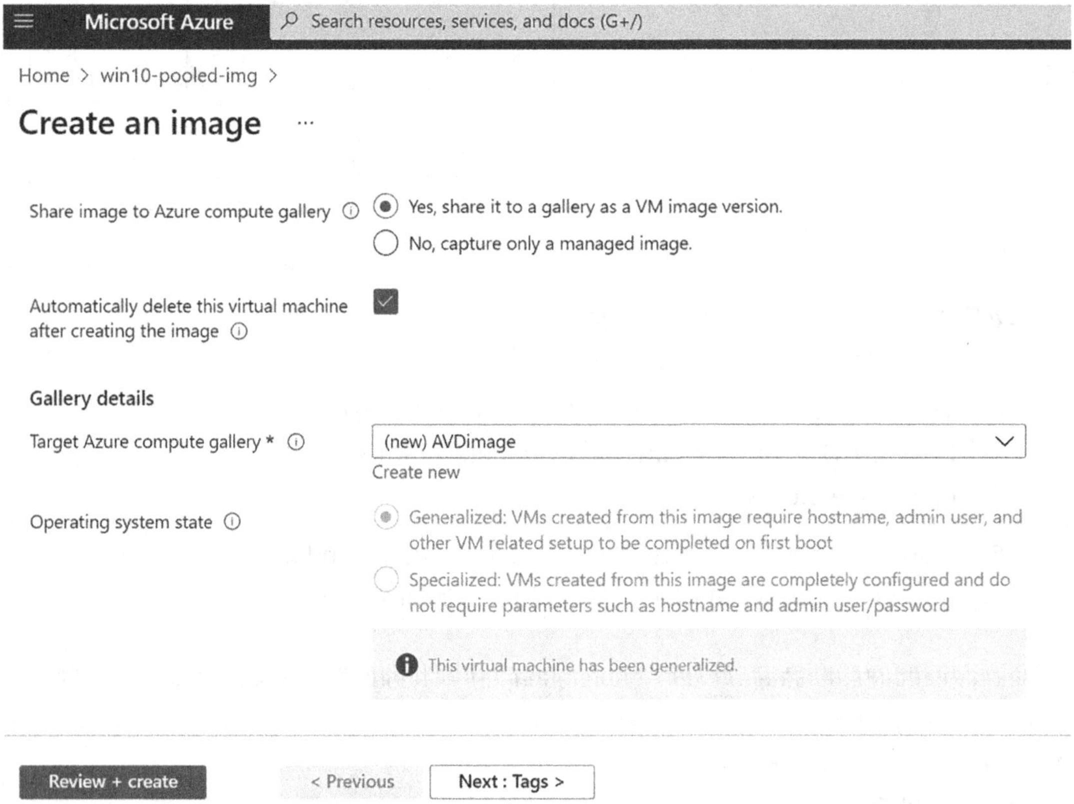

*Figure 7-3.*  *Creating an image*

11. Select image replication if you want to replicate the image to another region and click the "Review + create" button. See Figure 7-4.

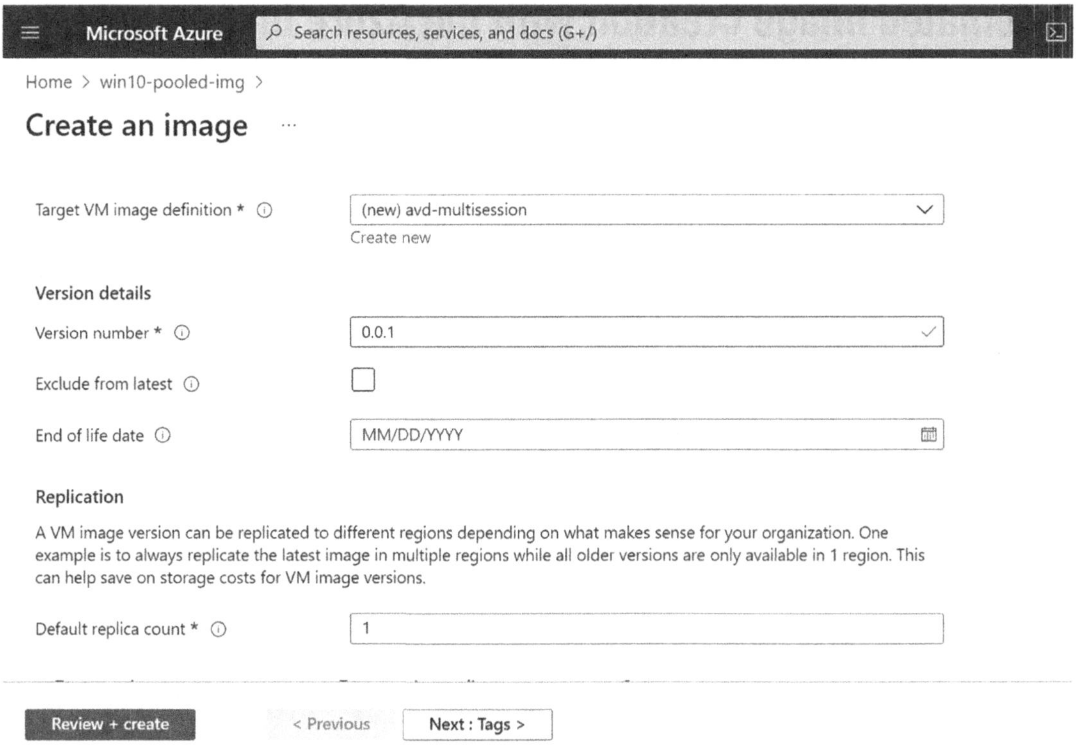

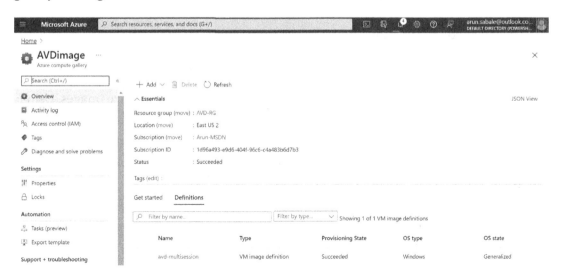

Figure 7-4. *Creating an image, step 2*

Once the image is created, you will be able to see the image in the shared image gallery. See Figure 7-5.

Figure 7-5. *Creating an image, image gallery*

# Automated Image Creation with the Azure Image Builder

Azure Image Builder (AIB) is a free, Azure-native tool that allows you to automate the image creation process, and you can still add customization with a PowerShell/Python/Shell script. AIB uses CLI and PowerShell commands to automate image creation with Microsoft.VirtualMachineImages provider. See Figure 7-6.

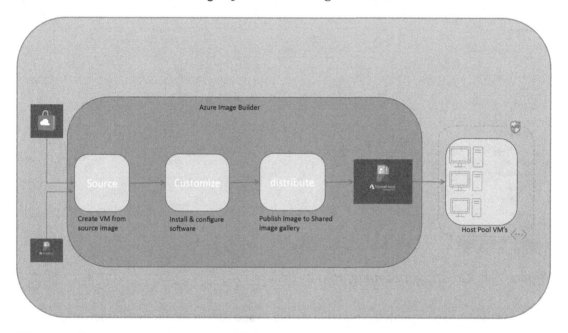

***Figure 7-6.*** *Creating an image, AIB flow*

AIB allows you to automate the source, customization, and distribution of the image to the shared image gallery.

With AIB, you can migrate your existing image customization pipeline to Azure while continuing to use existing scripts, commands, and processes to customize images. Using Image Builder, you can integrate your core applications into a VM image so your VMs can take on workloads immediately after creation. You can even add configurations to build images for Azure Virtual Desktop or as VHDs for use in Azure Stack or for ease of exporting.

Image Builder lets you start with Windows or Linux images from the Azure Marketplace or existing custom images and add your own customizations. You can also specify how you would like your resulting images hosted in the Azure Compute Gallery (formerly known as the Shared Image Gallery), as managed images or as VHDs.

# Creating and Using a Shared Image Gallery

A shared image gallery, which is now known as the Azure Compute Gallery, helps admins/operation teams to share images and application packages across subscriptions in your organization. The Azure Compute Gallery lets you store custom VM images and application packages and share them within or across regions. The image gallery also lets you choose a region to replicate the images and select storage residency (LRS, ZRS). You can create multiple galleries so that you can logically group resources and apply Azure role-based access control (Azure RBAC).

An Azure Compute Gallery provides the following:

- Global replication.

- Versioning and grouping of resources for easier management.

- Highly available resources with zone redundant storage (ZRS) accounts in regions that support availability zones. ZRS offers better resilience against zonal failures.

- Premium storage support (Premium_LRS).

- Sharing across subscriptions, and even between Active Directory (AD) tenants, using Azure RBAC.

- Scaling your deployments with resource replicas in each region.

You can share image and application with different users, service principals, or AD groups within your organization using the image gallery. Resources can be replicated to multiple regions for quicker scaling of your deployments.

# Image Management

A golden image is a copy of a full VM including any attached data disks (if any). You can create VMs from an image multiple times, and a copy of the VHD from the image is used to create a new VM disk. If you have multiple images that you need to maintain and would like to make them available throughout your company and let specific teams access specific images, then the Azure Image Gallery is your best option to manage multiple images with RBAC.

The following resources get created when you use the Azure Image Gallery to store images:

- *Image definition*: Image definitions are a logical grouping of image versions, and they carry information about the image and any requirements for using it to create VMs. There are three parameters for each image definition that are used in the combination: Publisher, Offer, and SKU. These parameters are used to find a specific image definition. This includes whether the image is Windows or Linux, release notes, and minimum and maximum memory requirements. It is a definition of a type of image.

- *Image version*: An image version is what you use to create a VM when using a gallery and image version, which allows you to store/create multiple versions of an image as needed for your environment. See Figure 7-7.

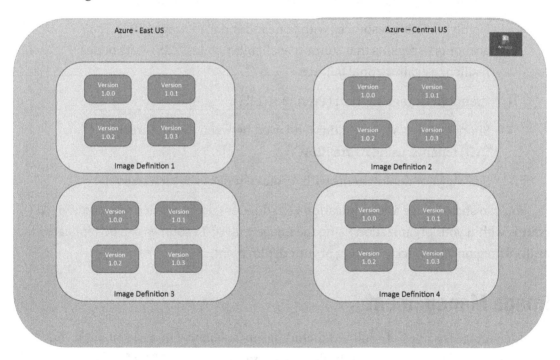

***Figure 7-7.*** *Azure image gallery version and definition*

# Generalized and Specialized Images

There are two operating system states supported by Azure Compute Gallery. Typically, images require that the VM used to create the image has been generalized before taking the image. Generalizing is a process that removes machine- and user-specific information from the VM. For Windows, the Sysprep tool is used. For Linux, you can use the `waagent -deprovision` or `-deprovision+user` parameter.

Specialized VMs have not been through a process to remove machine-specific information and accounts. Also, VMs created from specialized images do not have an `osProfile` associated with them. This means that specialized images will have some limitations in addition to some benefits.

- VMs and scale sets created from specialized images can be up and running quicker. Because they are created from a source that has already been through the first boot, VMs created from these images boot faster.

- Accounts that can be used to log into the VM can also be used on any VM created using the specialized image created from that VM.

- VMs will have the `computer name` of the VM the image was taken from. You should change the computer name to avoid collisions.

- The `osProfile` is how some sensitive information is passed to the VM, using `secrets`. This may cause issues using KeyVault, WinRM, and other functionality that uses `secrets` in the `osProfile`. In some cases, you can use Managed Service Identities (MSI) to work around these limitations.

# Azure Image Gallery Limits

There are limits, per subscription, for deploying resources using Azure Compute Gallery:

- 100 galleries per subscription per region
- 1,000 image definitions per subscription, per region
- 10,000 image versions per subscription per region
- 10 image version replicas per subscription per region

Any disk attached to the image must be less than or equal to 1 TB in size.

# Azure Image Gallery High Availability

Azure zone redundant storage (ZRS) provides resilience against an availability zone failure in the region. With the general availability of Azure Compute Gallery, you can choose to store your images in ZRS accounts in regions with availability zones. See Figure 7-8.

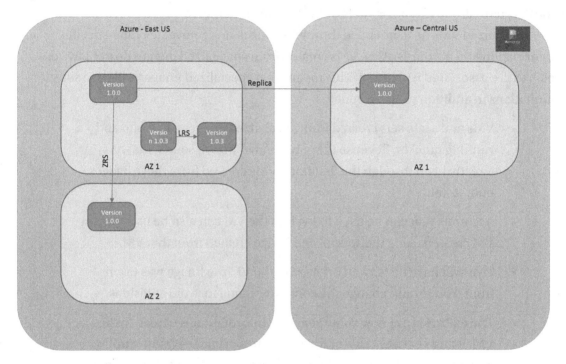

***Figure 7-8.*** *Azure image gallery zone redundant storage and image replication*

You can also choose the account type for each of the target regions. The default storage account type is Standard_LRS, but you can choose Standard_ZRS for regions with availability zones. See Figure 7-9.

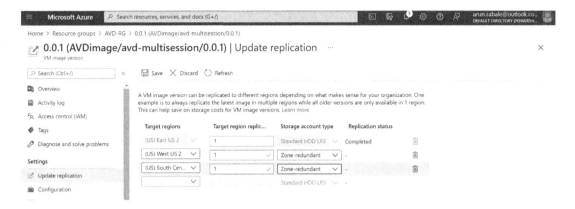

***Figure 7-9.*** *Azure image gallery zone redundant storage and image replication option*

## Steps to Create an Azure Image Gallery

You can create an Azure image gallery during the image capture process, but if you want to create an image gallery separately before capturing image, then these are the steps to do so:

1. Sign into the Azure portal at `https://portal.azure.com`.

2. Search for *Azure Compute Gallery* in the top search box and select Azure Compute Gallery in the results.

3. On the Azure Compute Gallery page, click Add.

4. On the "Create Azure compute gallery" page, select the correct subscription and resource group.

5. In Name, type the image gallery name based on the organization-specific naming standards and select the appropriate region for the image gallery. See Figure 7-10.

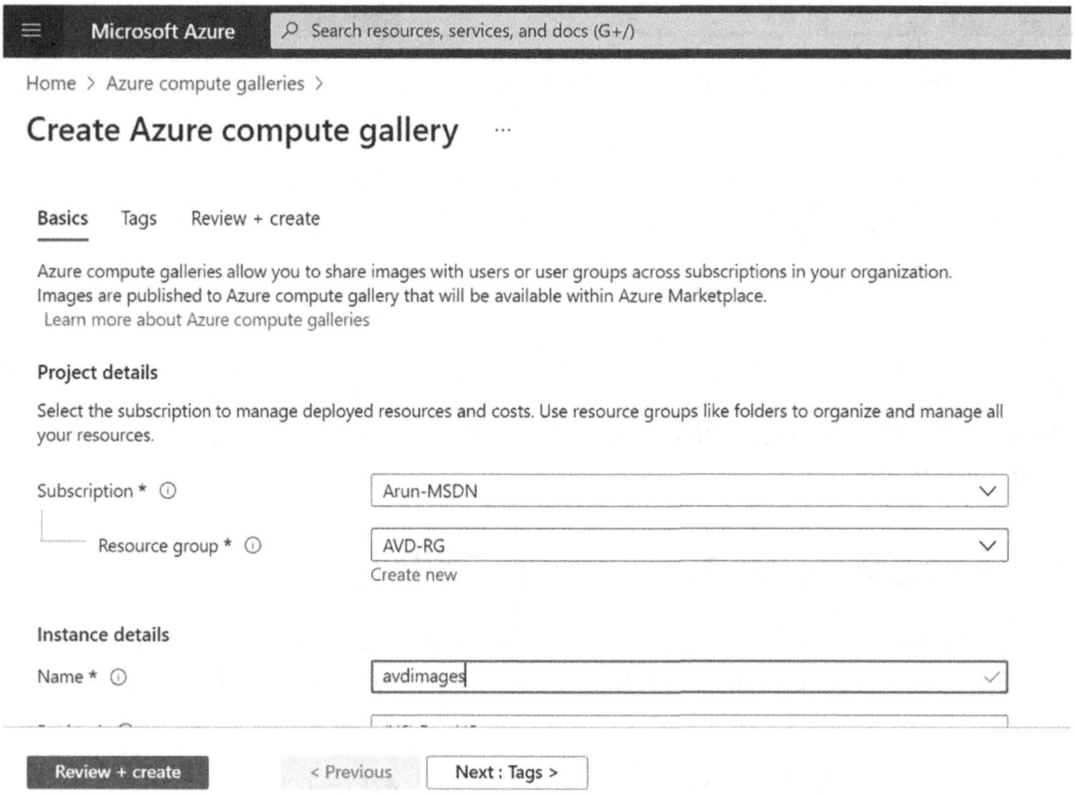

**Figure 7-10.**  *Azure image gallery creation*

6.  Click "Review + create."

7.  After validation passes, select Create to create the image gallery.

# Install Language Packs in Azure Virtual Desktop

Azure Virtual Desktop is a service that your users can deploy anytime, anywhere and access it from anywhere. That's why it's important that your users are able to customize which language their Windows 10 Enterprise multisession image displays. There are two ways you can accommodate the language needs of your users.

- Build separate host pools with a customized image for each language.

- Build a single host pool with different language and localization requirements for different users, but customize their images to ensure they can select whichever language they need. This method is a lot more efficient and cost-effective.

You can automate language pack installation with the following PowerShell script during the image creation process. You can use the following script sample to install the Spanish (Spain), French (France), and Chinese (PRC) language packs and satellite packages for Windows 10 Enterprise multisession, version 2004. The script integrates the language interface pack and all necessary satellite packages into the image. However, you can also modify this script to install other languages. Just make sure to run the script from an elevated PowerShell session, or else it won't work.

The script is available at https://github.com/Ar-Sa/Arun/blob/master/Powershell/Add%20language%20packs%20to%20a%20Windows%2010%20multisession%20image/Add-AVDLanguagePack.ps1.

```
########################################################
## Add Languages to running Windows Image for Capture##
########################################################

##Disable Language Pack Cleanup##
Disable-ScheduledTask -TaskPath "\Microsoft\Windows\AppxDeploymentClient\"
-TaskName "Pre-staged app cleanup"

##Set Language Pack Content Stores##
[string]$LIPContent = "E:"

##Spanish##
Add-AppProvisionedPackage -Online -PackagePath $LIPContent\es-es\
LanguageExperiencePack.es-es.Neutral.appx -LicensePath $LIPContent\es-es\
License.xml
Add-WindowsPackage -Online -PackagePath $LIPContent\Microsoft-Windows-
Client-Language-Pack_x64_es-es.cab
Add-WindowsPackage -Online -PackagePath $LIPContent\Microsoft-Windows-
LanguageFeatures-Basic-es-es-Package~31bf3856ad364e35~amd64~~.cab
Add-WindowsPackage -Online -PackagePath $LIPContent\Microsoft-Windows-
LanguageFeatures-Handwriting-es-es-Package~31bf3856ad364e35~amd64~~.cab
Add-WindowsPackage -Online -PackagePath $LIPContent\Microsoft-Windows-
LanguageFeatures-OCR-es-es-Package~31bf3856ad364e35~amd64~~.cab
```

```
Add-WindowsPackage -Online -PackagePath $LIPContent\Microsoft-Windows-
LanguageFeatures-Speech-es-es-Package~31bf3856ad364e35~amd64~~.cab
Add-WindowsPackage -Online -PackagePath $LIPContent\Microsoft-Windows-
LanguageFeatures-TextToSpeech-es-es-Package~31bf3856ad364e35~amd64~~.cab
Add-WindowsPackage -Online -PackagePath $LIPContent\Microsoft-Windows-
NetFx3-OnDemand-Package~31bf3856ad364e35~amd64~es-es~.cab
Add-WindowsPackage -Online -PackagePath $LIPContent\Microsoft-Windows-
InternetExplorer-Optional-Package~31bf3856ad364e35~amd64~es-es~.cab
Add-WindowsPackage -Online -PackagePath $LIPContent\Microsoft-Windows-
MSPaint-FoD-Package~31bf3856ad364e35~amd64~es-es~.cab
Add-WindowsPackage -Online -PackagePath $LIPContent\Microsoft-Windows-
Notepad-FoD-Package~31bf3856ad364e35~amd64~es-es~.cab
Add-WindowsPackage -Online -PackagePath $LIPContent\Microsoft-Windows-
PowerShell-ISE-FOD-Package~31bf3856ad364e35~amd64~es-es~.cab
Add-WindowsPackage -Online -PackagePath $LIPContent\Microsoft-Windows-
Printing-WFS-FoD-Package~31bf3856ad364e35~amd64~es-es~.cab
Add-WindowsPackage -Online -PackagePath $LIPContent\Microsoft-Windows-
StepsRecorder-Package~31bf3856ad364e35~amd64~es-es~.cab
Add-WindowsPackage -Online -PackagePath $LIPContent\Microsoft-Windows-
WordPad-FoD-Package~31bf3856ad364e35~amd64~es-es~.cab
$LanguageList = Get-WinUserLanguageList
$LanguageList.Add("es-es")
Set-WinUserLanguageList $LanguageList -force

##French##
Add-AppProvisionedPackage -Online -PackagePath $LIPContent\fr-fr\
LanguageExperiencePack.fr-fr.Neutral.appx -LicensePath $LIPContent\fr-fr\
License.xml
Add-WindowsPackage -Online -PackagePath $LIPContent\Microsoft-Windows-
Client-Language-Pack_x64_fr-fr.cab
Add-WindowsPackage -Online -PackagePath $LIPContent\Microsoft-Windows-
LanguageFeatures-Basic-fr-fr-Package~31bf3856ad364e35~amd64~~.cab
Add-WindowsPackage -Online -PackagePath $LIPContent\Microsoft-Windows-
LanguageFeatures-Handwriting-fr-fr-Package~31bf3856ad364e35~amd64~~.cab
Add-WindowsPackage -Online -PackagePath $LIPContent\Microsoft-Windows-
LanguageFeatures-OCR-fr-fr-Package~31bf3856ad364e35~amd64~~.cab
```

```
Add-WindowsPackage -Online -PackagePath $LIPContent\Microsoft-Windows-
LanguageFeatures-Speech-fr-fr-Package~31bf3856ad364e35~amd64~~.cab
Add-WindowsPackage -Online -PackagePath $LIPContent\Microsoft-Windows-
LanguageFeatures-TextToSpeech-fr-fr-Package~31bf3856ad364e35~amd64~~.cab
Add-WindowsPackage -Online -PackagePath $LIPContent\Microsoft-Windows-
NetFx3-OnDemand-Package~31bf3856ad364e35~amd64~fr-fr~.cab
Add-WindowsPackage -Online -PackagePath $LIPContent\Microsoft-Windows-
InternetExplorer-Optional-Package~31bf3856ad364e35~amd64~fr-FR~.cab
Add-WindowsPackage -Online -PackagePath $LIPContent\Microsoft-Windows-
MSPaint-FoD-Package~31bf3856ad364e35~amd64~fr-FR~.cab
Add-WindowsPackage -Online -PackagePath $LIPContent\Microsoft-Windows-
Notepad-FoD-Package~31bf3856ad364e35~amd64~fr-FR~.cab
Add-WindowsPackage -Online -PackagePath $LIPContent\Microsoft-Windows-
PowerShell-ISE-FOD-Package~31bf3856ad364e35~amd64~fr-FR~.cab
Add-WindowsPackage -Online -PackagePath $LIPContent\Microsoft-Windows-
Printing-WFS-FoD-Package~31bf3856ad364e35~amd64~fr-FR~.cab
Add-WindowsPackage -Online -PackagePath $LIPContent\Microsoft-Windows-
StepsRecorder-Package~31bf3856ad364e35~amd64~fr-FR~.cab
Add-WindowsPackage -Online -PackagePath $LIPContent\Microsoft-Windows-
WordPad-FoD-Package~31bf3856ad364e35~amd64~fr-FR~.cab
$LanguageList = Get-WinUserLanguageList
$LanguageList.Add("fr-fr")
Set-WinUserLanguageList $LanguageList -force

##Chinese(PRC)##
Add-AppProvisionedPackage -Online -PackagePath $LIPContent\zh-cn\
LanguageExperiencePack.zh-cn.Neutral.appx -LicensePath $LIPContent\zh-cn\
License.xml
Add-WindowsPackage -Online -PackagePath $LIPContent\Microsoft-Windows-
Client-Language-Pack_x64_zh-cn.cab
Add-WindowsPackage -Online -PackagePath $LIPContent\Microsoft-Windows-
LanguageFeatures-Basic-zh-cn-Package~31bf3856ad364e35~amd64~~.cab
Add-WindowsPackage -Online -PackagePath $LIPContent\Microsoft-Windows-
LanguageFeatures-Fonts-Hans-Package~31bf3856ad364e35~amd64~~.cab
Add-WindowsPackage -Online -PackagePath $LIPContent\Microsoft-Windows-
LanguageFeatures-Handwriting-zh-cn-Package~31bf3856ad364e35~amd64~~.cab
```

```
Add-WindowsPackage -Online -PackagePath $LIPContent\Microsoft-Windows-
LanguageFeatures-OCR-zh-cn-Package~31bf3856ad364e35~amd64~~.cab
Add-WindowsPackage -Online -PackagePath $LIPContent\Microsoft-Windows-
LanguageFeatures-Speech-zh-cn-Package~31bf3856ad364e35~amd64~~.cab
Add-WindowsPackage -Online -PackagePath $LIPContent\Microsoft-Windows-
LanguageFeatures-TextToSpeech-zh-cn-Package~31bf3856ad364e35~amd64~~.cab
Add-WindowsPackage -Online -PackagePath $LIPContent\Microsoft-Windows-
NetFx3-OnDemand-Package~31bf3856ad364e35~amd64~zh-cn~.cab
Add-WindowsPackage -Online -PackagePath $LIPContent\Microsoft-Windows-
InternetExplorer-Optional-Package~31bf3856ad364e35~amd64~zh-cn~.cab
Add-WindowsPackage -Online -PackagePath $LIPContent\Microsoft-Windows-
MSPaint-FoD-Package~31bf3856ad364e35~amd64~zh-cn~.cab
Add-WindowsPackage -Online -PackagePath $LIPContent\Microsoft-Windows-
Notepad-FoD-Package~31bf3856ad364e35~amd64~zh-cn~.cab
Add-WindowsPackage -Online -PackagePath $LIPContent\Microsoft-Windows-
PowerShell-ISE-FOD-Package~31bf3856ad364e35~amd64~zh-cn~.cab
Add-WindowsPackage -Online -PackagePath $LIPContent\Microsoft-Windows-
Printing-WFS-FoD-Package~31bf3856ad364e35~amd64~zh-cn~.cab
Add-WindowsPackage -Online -PackagePath $LIPContent\Microsoft-Windows-
StepsRecorder-Package~31bf3856ad364e35~amd64~zh-cn~.cab
Add-WindowsPackage -Online -PackagePath $LIPContent\Microsoft-Windows-
WordPad-FoD-Package~31bf3856ad364e35~amd64~zh-cn~.cab
$LanguageList = Get-WinUserLanguageList
$LanguageList.Add("zh-cn")
Set-WinUserLanguageList $LanguageList -force
```

The script might take a while depending on the number of languages you need to install.

## Enable Languages in the Windows Settings App

Once you deploy the host pool, you have to add the language to each user's language list so they can select their preferred language in the Settings menu. You can set up the following script as an automated task or logon script that activates when the user signs into their session:

```
$LanguageList = Get-WinUserLanguageList
$LanguageList.Add("es-es")
$LanguageList.Add("fr-fr")
$LanguageList.Add("zh-cn")
Set-WinUserLanguageList $LanguageList -force
```

After a user changes their language settings, they'll need to sign out of their Azure Virtual Desktop session and sign in again for the changes to take effect.

# Summary

In this chapter, you learned about creating a Azure Virtual Desktop image and publishing the image to the shared image gallery. We also talked about options to automate the image creation process, manage the image versions, and create image replicas in different regions. Since you know everything about image creation, the next chapter will cover Azure Virtual Desktop session host creation.

# CHAPTER 8

# Create and Configure Host Pools and Session Hosts

In this chapter, you will learn how to set up pooled and personal session hosts; set up host pools using the Azure portal, PowerShell, Azure CLI, Azure Resource Manager (ARM) templates; and configure host pool settings such as USB redirect and audio redirect. Also, you will learn about the recommended process to assign users to host pools, including pooled and personal desktops.

Finally, you will look at OS patching options and recommendations and how to apply security and compliance settings on the session host.

Let's get started with pooled and personal host pool/session host creation.

## Create a Host Pool by Using the Azure Portal

There are two different types of host pools that Azure Virtual Desktop offers, and each host pool creation process is little different, so we are going to learn how to create both personal and pooled host pools using the Azure portal. Let's understand the host pool types before we begin with the host pool creation.

- *Host pool*: A host pool is a collection of Azure virtual machines (VMs) that act as session hosts for AVD. Users obtain access to host pools by being allocated to a host pool via an assigned application group.

© Arun Sabale and Balu N Ilag 2022
A. Sabale and B. N. Ilag, *Microsoft Azure Virtual Desktop Guide*,
https://doi.org/10.1007/978-1-4842-8063-8_8

- *Pooled*: You can configure a pooled host pool where several users sign in and share a VM. Typically, none of those users would be a local administrator on the pooled VM. With pooled VMs, you can use one of the recommended images that includes a Windows 10 Enterprise multisession. This operating system is exclusive to AVD. You can also create/use your own custom image.

- *Personal*: A personal host pool is where each user has their own dedicated VM. Those users would typically be local administrators for the VM. This enables the user to install or uninstall apps without impacting other users.

Let's see how you can create both host pool types from the Azure portal.

# Personal Host Pool Creation Using the Azure Portal

A personal virtual desktop is a virtual machine hosted on a Remote Desktop virtualization host and assigned to a dedicated user. A personal virtual desktop is one VM per user assignment and retains all changes made by the user. The Remote Desktop (RD) Connection Broker Manager can be used to assign an unassigned virtual machine to a new user. The assignment is stored in Active Directory (AD) and stays intact even after the user logs off from the personal virtual desktop. An administrator can reassign a personal virtual desktop or make changes to the assignment through the RD Connection Broker Manager.

Let's begin with creating the personal desktop from the Azure portal. Follow these steps:

1. Log in to `portal.Azure.com` with an appropriate account. The login account should have contributor or an equivalent permission so that you can create virtual desktop resources in Azure.

2. Use the top search box to navigate to Azure Virtual Desktop.

3. On the Azure Virtual Desktop page, click the "Create a host pool" button to get started. See Figure 8-1.

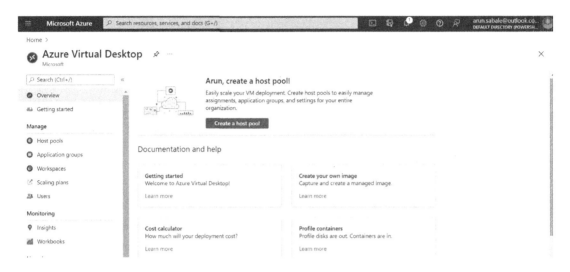

***Figure 8-1.*** *Azure Virtual DesktopHost pool creation*

4.  On the Basic tab you will enter common details such as a resource
    group, a host pool name, and the location. Set the host pool type
    to Personal and the assignment type to Automatic/Direct based
    on your requirements.

    *Automatic assignment*: You must assign the user to the personal
    desktop host pool, and this option will assign the next available
    VM automatically to a new user at the first login. The assignment
    will be permanent after the first login.

    *Direct assignment*: When you use direct assignment, you must
    assign the user to both the personal desktop host pool and a
    specific session host before they can connect to their personal
    desktop.

    Click the Next button and go to the Virtual Machines tab. See
    Figure 8-2.

213

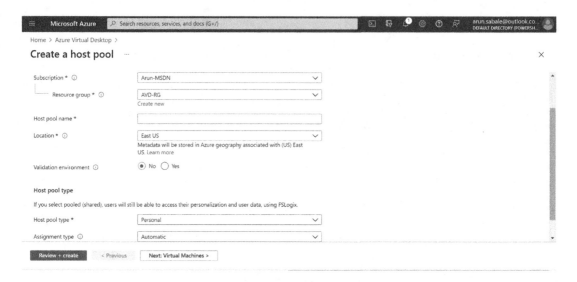

***Figure 8-2.*** *Azure Virtual Desktop, personal host pool creation*

5.  On the Virtual Machines tab, you can create a session host, or you
    can add a session host after the host pool creation. If you select
    virtual machine creation, then enter all the required details for the
    virtual machine, as shown here:

    *Name prefix*: This will be the prefix for the VM in the host pool,
    and the suffix will be added by Azure Virtual Desktop at the end of
    the name.

    *VM location*: You can choose a different region for virtual
    machines than the host pool, especially if you want metadata
    to be stored in a particular geography, but you want the virtual
    machines closer to the user.

    *Availability zone*: Azure offers a range of options for managing the
    availability and resiliency for your applications. Architect your
    solution to use replicated virtual machines in availability zones
    or availability sets to protect your apps and data from data center
    outages and maintenance events. See Figure 8-3.

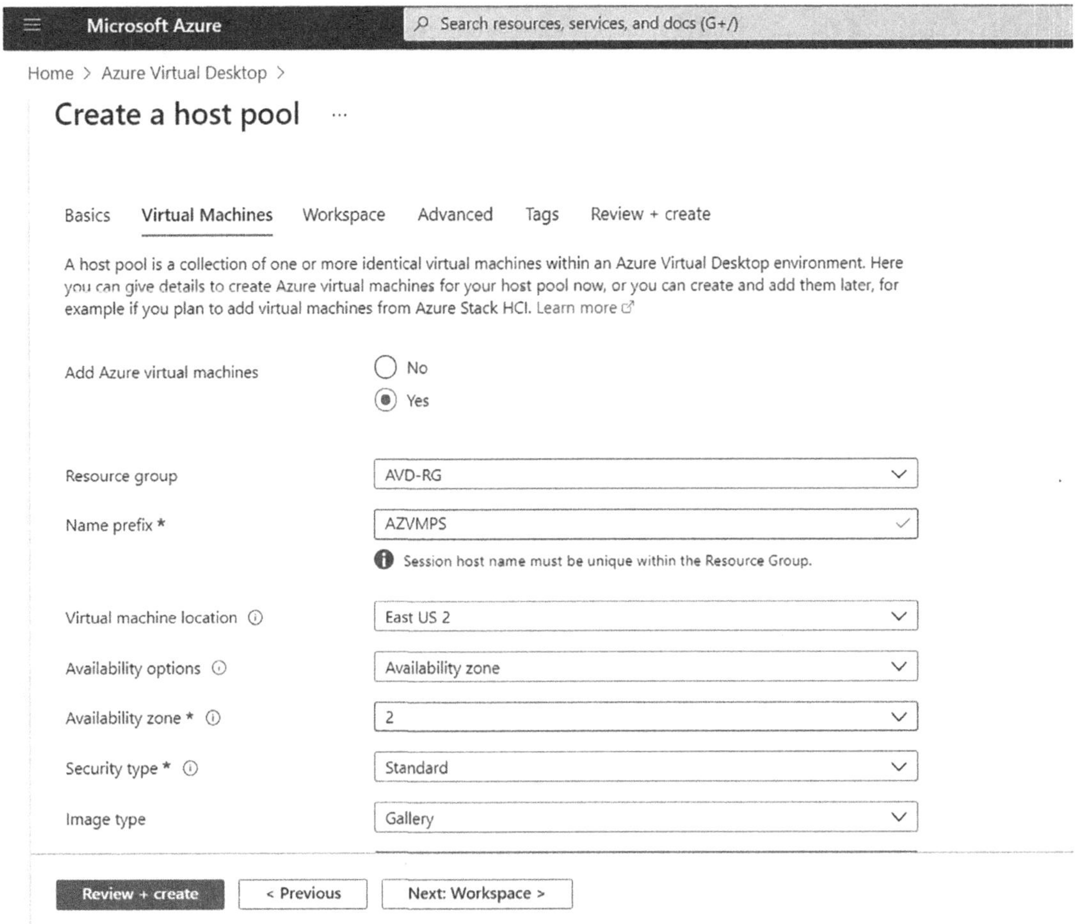

**Figure 8-3.** *Azure Virtual Desktop, personal hostpool creation, Virtual Machines tab*

*Image and size*: You can select the size and image based on the assessment and your organization's requirements (refer to Chapter 2).

*VNet and security*: Select the existing virtual network you created in an earlier chapter (refer to Chapter 3 for details) See Figure 8-4.

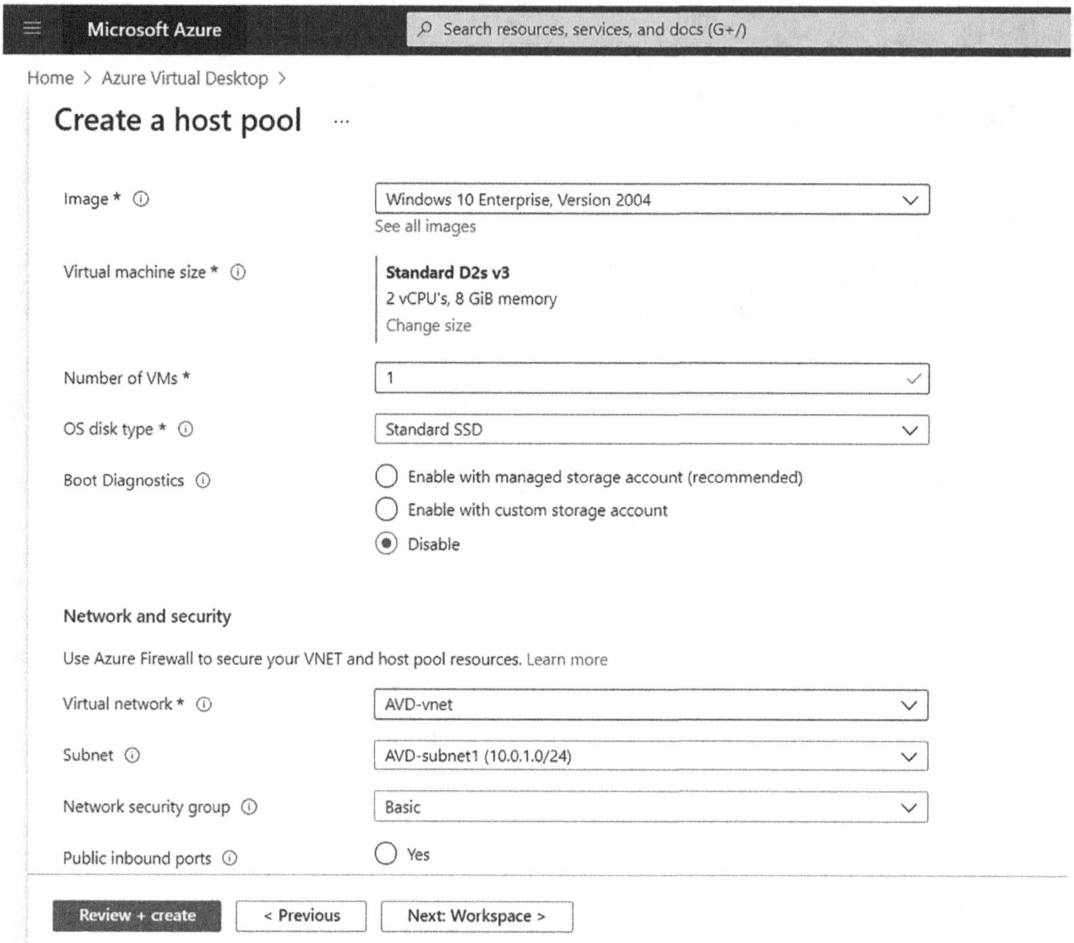

**Figure 8-4.** *Azure Virtual Desktop, personal host pool creation, VM size and Network tab*

*Domain join*: You can select Active Directory (on-premises) and enter the domain join OU plus credentials. If you are using Azure ADDS, then the default computer OU for domain join is `OU=AADDC Computers,DC=powershelltalk,DC=com` (replace `powershelltalk` with your correct domain name).

Azure Active Directory is not recommended for production as it will just register the session host to Azure without requiring an organizational account to sign in to the device. If you select Azure Active Directory, then you may not be prompted for credentials as the session host will get registered to Azure Active Directory with the Azure portal's logged-in credential. See Figure 8-5.

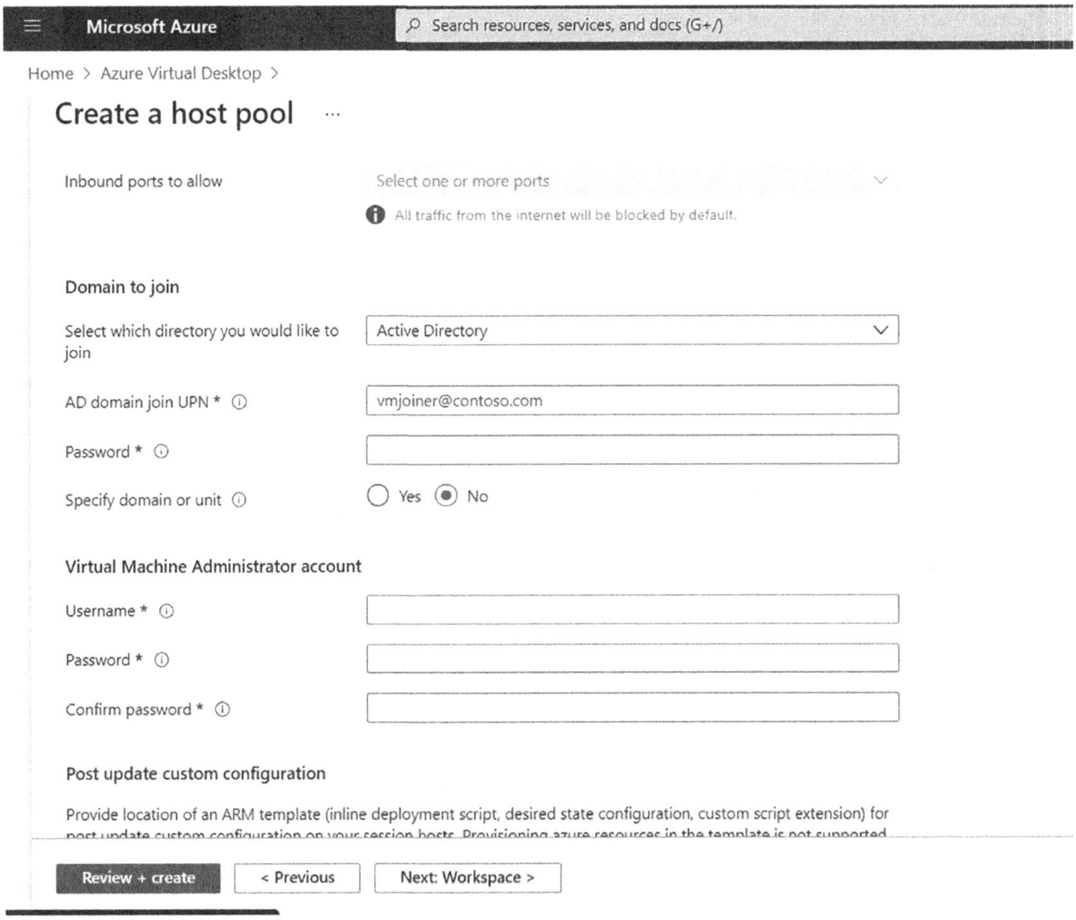

**Figure 8-5.** *Azure Virtual Desktop, personal hostpool creation, Domain join tab*

6.  Click the Next button and go to the Workspace tab. On the Workspace tab, select the existing workspace or create a new one for the host pool. See Figure 8-6.

217

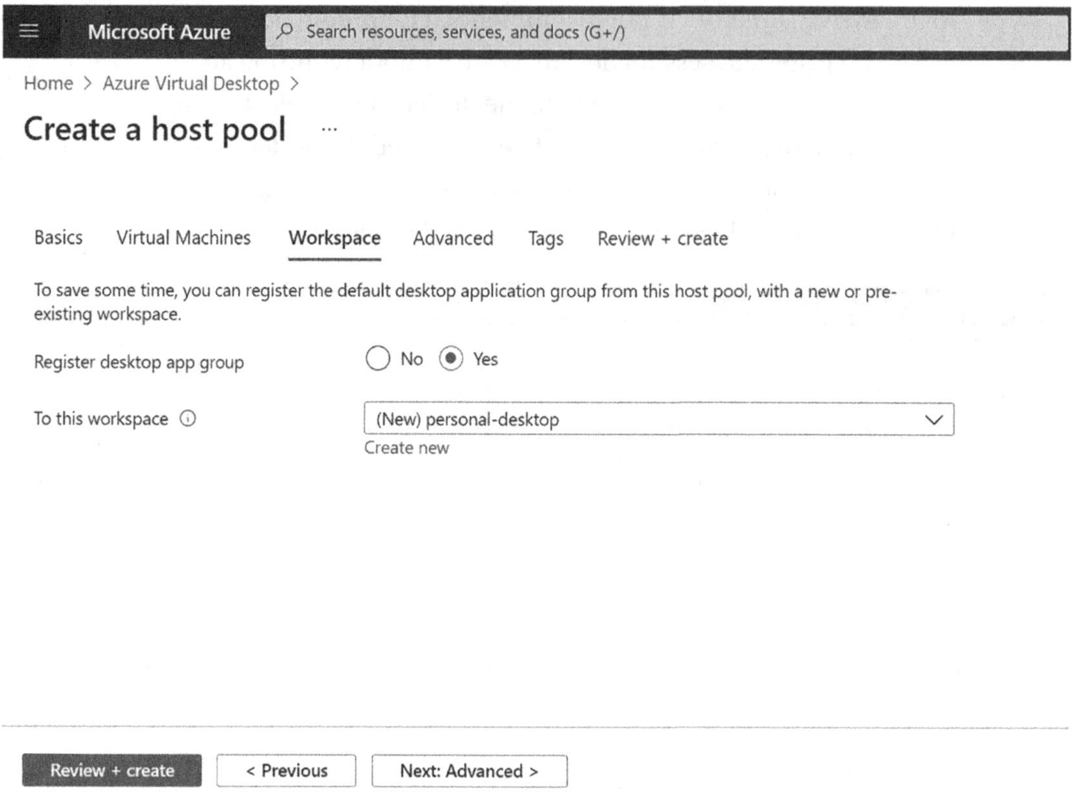

**Figure 8-6.** *Azure Virtual Desktop, personal hostpool creation, Workspace tab*

7.  Next is the Advanced tab on which you can define the Azure
    Virtual Desktop diagnostic log location; you can store diagnostic
    logs in log analytics, storage accounts, and event hubs. The
    diagnostic log contains all the connection information such as
    successful connections, failed connections, and AVD host pool
    health, so it is recommended to enable diagnostic logs. If you are
    planning to create an Azure dashboard for AVD, then you can use
    log analytics to store all the diagnostic logs. See Figure 8-7.

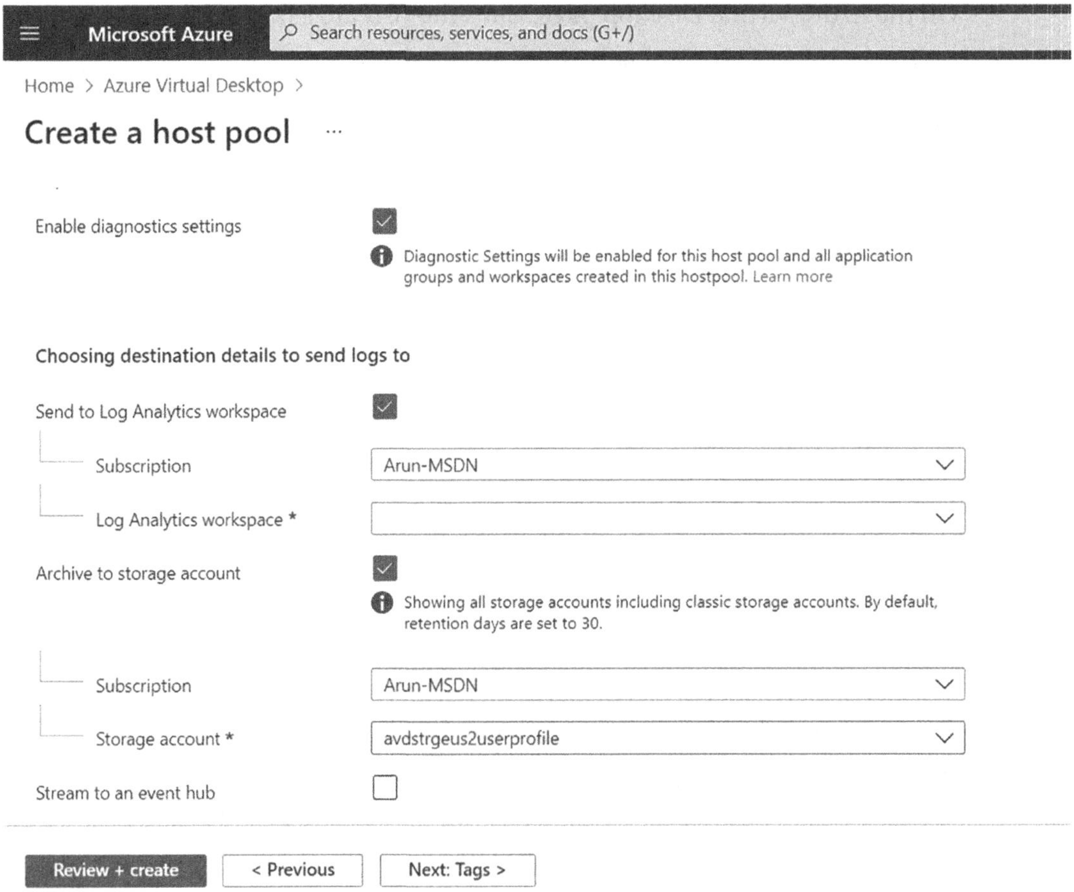

**Figure 8-7.** *Azure Virtual Desktop, personal hostpool creation, diagnostics*

8.  Click the "Review + create" button and then the Create button to
    create your host pool.

# Pooled Host Pool Creation Using the Azure Portal

Follow these steps:

1.  Log in to `portal.azure.com` with an appropriate account.
    The login account should have contributor permission or an
    equivalent permission so that you can create virtual desktop
    resources in Azure.

2.  Use the top search box to navigate to Azure Virtual Desktop.

3.  On the Azure Virtual Desktop page, Click the "Create a host pool" button to get started. See Figure 8-8.

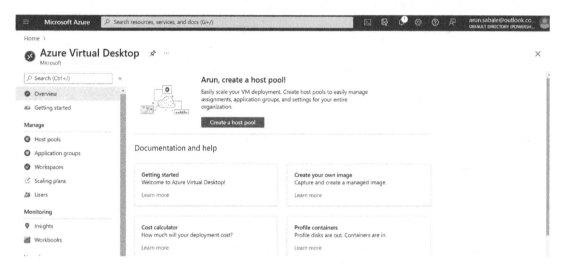

***Figure 8-8.*** *Azure Virtual Desktop, pooled host pool creation*

4.  On the Basics tab you will enter common details such as a resource group, a host pool name, and the location. Set the host pool type to Pooled and the load balancing type to Depth first or Breadth first, based on your requirements.

    -   *Pooled session load balancing algorithm*: Session host load balancing is achieved by either the depth-first or breadth-first algorithm. The broker decides how new incoming sessions are to be distributed across the VMs in a host pool.

    -   *Breadth-first*: This is the default configuration for new nonpersistent host pools. It distributes new user sessions across all available session hosts in the host pool. When you configure the breadth-first load balancing, you may set a maximum session limit per session host in the host pool.

    -   *Depth-first*: This distributes new user sessions to an available session host with the highest number of connections, but that has not reached its maximum session limit threshold. When you configure the depth-first load balancing, you must set a maximum session limit per session host in the host pool.

- *Max session limit*: This is the maximum number of users who have concurrent sessions on a session host. When setting a host pool to have depth-first load balancing or when you're planning to use autoscaling, you must set an appropriate max session limit according to the configuration of your deployment and capacity of your VMs. It is important to calculate the max session limit per session host properly to avoid performance issues in production (refer to Chapter 2 for more details).

Table 8-1 shows an example of the maximum users per vCPU.

***Table 8-1.*** *Azure Virtual Desktop Usage Profile*

| Workload Type | Maximum Users/ vCPU | Example Azure Instances | Profile Storage Minimum |
|---|---|---|---|
| Light | 6 | D8s_v4, F8s_v2, D8as_v4, D16s_v4, F16s_v2, D16as_v4 | 30 GB |
| Medium | 4 | D8s_v4, F8s_v2, D8as_v4, D16s_v4, F16s_v2, D16as_v4 | 30 GB |
| Heavy | 2 | D8s_v4, F8s_v2, D8as_v4, D16s_v4, F16s_v2, D16as_v4 | 30 GB |
| Power | 1 | D8s_v4, F8s_v2, D8as_v4, D16s_v4, F16s_v2, D16as_v4, NV12, NVv4 | 30 GB |

It is always recommended to consider application/software recommendations and operating system requirements while deciding the usage profile for the pooled desktop.

Click the Next button and go to the Virtual Machines tab. See
Figure 8-9.

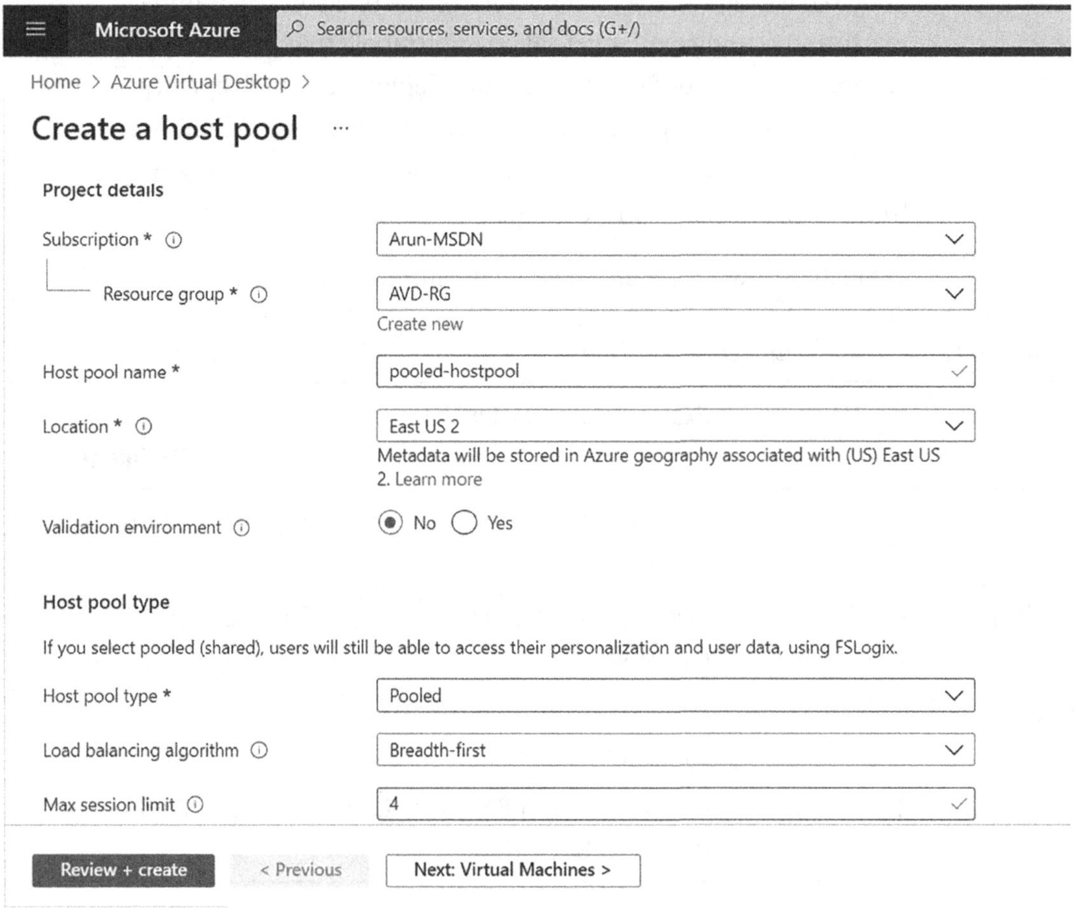

*Figure 8-9. Azure Virtual Desktop pooled hostpool creation, step 1*

5. On the Virtual Machines tab, you can a create session host or you
   can add a session host after the host pool creation. If you select to
   create a virtual machine, then enter all the required details for the
   virtual machine, as shown here:

   • *Name prefix*: This will be the prefix for the VM in the host pool,
     and a suffix will be added by Azure Virtual Desktop at the end of
     the name.

- *VM Location*: You can choose a different region for virtual machines than the host pool, especially if you want metadata to be stored in a particular geography, but you want the virtual machines closer to the user.

- *Availability zone*: Azure offers a range of options for managing the availability and resiliency of your applications. Architect your solution to use replicated virtual machines in availability zones or availability sets to protect your apps and data from data center outages and maintenance events. See Figure 8-10.

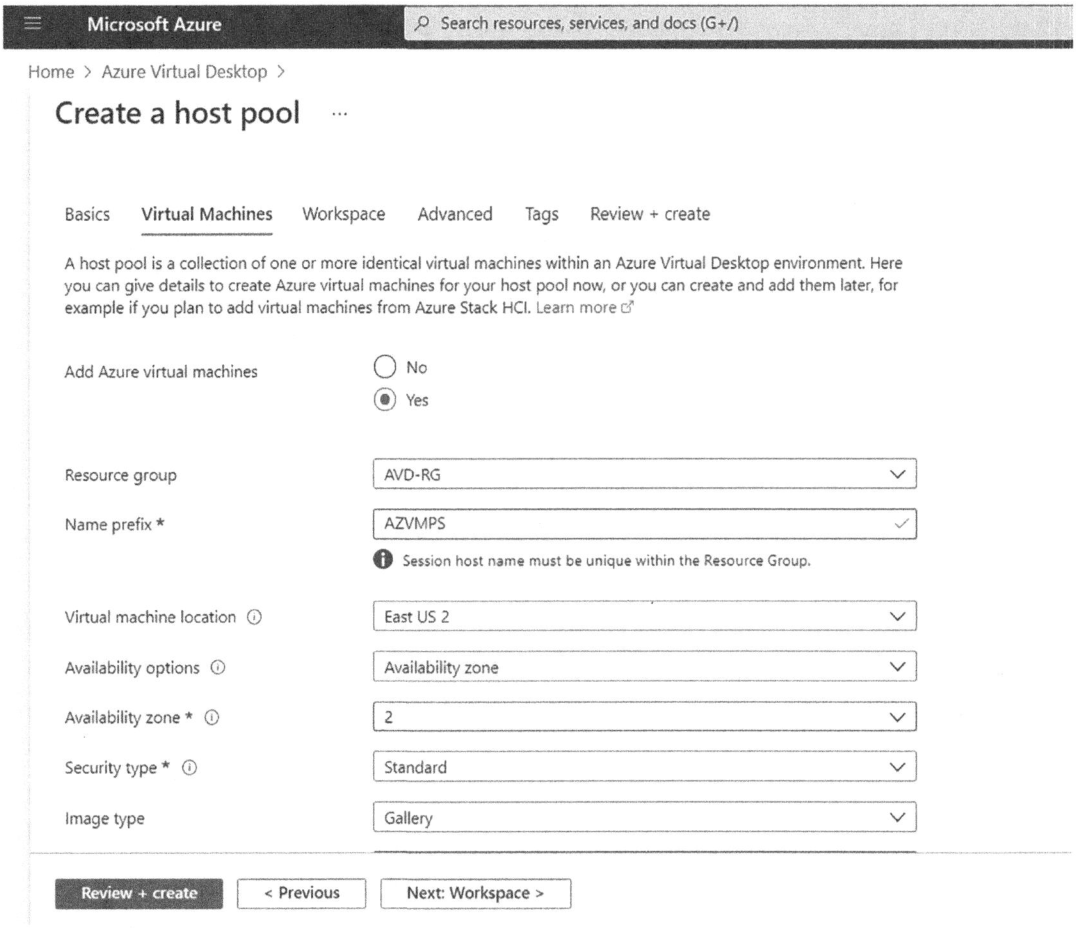

*Figure 8-10.* *Azure Virtual Desktop pooled hostpool creation, Virtual Machines tab*

*Image and size*: You can select the size and multisession image based on the assessment and your organization requirement (refer to Chapter 2).

*VNet and security*: Select the existing virtual network you created in an earlier chapter (refer to Chapter 4 for details). See Figure 8-11.

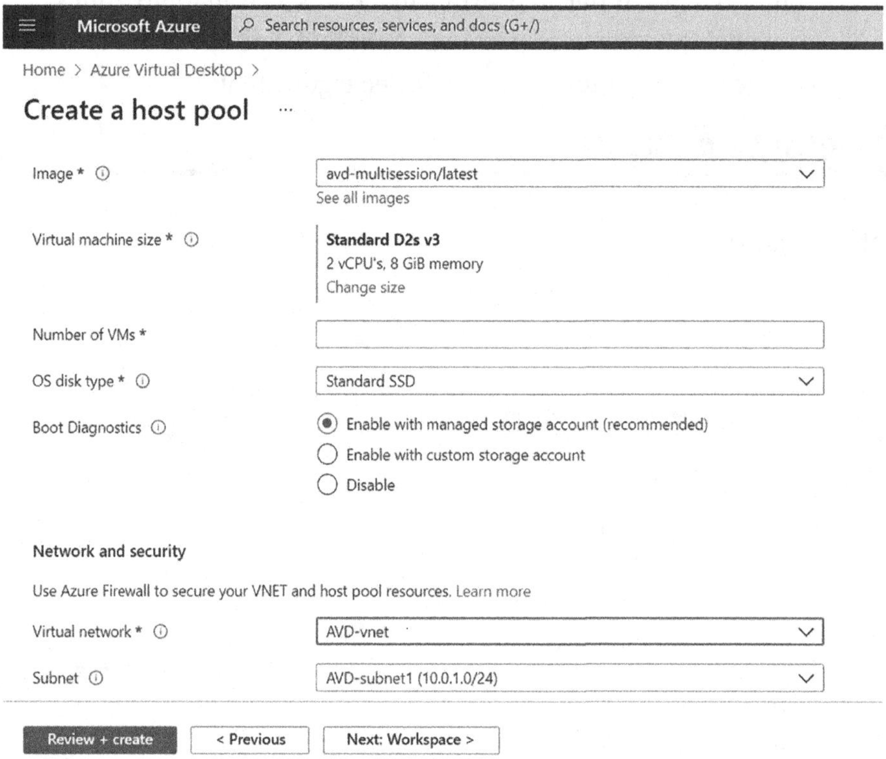

*Figure 8-11.*  *Azure Virtual Desktop, pooled hostpool creation, VM size and network tab*

*Domain join*: You can select Active Directory (on-premises) and enter the domain join OU and credentials. If you select Azure Active Directory, then you may not be prompted for credentials. See Figure 8-12.

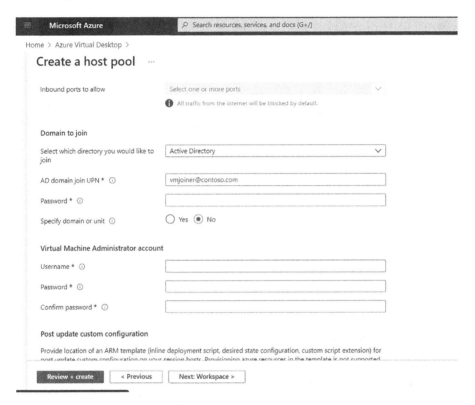

***Figure 8-12.*** *Azure Virtual Desktop, pooled hostpool creation, Domain join tab*

6.  Click the Next button and go to the Workspace tab on which you select the existing workspace or create a new one for the host pool. See Figure 8-13.

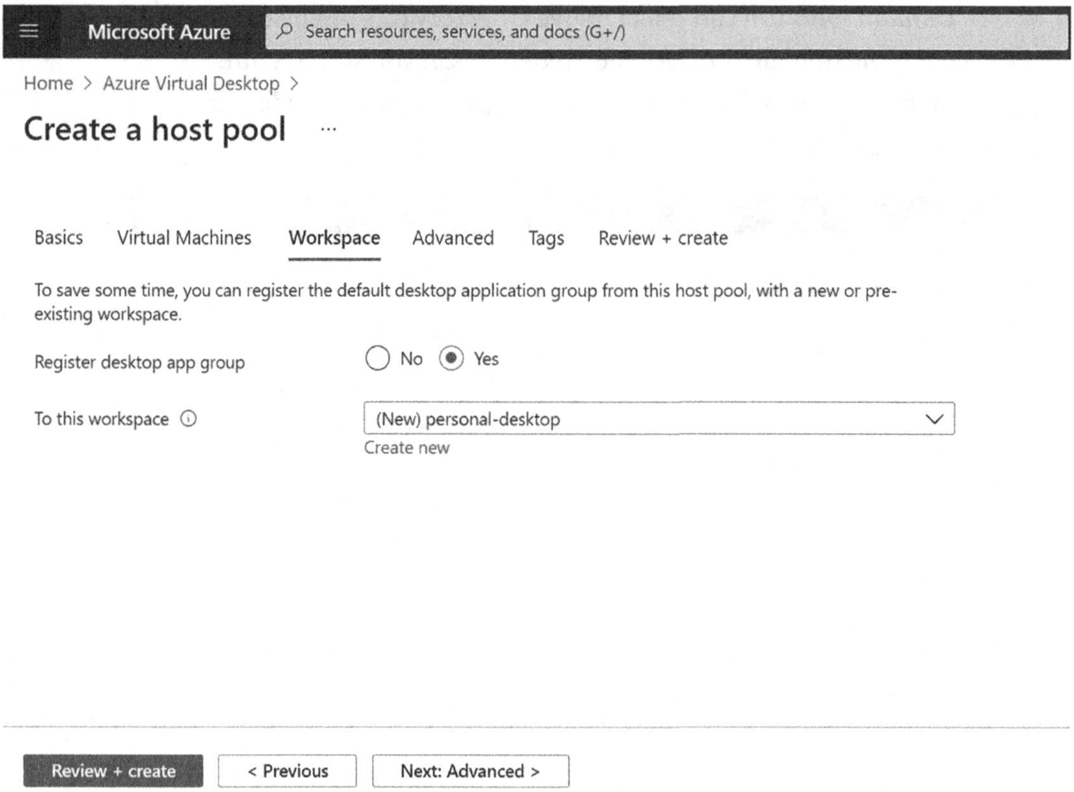

**Figure 8-13.** *Azure Virtual Desktop pooled hostpool creation, Workspace tab*

7.  The next tab is Advanced, where you can define the Azure Virtual
    Desktop diagnostic log location; you can store diagnostic logs in
    log analytics, a storage account, and an event hub. The diagnostic
    log contains all the connection information such as successful
    connections, failed connections, and AVD host pool health, so it is
    recommended to enable the diagnostic logs. If you are planning to
    create an Azure dashboard for AVD, you can use the log analytics
    to store all the diagnostic logs. See Figure 8-14.

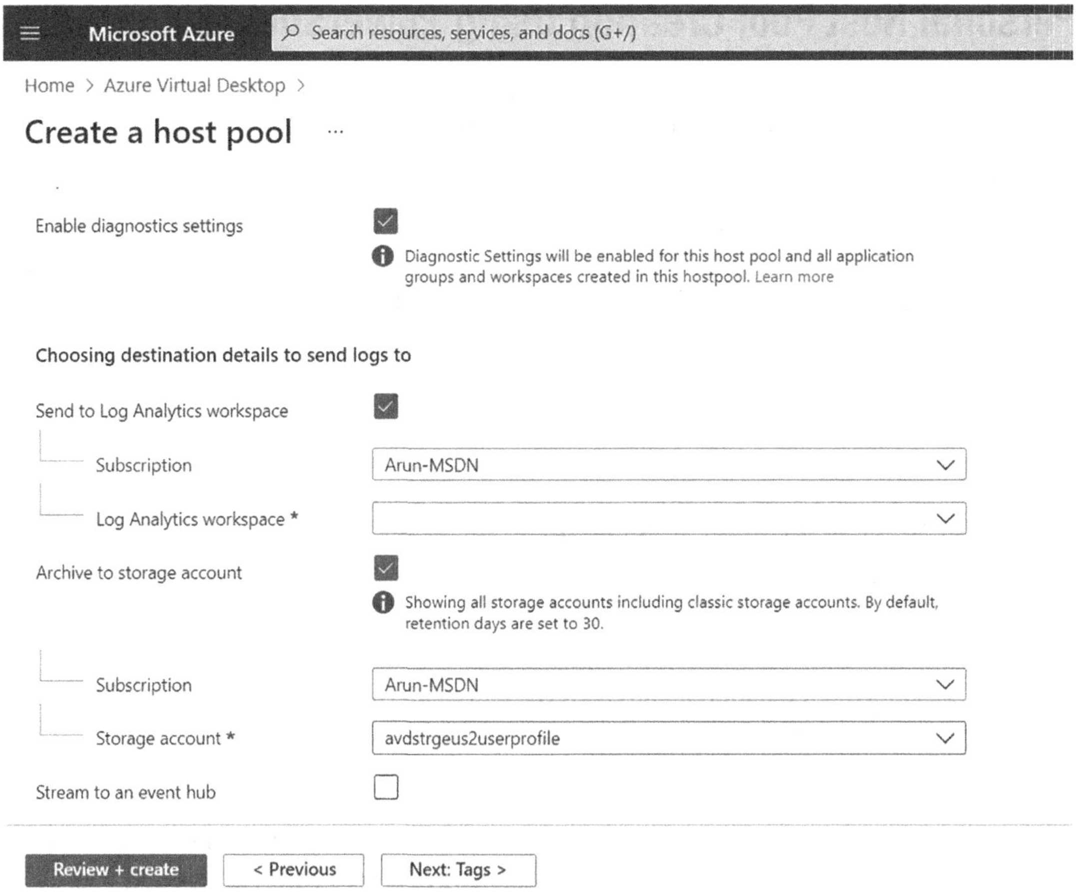

*Figure 8-14.* *Azure Virtual Desktop pooled hostpool creation, diagnostics*

8.  Click the "Review + create" button and then the Create button to create your host pool. See Figure 8-15.

# Automate the Creation of Azure Virtual Desktop Host and Host Pools

The following sections cover creation of azure virtual desktop including session host, hostpool and hostpool config using Powershell, Azure CLI, ARM. If you are thinking about automating Azure Virtual Desktop deployment then this section will help you to understand all automation options.

# Personal Host Pool Creation Using PowerShell/CLI or ARM

In this section, you will see the automation options for creating a personal host pool. The PowerShell module `Az.DesktopVirtualization` allows you to create a personal host pool as well as add a session host in the personal host pool.

I always recommend using the Azure Resource Manager (ARM) template wherever it is possible to get additional benefits from IAC.

Let's get started with the steps for PowerShell and ARM. The following are the resources that need to be created as part of an Azure Virtual Desktop host pool:

- Resource group to group all host pool–related resources

- AVD workspace to group multiple host pools

- Personal host pool and app group

- VM/session host creation

- Domain join extension

- Azure ARM `JsonADDomainExtension` extension to join a VM to the host pool with a host pool token

The full PowerShell and ARM code to create an Azure Virtual Desktop personal desktop can be found at `https://github.com/Ar-Sa/Arun/blob/master/PowerShell/PowerShell%20and%20ARM%20to%20create%20Azure%20virtual%20desktop%20personal%20desktop/New-AVDPersonalHostpool.ps1`.

First you have to log in to Azure using the `Connect-AzAccount` command and select the correct subscription in which you want to create the Azure Virtual Desktop host pool. You can create a new resource group and the AVD workspace using the following PowerShell command, or if you already have a resource group and workspace, then you can skip this step. The following command also checks if the resource group and workspace are already present in the selected subscription, and if it is, then PowerShell will skip the resource creation. See Figure 8-15.

```
68
69   #region create RG
70   $RGDetail = Get-AzResourceGroup -Name $ResourceGroupName -Location $location -ErrorAction SilentlyContinue
71   if($RGDetail)
72   {
73       Write-Output "RG $ResourceGroupName already exist"
74   }
75   else{
76       $RGDetail1 = New-AzResourceGroup -Name $ResourceGroupName -Location $location
77       Write-Output "RG $ResourceGroupName created"
78   }
79   #endregion
80
81
82   #region create workspace
83   $WorkspaceName= "W-"+$HostPoolName
84   $ErrorActionPreference= "SilentlyContinue"
85   $WPDetail = get-AzWvdWorkspace -Name $WorkspaceName -ResourceGroupName $ResourceGroupName
86   $ErrorActionPreference= "Continue"
87   if($WPDetail)
88   {
89       Write-Output "WorkspaceName $WorkspaceName already exist"
90   }
91   else{
92       $WorkspaceDetail = New-AzWvdWorkspace -Name $WorkspaceName -ResourceGroupName $ResourceGroupName -Location $location
93       Write-Output "WorkspaceName $WorkspaceName created"
94   }
95   #endregion
```

***Figure 8-15.*** *Azure Virtual Desktop workspace creation via PowerShell*

The cmdlet New-AzWvdHostPool will create the host pool, and you can use the New-AzWvdApplicationGroup cmdlet to create a desktop application group. Additionally, Register-AzWvdApplicationGroup will register the desktop app group with the workspace. You can either create a workspace with this cmdlet or use an existing workspace.

The cmdlet New-AzWvdRegistrationInfo creates a registration token to authorize a session host to join the host pool and save it to the $token variable. You can specify how long the registration token is valid by using the -ExpirationTime parameter. The token's expiration date can be no less than an hour and no more than one month. If you set -ExpirationTime outside of that limit, the cmdlet won't create the token. Note that ExpirationTime accepts the date and time in a specific format, so you have to convert the value to a string in the yyyy-MM-ddTHH:mm:ss.fffffffZ format. See Figure 8-16.

```
96
97    #region create Hostpool
98    $appGroup= $HostPoolName+"-app"
99    $ErrorActionPreference= "SilentlyContinue"
100   $hpDetail = get-AzWvdHostPool -Name $HostPoolName -ResourceGroupName $ResourceGroupName
101   $ErrorActionPreference= "Continue"
102   if($hpDetail)
103   {
104       Write-Output "HostPoolName $HostPoolName already exist"
105   }
106   else{
107       $hpDetail1 =  New-AzWvdHostPool -ResourceGroupName $resourcegroupname -Name $HostPoolName -WorkspaceName `
108       $WorkspaceName -HostPoolType $HostpoolType -LoadBalancerType $loadBalancerType -Location $location `
109       -DesktopAppGroupName $appGroup -PreferredAppGroupType $ApplicationGroupType
110       Write-Output "HostPoolName $HostPoolName created"
111   }
112   #endregion
113
114
115
116   #region get registration token
117   $token = (new-AzWvdRegistrationInfo -HostPoolName $HostPoolName -ResourceGroupName $ResourceGroupName `
118   -ExpirationTime $((get-date).ToUniversalTime().AddDays(1).ToString('yyyy-MM-ddTHH:mm:ss.fffffffZ'))).Token
119   #endregion
120
```

***Figure 8-16.*** *Azure Virtual Desktop host pool creation via PowerShell*

The next step is to create the session host and register it with the host pool with the correct token we generated earlier. The New-AzResourceDeployment cmdlet will trigger the ARM template from the URI https://raw.githubusercontent.com/Ar-Sa/Arun/master/PowerShell/PowerShell%20and%20ARM%20to%20create%20Azure%20virtual%20desktop%20personal%20desktop/New-personalAVDTemplate.json, and the ARM template will take care of creating the session host, domain joining, and registering session host with a host pool. You can add customization in the ARM template to make the VM/session host compliant as per your requirements. See Figure 8-17.

```
126    #calling ARM template to create session host and register to hostpool
127
128    $tagsObject = @{...}
132
133    $Parameters = [ordered]@{
134            "imageReferenceID"          = "$imageID"
135            "rdshPrefix" = "$rdshNamePrefix"
136            "rdshVMDiskType"            = "StandardSSD_LRS"
137            "rdshVmSize"    = "$rdshVmSize"
138            "administratorAccountUsername"     = "$DomainUser"
139            "administratorAccountPassword"     = "$DomainPass"
140            "Domain"        = "$Domain"
141            "ouPath"            = "$DomainOU"
142            "existingSubnetName"            = "$existingSubnetName"
143            "networkInterfaceTags"            = $tagsObject
144            "virtualMachineTags"        = $tagsObject
145            "vmInitialNumber"        = 1
146            "hostpoolToken"        = $token
147            "hostpoolName" = "$HostPoolName"
148            "vmLocation"        = "$location"
149            "virtualNetworkResourceGroupName" = "$virtualNetworkResourceGroupName"
150            "existingVnetName" = "$existingVnetName"
151            "rdshNumberOfInstances"=$HostCount
152            }
153
154    New-AzResourceGroupDeployment -TemplateUri "https://github.com/Ar-Sa/Arun/blob/26b748a5a90e3fa9397d6b56f818ec744319cd
155    -TemplateParameterObject $Parameters -ResourceGroupName $ResourceGroupName -Name $HostPoolName
```

***Figure 8-17.*** *Azure Virtual Desktop creation via PowerShell and ARM*

The PowerShell script/runbook is available at https://raw.githubusercontent.com/Ar-Sa/Arun/master/PowerShell/PowerShell%20and%20ARM%20to%20create%20Azure%20virtual%20desktop%20personal%20desktop/New-AVDPersonalHostpool.ps1.

```
1.    <#
2.        .DESCRIPTION
3.            Runbook to Create AVD personal host pool
4.
5.        .NOTES
6.            AUTHOR: Arun sabale
7.            LASTEDIT: Dec 05, 2021
8.    #>
9.
10.   param(
11.
```

```
12.        [Parameter(mandatory = $false)]
13.        [string]$Host poolType = "pooled", #Personal / Pooled
14.
15.        [Parameter(mandatory = $false)]
16.        [string]$loadBalancerType = "BreadthFirst",#<for pooled-
           BreadthFirst|DepthFirst & for personal - Persistent>
17.
18.        [Parameter(mandatory = $true)]
19.        [string]$Host poolName = "avdhost pool2",
20.
21.        [Parameter(mandatory = $true)]
22.        [string]$ResourceGroupName = "AVD-RG",
23.
24.        [Parameter(mandatory = $true)]
25.        [int]$HostCount = 2,
26.
27.        [Parameter(mandatory = $true)]
28.        [string]$rdshNamePrefix = "Azeus2pl",
29.
30.        [Parameter(mandatory = $true)]
31.        [string]$rdshVmSize = "Standard_D4s_v3",
32.
33.        [Parameter(mandatory = $true)]
34.        [string]$existingVNetName = "AVD-vnet",
35.
36.        [Parameter(mandatory = $true)]
37.        [string]$existingSubnetName = "AVD-subnet1",
38.
39.        [Parameter(mandatory = $true)]
40.        [string]$virtualNetworkResourceGroupName= "AVD-RG",
41.
42.        [Parameter(mandatory = $true)]
43.        [string]$location = "eastus2",
44.
45.        [Parameter(mandatory = $false)]
```

```
46.        [string]$ApplicationGroupType = "Desktop",   #Desktop or RemoteApp
47.
48.        [Parameter(mandatory = $true)]
49.        [string]$DomainPass = "********",
50.
51.        [Parameter(mandatory = $true)]
52.        [string]$DomainUser = "admin*@powershelltalk.com",
53.
54.        [Parameter(mandatory = $true)]
55.        [string]$Domain = "powershelltalk.com",
56.
57.        [Parameter(mandatory = $true)]
58.        [string]$DomainOU = "OU=AADDC Computers,DC=powershelltalk,DC=com",
59.
60.        [Parameter(mandatory = $false)]
61.        [string]$MaxSessionLimit=4, #applicable only if pooled host pool
62.
63.        [Parameter(mandatory = $false)]
64.        [string]$CustomRdpProperty="drivestoredirect:s:;audiomode:i:0;
           videoplaybackmode:i:1;redirectclipboard:i:1;redirectprinters:
           i:1;devicestoredirect:s:*;redirectcomports:i:1;redirectsmart
           cards:i:1;usbdevicestoredirect:s:*;enablecredsspsupport:i:1;
           use multimon:i:1;audiocapturemode:i:1;encode redirected video
           capture:i:1;redirected video capture encoding quality:i:1;
           camerastoredirect:s:*",   #https://docs.microsoft.com/en-us/
           windows-server/remote/remote-desktop-services/clients/rdp-files
65.
66.        [Parameter(mandatory = $true)]
67.        [string]$imageID = "/subscriptions/1d96a493-e9d6-404f-96c6-
           c4a483b6d7b3/resourceGroups/AVD-RG/providers/Microsoft.Compute/
           galleries/AVDimage/images/avd-multisession/versions/0.0.1"
68.
69.    )
70.
71.  try{
```

```
72.
73.    #login to Azure - make sure you login to correct Azure
       subscription via connect-AzAccount or using below commented code
74.
75.    #$SPNKey = ConvertTo-SecureString "$password" -AsPlainText -Force
76.    #$psCred = New-Object System.Management.Automation.
       PSCredential($userid , $SPNKey)
77.    #connect-AzAccount -Credential $psCred
78.    #Select-AzSubscription 1d96a493-e9d6-404f-96c6-c4a483b6d7b3
79.
80.    #region create RG
81.    $RGDetail = Get-AzResourceGroup -Name $ResourceGroupName
       -Location $location -ErrorAction SilentlyContinue
82.    if($RGDetail)
83.    {
84.        Write-Output "RG $ResourceGroupName already exist"
85.    }
86.    else{
87.        $RGDetail1 = New-AzResourceGroup -Name $ResourceGroupName
           -Location $location
88.        Write-Output "RG $ResourceGroupName created"
89.    }
90.    #endregion
91.
92.
93.    #region create workspace
94.    $WorkspaceName= "W-"+$Host poolName
95.    $ErrorActionPreference= "SilentlyContinue"
96.    $WPDetail = get-AzWvdWorkspace -Name $WorkspaceName
       -ResourceGroupName $ResourceGroupName
97.    $ErrorActionPreference= "Continue"
98.    if($WPDetail)
99.    {
100.       Write-Output "WorkspaceName $WorkspaceName already exist"
101.   }
```

```
102.        else{
103.            $WorkspaceDetail = New-AzWvdWorkspace -Name $WorkspaceName
                -ResourceGroupName $ResourceGroupName `
104.            -Location $location
105.            Write-Output "WorkspaceName $WorkspaceName created"
106.        }
107.        #endregion
108.

109.        #region create Host pool
110.        $appGroup= $Host poolName+"-app"
111.        $ErrorActionPreference= "SilentlyContinue"
112.        $hpDetail = get-AzWvdHost pool -Name $Host poolName
                -ResourceGroupName $ResourceGroupName
113.        $ErrorActionPreference= "Continue"
114.        if($hpDetail)
115.        {
116.            Write-Output "Host poolName $Host poolName already exist"
117.        }
118.        else{
119.

120.            $hpDetail1 =  New-AzWvdHost pool -ResourceGroupName
                $resourcegroupname -Name $Host poolName `
121.            -MaxSessionLimit $MaxSessionLimit -Host poolType $Host
                poolType -LoadBalancerType $loadBalancerType `
122.            -Location $location -PreferredAppGroupType $Application
                GroupType -CustomRdpProperty $CustomRdpProperty
123.

124.            Write-Output "Host poolName $Host poolName created"
125.

126.        }
127.        #endregion
128.

129.        #region create desktop App group
130.        $ErrorActionPreference= "SilentlyContinue"
```

```
131.     $agDetail = get-AzWvdApplicationGroup -ResourceGroupName
         $ResourceGroupName -Name $appGroup
132.     $ErrorActionPreference= "Continue"
133.     if($agDetail)
134.     {
135.         Write-Output "App group $appGroup already exist"
136.     }
137.     else{
138.
139.         $dag = New-AzWvdApplicationGroup -Name $appGroup -Resource
            GroupName $resourcegroupname `
140.         -Host poolArmPath $hpDetail1.Id -Location $location
            -ApplicationGroupType $ApplicationGroupType
141.
142.         $reg = Register-AzWvdApplicationGroup -ResourceGroupName
            $ResourceGroupName -WorkspaceName `
143.         $WorkspaceName -ApplicationGroupPath $dag.id
144.         Write-Output "App group $appGroup created"
145.
146.     }
147.     #endregion
148.
149.
150.     #region get registration token
151.     $token = (new-AzWvdRegistrationInfo -Host poolName $Host
         poolName -ResourceGroupName $ResourceGroupName `
152.     -ExpirationTime $((get-date).ToUniversalTime().AddDays(1).
         ToString('yyyy-MM-ddTHH:mm:ss.fffffffZ'))).Token
153.     #endregion
154.
155.
156.     #region create session host
157.
158.     Write-Output "creating vm .."
159.
```

```
160.        #calling ARM template
161.
162.        $tagsObject = @{
163.                'Host pool'      = $Host poolName
164.                'size'       = $rdshVmSize
165.            }
166.
167.        $Parameters = [ordered]@{
168.                    "imageReferenceID"       = "$imageID"
169.                    "rdshPrefix" = "$rdshNamePrefix"
170.                    "rdshVMDiskType"          = "StandardSSD_LRS"
171.                    "rdshVmSize"   = "$rdshVmSize"
172.                    "administratorAccountUsername"
                        = "$DomainUser"
173.                    "administratorAccountPassword"
                        = "$DomainPass"
174.                    "Domain"          = "$Domain"
175.                    "ouPath"             = "$DomainOU"
176.                    "existingSubnetName"
                        = "$existingSubnetName"
177.                    "networkInterfaceTags"
                        = $tagsObject
178.                    "virtualMachineTags"          = $tagsObject
179.                    "vmInitialNumber"           = 1
180.                    "host poolToken"          = $token
181.                    "host poolName" = "$Host poolName"
182.                    "vmLocation"         = "$location"
183.                    "virtualNetworkResourceGroupName" =
                        "$virtualNetworkResourceGroupName"
184.                     "existingVNetName" = "$existingVNetName"
185.                     "rdshNumberOfInstances"=$HostCount
186.                    }
187.
188.
```

```
189.         New-AzResourceGroupDeployment -TemplateUri "https://
             raw.githubusercontent.com/Ar-Sa/Arun/master/PowerShell/
             PowerShell%20and%20ARM%20to%20create%20Azure%20virtual%20
             desktop%20personal%20desktop/New-personalAVDTemplate.json" `
190.         -TemplateParameterObject $Parameters -ResourceGroupName
             $ResourceGroupName -Name $Host poolName
191.     #endregion
192.  }
193. catch
194. {
195. Write-Output "failed to create host pool"
196. Write-Error "failed to create host pool"
197. }
```

ARM Template - https://raw.githubusercontent.com/Ar-Sa/Arun/master/
PowerShell/PowerShell%20and%20ARM%20to%20create%20Azure%20virtual%20
desktop%20personal%20desktop/New-personalAVDTemplate.json

```
1.   {
2.         "$schema": "https://schema.management.Azure.com/schemas/
             2015-01-01/deploymentTemplate.json#",
3.         "contentVersion": "1.0.0.0",
4.         "parameters": {
5.             "artifactsLocation": {
6.                 "defaultValue": "https://wvdportalstorageblob.blob.
                     core.windows.net/galleryartifacts/Configuration.zip",
7.                 "type": "String",
8.                 "metadata": {
9.                     "description": "The base URI where artifacts
                         required by this template are located."
10.                }
11.            },
12.            "imageReferenceID": {
13.                "type": "String",
```

```
14.              "metadata": {
15.                  "description": "imageReferenceID"
16.              }
17.          },
18.          "rdshPrefix": {
19.              "defaultValue": "[take(toLower(resourceGroup().
                 name),10)]",
20.              "type": "String",
21.              "metadata": {
22.                  "description": "This prefix will be used in
                     combination with the VM number to create the VM
                     name. This value includes the dash, so if using
                     "rdsh" as the prefix, VMs would be named "rdsh-0",
                     "rdsh-1", etc. You should use a unique prefix to
                     reduce name collisions in Active Directory."
23.              }
24.          },
25.          "rdshNumberOfInstances": {
26.              "type": "Int",
27.              "defaultValue": 1,
28.              "metadata": {
29.                  "description": "Number of session hosts that will
                     be created and added to the host pool."
30.              }
31.          },
32.          "rdshVMDiskType": {
33.              "allowedValues": [
34.                  "Premium_LRS",
35.                  "StandardSSD_LRS",
36.                  "Standard_LRS"
37.              ],
38.              "type": "String",
39.              "metadata": {
40.                  "description": "The VM disk type for the VM: HDD
                     or SSD."
```

```
41.                  }
42.              },
43.              "rdshVmSize": {
44.                  "defaultValue": "Standard_d4hs_v3",
45.                  "type": "String",
46.                  "metadata": {
47.                      "description": "The size of the session host VMs."
48.                  }
49.              },
50.              "enableAcceleratedNetworking": {
51.                  "defaultValue": false,
52.                  "type": "Bool",
53.                  "metadata": {
54.                      "description": "Enables Accelerated Networking
                         feature, notice that VM size must support it,
                         this is supported in most of general purpose and
                         compute-optimized instances with 2 or more vCPUs,
                         on instances that supports hyperthreading it is
                         required minimum of 4 vCPUs."
55.                  }
56.              },
57.              "administratorAccountUsername": {
58.                  "type": "String",
59.                  "metadata": {
60.                      "description": "The username for the admin."
61.                  }
62.              },
63.              "administratorAccountPassword": {
64.                  "type": "SecureString",
65.                  "metadata": {
66.                      "description": "The password that corresponds to
                         the existing domain username."
67.                  }
68.              },
```

```
69.                "existingSubnetName": {
70.                    "type": "String",
71.                    "metadata": {
72.                        "description": "The unique id of the subnet for
                            the nics."
73.                    }
74.                },
75.                "vmLocation": {
76.                    "type": "string",
77.                    "metadata": {
78.                        "description": "The location of the session
                            host VMs."
79.                    }
80.                },
81.                "networkInterfaceTags": {
82.                    "defaultValue": {},
83.                    "type": "Object",
84.                    "metadata": {
85.                        "description": "The tags to be assigned to the
                            network interfaces"
86.                    }
87.                },
88.                "virtualMachineTags": {
89.                    "defaultValue": {},
90.                    "type": "Object",
91.                    "metadata": {
92.                        "description": "The tags to be assigned to the
                            virtual machines"
93.                    }
94.                },
95.                "vmInitialNumber": {
96.                    "defaultValue": 0,
97.                    "type": "Int",
```

```
98.              "metadata": {
99.                  "description": "VM name prefix initial number."
100.             }
101.         },
102.         "hostpoolToken": {
103.             "type": "String",
104.             "metadata": {
105.                 "description": "The token for adding VMs to the
                     host pool"
106.             }
107.         },
108.         "hostpoolName": {
109.             "type": "String",
110.             "metadata": {
111.                 "description": "The name of the host pool"
112.             }
113.         },
114.         "ouPath": {
115.             "defaultValue": "",
116.             "type": "String",
117.             "metadata": {
118.                 "description": "OUPath for the domain join"
119.             }
120.         },
121.         "domain": {
122.             "defaultValue": "",
123.             "type": "String",
124.             "metadata": {
125.                 "description": "Domain to join"
126.             }
127.         },
128.
129.         "virtualNetworkResourceGroupName": {
130.             "type": "string",
```

```
131.                    "metadata": {
132.                        "description": "The resource group containing the
                            existing virtual network."
133.                    }
134.                },
135.                "existingVNetName": {
136.                    "type": "string",
137.                    "metadata": {
138.                        "description": "The name of the virtual network
                            the VMs will be connected to."
139.                    }
140.                }
141.            },
142.            "variables": {
143.                "subnet-id": "[resourceId(parameters('virtualNetwork
                    ResourceGroupName'),'Microsoft.Network/virtualNetworks/
                    subnets',parameters('existingVNetName'), parameters
                    ('existingSubnetName'))]",
144.                "existingDomainUsername": "[first(split(parameters
                    ('administratorAccountUsername'), '@'))]",
145.                "domain": "[if(equals(parameters('domain'), ''), last
                    (split(parameters('administratorAccountUsername'), '@')),
                    parameters('domain'))]",
146.                "storageAccountType": "[parameters('rdshVMDiskType')]"
147.            },
148.            "resources": [
149.
150.
151.                {
152.                    "type": "Microsoft.Network/networkInterfaces",
153.                    "apiVersion": "2018-11-01",
154.                    "name": "[concat(parameters('rdshPrefix'), add
                        (copyindex(), parameters('vmInitialNumber')),
                        '-nic')]",
155.                    "location": "[parameters('vmLocation')]",
```

```
156.                    "dependsOn": [
157.                    ],
158.                    "tags": "[parameters('networkInterfaceTags')]",
159.                    "properties": {
160.                        "ipConfigurations": [
161.                            {
162.                                "name": "ipconfig",
163.                                "properties": {
164.                                    "privateIPAllocationMethod":
                                     "Dynamic",
165.                                    "subnet": {
166.                                        "id": "[variables('subnet-id')]"
167.                                    }
168.                                }
169.                            }
170.                        ],
171.                        "enableAcceleratedNetworking": "[parameters
                            ('enableAcceleratedNetworking')]"
172.                    },
173.                    "copy": {
174.                        "name": "rdsh-nic-loop",
175.                        "count": "[parameters('rdshNumberOfInstances')]"
176.                    }
177.                },
178.                {
179.                    "type": "Microsoft.Compute/virtualMachines",
180.                    "apiVersion": "2018-10-01",
181.                    "name": "[concat(parameters('rdshPrefix'),
                        add(copyindex(), parameters('vmInitialNumber')))]",
182.                    "location": "[parameters('vmLocation')]",
183.                    "dependsOn": [
184.                        "[concat('Microsoft.Network/networkInterfaces/',
                            parameters('rdshPrefix'), add(copyindex(),
                            parameters('vmInitialNumber')), '-nic')]"
185.                    ],
```

```
186.                    "tags": "[parameters('virtualMachineTags')]",
187.                    "properties": {
188.                        "hardwareProfile": {
189.                            "vmSize": "[parameters('rdshVmSize')]"
190.                        },
191.                        "osProfile": {
192.                            "computerName": "[concat(parameters
                               ('rdshPrefix'), add(copyindex(), parameters
                               ('vmInitialNumber')))]",
193.                            "adminUsername": "[variables('existingDomainU
                               sername')]",
194.                            "adminPassword": "[parameters('administrator
                               AccountPassword')]"
195.                        },
196.                        "storageProfile": {
197.                            "imageReference": {
198.                                "id": "[parameters('imageReferenceID')]"
199.                            },
200.                            "osDisk": {
201.                                "createOption": "FromImage",
202.                                "name": "[concat(parameters('rdshPrefix'),
                                   add(copyindex(), parameters
                                   ('vmInitialNumber')), '-OsDisk')]",
203.                                "managedDisk": {
204.                                    "storageAccountType": "[variables
                                       ('storageAccountType')]"
205.                                }
206.                            }
207.                        },
208.                        "networkProfile": {
209.                            "networkInterfaces": [
```

```
210.                                {
211.                                    "id": "[resourceId('Microsoft.
                                        Network/networkInterfaces', concat
                                        (parameters('rdshPrefix'),
                                        add(copyindex(), parameters
                                        ('vmInitialNumber')), '-nic'))]"
212.                                }
213.                            ]
214.                        },
215.                        "diagnosticsProfile": {
216.                            "bootDiagnostics": {
217.                                "enabled": false
218.                            }
219.                        },
220.                        "licenseType": "Windows_Client"
221.                    },
222.                    "copy": {
223.                        "name": "rdsh-vm-loop",
224.                        "count": "[parameters('rdshNumberOfInstances')]"
225.                    }
226.                },
227.                {
228.                    "type": "Microsoft.Compute/virtualMachines/extensions",
229.                    "apiVersion": "2018-10-01",
230.                    "name": "[concat(parameters('rdshPrefix'),
                        add(copyindex(), parameters('vmInitialNumber')), '/',
                        'joindomain')]",
231.                    "location": "[parameters('vmLocation')]",
232.                    "dependsOn": [
233.                        "rdsh-vm-loop"
234.                    ],
235.                    "properties": {
236.                        "publisher": "Microsoft.Compute",
237.                        "type": "JsonADDomainExtension",
238.                        "typeHandlerVersion": "1.3",
```

```
239.                    "autoUpgradeMinorVersion": true,
240.                   "settings": {
241.                       "name": "[variables('domain')]",
242.                       "ouPath": "[parameters('ouPath')]",
243.                       "user": "[parameters('administratorAccount
                           Username')]",
244.                       "restart": "true",
245.                       "options": "3"
246.                   },
247.                   "protectedSettings": {
248.                       "password": "[parameters('administrator
                           AccountPassword')]"
249.                   }
250.               },
251.               "copy": {
252.                   "name": "rdsh-domain-join-loop",
253.                   "count": "[parameters('rdshNumberOfInstances')]"
254.               }
255.           },
256.           {
257.               "type": "Microsoft.Compute/virtualMachines/
                   extensions",
258.               "apiVersion": "2018-10-01",
259.               "name": "[concat(parameters('rdshPrefix'), add
                   (copyindex(), parameters('vmInitialNumber')), '/',
                   'dscextension')]",
260.               "location": "[parameters('vmLocation')]",
261.               "dependsOn": [
262.                   "rdsh-domain-join-loop"
263.               ],
264.               "properties": {
265.                   "publisher": "Microsoft.PowerShell",
266.                   "type": "DSC",
267.                   "typeHandlerVersion": "2.73",
268.                   "autoUpgradeMinorVersion": true,
```

```
269.                        "settings": {
270.                            "modulesUrl": "[parameters
                                 ('artifactsLocation')]",
271.                            "configurationFunction": "Configuration.ps1
                                 \\AddSessionHost",
272.                            "properties": {
273.                                "hostPoolName": "[parameters('hostpool
                                     Name')]",
274.                                "registrationInfoToken": "[parameters
                                     ('hostpoolToken')]"
275.                            }
276.                        }
277.                    },
278.                    "copy": {
279.                        "name": "rdsh-dsc-loop",
280.                        "count": "[parameters('rdshNumberOfInstances')]"
281.                    }
282.                }
283.            ],
284.            "outputs": {}
285.        }
```

# Pooled Host Pool Creation Using PowerShell/CLI and ARM

Pooled desktop is different then personal desktop and thats why you need
additional detail for automation/script to create pooled hostpool. Since
everything is possible with automation, we can use PowerShell and ARM in
such a way that they can create pooled as well as personal desktops, and you
must make sure you are passing the correct parameter required for the pooled
desktop using the same PowerShell and ARM versions mentioned in earlier
section (section - personal Host Pool Creation Using PowerShell/CLI and ARM).

Here are the parameters required for a pooled desktop:

- $HostpoolType must set to pooled as follows so that the script will create the pooled host pool:

$HostpoolType = "pooled"

- $loadBalancerType can be BreadthFirst or DepthFirst for a pooled host pool. Change the value in the script param as shown here:

$loadBalancerType = "BreadthFirst"

- The $MaxSessionLimit parameter is required only for pooled host pools, and it will define the number of concurrent sessions per VM/ session hosts on the pooled host pool. Make sure you are changing values before triggering PowerShell and ARM. See Figure 8-18.

$MaxSessionLimit=4

```
10  ⊟param(
11
12       [Parameter(mandatory = $false)]
13       [string]$HostpoolType = "pooled", #Personal / Pooled
14
15       [Parameter(mandatory = $false)]
16       [string]$loadBalancerType = "BreadthFirst",#<for pooled- BreadthFirst|DepthFirst & for personal - Persistent>
17
18       [Parameter(mandatory = $false)]
19       [string]$MaxSessionLimit=4, #applicable only if pooled hostpool
20
21       [Parameter(mandatory = $true)]
22       [string]$HostPoolName = "avdhostPool2",
23
24       [Parameter(mandatory = $true)]
25       [string]$ResourceGroupName = "AVD-RG",
26
27       [Parameter(mandatory = $true)]
28       [int]$HostCount = 2,
```

*Figure 8-18.* *Azure Virtual Desktop creation via PowerShell plus ARM*

Follow the same steps mentioned here for the personal host pool creation and create a pooled host pool just by changing the host pool type, load balancing type, and the max session limit parameter in the PowerShell mentioned in the previous section.

# Configure Host Pool Settings

Customizing a host pool's Remote Desktop Protocol (RDP) properties, such as multimonitor experience and audio/video redirection, allows you to set up an optimal experience for your users, based on their needs. It also allows you to set up Azure Virtual Desktop as per your organization's compliance requirements. You can set the RDP properties at the time of the host pool creation using PowerShell automation (described earlier), or if you would like to change the default RDP file properties, you can customize the RDP properties in Azure Virtual Desktop either by using the Azure portal or by using the `-CustomRdpProperty` parameter in the `Update-AzWvdHostPool` cmdlet.

By default, the `CustomRdpProperty` field is null in the Azure portal. A null `CustomRdpProperty` field will apply all the default RDP properties to your host pool.

Table 8-2 includes the list of important RDP file settings that you can use with the Remote Desktop clients. When configuring settings, check the client comparisons to see which redirections each client supports.

*Table 8-2.* *RDP Setting for Azure Virtual Desktop*

**SESSION BEHAVIOR**

| RDP Setting | Description | Values | Default Value |
|---|---|---|---|
| `autoreconnection enabled:i:value` | Determines whether the client will automatically try to reconnect to the remote computer if the connection is dropped, such as when there's a network connectivity interruption. | 0: Client does not automatically try to reconnect<br><br>1: Client automatically tries to reconnect | 1 |
| `bandwidthautodetect: i:value` | Determines whether to use automatic network bandwidth detection. Requires `bandwidthautodetect` to be set to 1. | 0: Disables automatic network type detection<br><br>1: Enables automatic network type detection | 1 |
| `networkautodetect: i:value` | Determines whether the automatic network type detection is enabled | 0: Doesn't use automatic network bandwidth detection<br><br>1: Uses automatic network bandwidth detection | 1 |
| `compression: i:value` | Determines whether bulk compression is enabled when it is transmitted by RDP to the local computer | 0: Disables RDP bulk compression<br><br>1: Enables RDP bulk compression | 1 |

| | | |
|---|---|---|
| videoplaybackmode: i:value | Determines if the connection will use RDP-efficient multimedia streaming for video playback | 0: Doesn't use RDP efficient multimedia streaming for video playback<br><br>1: Uses RDP-efficient multimedia streaming for video playback when possible | 1 |
| **DEVICE REDIRECTION** | | |
| audiocapturemode: i:value | Microphone redirection:<br><br>Indicates whether audio input redirection is enabled | 0: Disables audio capture from the local device<br><br>1: Enables audio capture from the local device and redirection to an audio application in the remote session | 0 |
| encode redirected video capture:i:value | Enables or disables encoding of redirected video | 0: Disables encoding of redirected video<br><br>1: Enables encoding of redirected video | 1 |
| redirected video capture encoding quality:i:value | Controls the quality of encoded video | 0: High-compression video; quality may suffer when there is a lot of motion<br><br>1: Medium compression<br><br>2: Low-compression video with high picture quality | 0 |

*(continued)*

251

*Table 8-2.* (*continued*)

**DEVICE REDIRECTION**

| RDP Setting | Description | Values | Default Value |
|---|---|---|---|
| `audiomode:i:value` | Audio output location: | 0: Plays sounds on the local computer (plays on this computer)<br>1: Plays sounds on the remote computer (plays on remote computer)<br>2: Does not play sounds | 0 |
| `camerastoredirect:s:value` | Camera redirection:<br>Configures which cameras to redirect; this setting uses a semicolon-delimited list of KSCATEGORY_VIDEO_CAMERA interfaces of cameras enabled for redirection. | *: Redirects all cameras<br>List of cameras, such as `camerastoredirect:s:\?\ usb#vid_0bda&pid_58b0&mi`<br>Can exclude a specific camera by prepending the symbolic link string with - | Don't redirect any cameras |
| **devicestoredirect: s:value** | Plug and play device redirection:<br>Determines which devices on the local computer will be redirected and available in the remote session | *: Redirects all supported devices, including ones that are connected later<br>Valid hardware ID for one or more devices<br>DynamicDevices: Redirects all supported devices that are connected later | Don't redirect any devices |

| drivestoredirect:<br>s:value | Drive/storage redirection:<br>Determines which disk drives on the local computer will be redirected and available in the remote session | No value specified: don't redirect any drives | Don't redirect any drives |
| --- | --- | --- | --- |
| | | *: Redirects all disk drives, including drives that are connected later | |
| | | DynamicDrives: redirects any drives that are connected later | |
| | | The drive and labels for one or more drives, such as `drivestoredirect:s:C:;E:;:` Redirects the specified drive(s) | |
| keyboardhook:<br>i:value | Determines when Windows key combinations (Windows key, Alt+Tab) are applied to the remote session for desktop connections | 0: Windows key combinations applied on the local computer | 2 |
| | | 1: Windows key combinations applied on the remote computer when in focus | |
| | | 2: Windows key combinations applied on the remote computer in full-screen mode only | |
| redirectclipboard:<br>i:value | Clipboard redirection:<br>Determines whether clipboard redirection is enabled | 0: Clipboard on local computer isn't available in remote session | 1 |
| | | 1: Clipboard on local computer is available in remote session | |

*(continued)*

253

*Table 8-2.* (*continued*)

**DEVICE REDIRECTION**

| RDP Setting | Description | Values | Default Value |
|---|---|---|---|
| **redirectcomports: i:value** | COM ports redirection: | 0: COM ports on the local computer are not available in the remote session | 0 |
| | Determines whether COM (serial) ports on the local computer will be redirected and available in the remote session | 1: COM ports on the local computer are available in the remote session | |
| **redirectprinters: i:value** | Printer redirection: | 0: The printers on the local computer not available in the remote session | 1 |
| | Determines whether printers configured on the local computer will be redirected and available in the remote session | 1: The printers on the local computer available in the remote session | |
| **redirectsmartcards: i:value** | Smart card redirection: | 0: The smart card device on the local computer is not available in the remote session | 1 |
| | Determines whether smart card devices on the local computer will be redirected and available in the remote session | 1: The smart card device on the local computer is available in the remote session | |

| | | | |
|---|---|---|---|
| **usbdevicestoredirect: s:value** | USB redirection | *: Redirects all USB devices that are not already redirected by another high-level redirection<br><br>{Device Setup Class GUID}: Redirects all devices that are members of the specified device setup class<br><br>USBInstanceID: Redirects a specific USB device identified by the instance ID | Don't redirect any USB devices |

**DISPLAY SETTINGS**

| | | | |
|---|---|---|---|
| use multimon: i:value | Determines whether the remote session will use one or multiple displays from the local computer | 0: Doesn't enable multiple display support<br><br>1: Enables multiple display support | 1 |
| selectedmonitors: s:value | Specifies which local displays to use from the remote session; the selected displays must be contiguous; requires use of multimon to be set to 1<br><br>Available only on the Windows Inbox (MSTSC) and Windows Desktop (MSRDC) clients | Comma separated list of machine-specific display IDs; IDs can be retrieved by calling mstsc.exe /l. The first ID listed will be set as the primary display in the session | All displays |

*(continued)*

255

*Table 8-2.* (*continued*)

**DISPLAY SETTINGS**

| RDP Setting | Description | Values | Default Value |
|---|---|---|---|
| `maximizetocurrent displays::i:value` | Determines which display the remote session goes full-screen on when maximizing; requires use `multimon` to be set to 1 | 0: Session goes full-screen on the displays initially selected when maximizing | 0 |
| | | 1: Session dynamically goes full-screen on the displays touched by the session window when maximizing | |
| | Available only on the Windows Desktop (MSRDC) client | | |
| `singlemoninwindowed mode:i:value` | Determines whether a multidisplay remote session automatically switches to single display when exiting full-screen; requires use `multimon` to be set to 1 | 0: Session retains all displays when exiting full-screen | 0 |
| | | 1: Session switches to single display when exiting full-screen | |
| | Available only on the Windows Desktop (MSRDC) client | | |

| | | |
|---|---|---|
| `screen mode id:`<br>`i:value` | Determines whether the remote session window appears full-screen when you launch the connection | 1: The remote session will appear in a window<br><br>2: The remote session will appear full-screen | 2 |
| `smart sizing:`<br>`i:value` | Determines whether the local computer scales the content of the remote session to fit the window size | 0: The local window content won't scale when resized<br><br>1: The local window content will scale when resized | 0 |
| `dynamic`<br>`resolution:i:value` | Determines whether the resolution of the remote session is automatically updated when the local window is resized | 0: Session resolution remains static for the duration of the session<br><br>1: Session resolution updates as the local window resizes | 1 |

*(continued)*

257

*Table 8-2.* (*continued*)

**DISPLAY SETTINGS**

| RDP Setting | Description | Values | Default Value |
|---|---|---|---|
| `desktop size id:i:value` | Specifies the dimensions of the remote session desktop from a set of predefined options. This setting is overridden if `desktopheight` and `desktopwidth` are specified. | -0: 640×480<br><br>- 1: 800×600<br><br>- 2: 1024×768<br><br>- 3: 1280×1024<br><br>- 4: 1600×1200 | Match the local computer |
| `desktopheight: i:value` | Specifies the resolution height (in pixels) of the remote session | Numerical value between 200 and 8192 | Match the local computer |
| `desktopwidth: i:value` | Specifies the resolution width (in pixels) of the remote session | Numerical value between 200 and 8192 | Match the local computer |
| `desktopscalefactor: i:value` | Specifies the scale factor of the remote session to make the content appear larger | Numerical value from the following list: 100, 125, 150, 175, 200, 250, 300, 400, 500 | Match the local computer |

Here is a PowerShell example to update the custom RDP properties.

You can update multiple RDP properties by using the `update-AzWvdHostpool` command as follows:

```
$CustomRdpProperty="drivestoredirect:s:;audiomode:i:0;videoplaybackmode:i:1"

Update-AzWvdHostPool -ResourceGroupName <resourcegroupname> -Name
<hostpoolname> -CustomRdpProperty $CustomRdpProperty
```

# Assign Users to Host Pools

There are multiple ways to assign the user to a Azure Virtual Desktop host pool; you can use the Azure portal, PowerShell, or the CLI to add users to the host pool.

Follow these steps to add a user on the pooled or personal host pool:

1. Log in to the Azure portal with the appropriate credentials that have permissions on the host pool and application group.

2. Go to Azure Virtual Desktop and click the host pool on which you want to add users. See Figure 8-19.

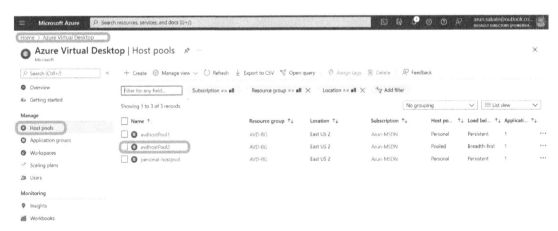

***Figure 8-19.*** *Azure Virtual Desktop, user or group assignment*

3.  Click the Applications in the left pane and then click the
    application group name. See Figure 8-20.

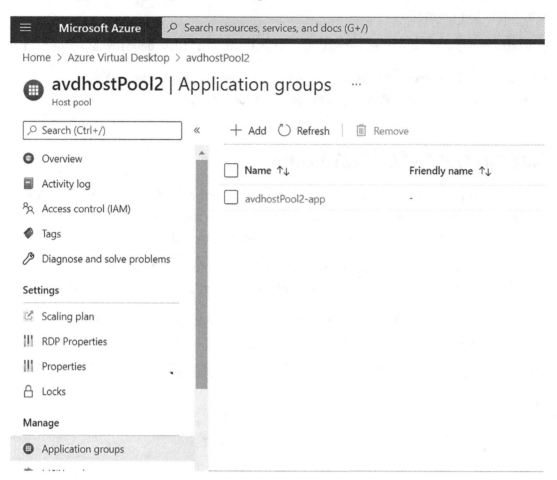

*Figure 8-20.* *Azure Virtual Desktop, Application groups tab*

4.  On the Application groups page, click Assignment and then the
    Add button at the top. See Figure 8-21.

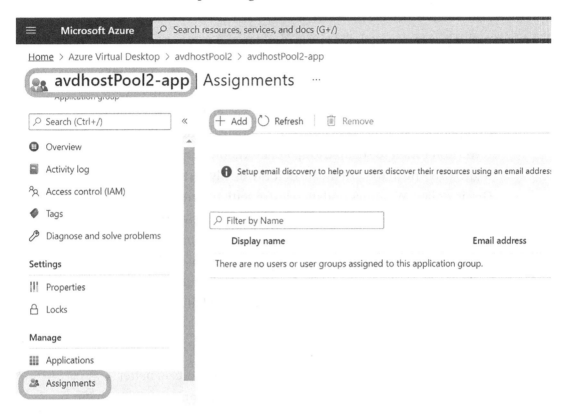

*Figure 8-21.* *Azure Virtual Desktop, application group assignment*

5.  In the Add User pop-up, you can add a single user ID or group.
    The user or group must be synced/present in Azure AD. Click Save
    to add the user or group on the host pool and then you can use
    the Remote Desktop client on Windows/the Web/Mac and access
    Azure Virtual Desktop.

---

**Note**    If you are using the direct assignment type on the personal host pool, then
you must assign the user to the session host in addition to the previous steps.

---

# Apply OS and Application Updates to a Running Azure Virtual Desktop Host

There are multiple ways to patch the virtual desktop environment.

- *Group Policy*: You can configure Group Policy to set the Windows update or registry setting. The Group Policy can found under Computer Configuration ➤ Administrative Templates ➤ Windows Components ➤ Windows Update ➤ Configure Automatic Updates. If you don't want to set up Group Policy, then you can try the registry setting in the VM image or individually on each VM or using Group Policy. Windows update registry settings are available at HKEY_LOCAL_MACHINE ➤ SOFTWARE ➤ Policies ➤ Microsoft ➤ Windows ➤ WindowsUpdate ➤ AU. The main problem with this option is the VM reboot; you cannot simply reboot the VM anytime and kick the user session off the host pool. Unfortunately, users can't reboot the VM by themselves after a patch installation, because of the default limited permissions. So, in short, this is not a good option for an Azure Virtual Desktop production environment.

- *SCCM/Intune/Azure update management*: These are all better options to patch an Azure Virtual Desktop environment, with specific maintenance windows, and you can always create different schedules and a different group of session hosts so that all the sessions will not be down at the same time. Additionally, you can test the patches on a dev environment to observe the impact on the application/services and then install them in production to avoid any outages in the production environment.

It is always recommended to update the session host image frequently so that you will not have any noncompliant VMs when you create a new session host using the image. You can refer to the image creation steps for all the details.

# Apply Security and Compliance Settings to Session Hosts

Azure Virtual Desktop is a managed virtual desktop service that includes many security capabilities for keeping your organization safe. In an Azure Virtual Desktop deployment, Microsoft manages portions of the services on the customer's behalf. The service has many built-in advanced security features, such as Reverse Connect, that reduce the risk involved with having remote desktops accessible from anywhere. Still, there are additional steps you can take to keep your Azure Virtual Desktop deployments secure.

The main difference between traditional on-premises Virtual Desktop Infrastructures (VDIs) and Azure Virtual Desktop is the security responsibilities. The customer is fully responsible for traditional on-premises VDI security, but, for most of the cloud services, these responsibilities are shared between the you and the cloud provider. When you use Azure Virtual Desktop, the physical host, network, and data center environment are already secured by the provider. The following are the best practices you can implement for Azure Virtual Desktop.

You can apply most of the security and compliance settings on the Azure Virtual Desktop session host by using Group Policy or using the session host image.

- *Enable Microsoft Defender for the cloud*: It is recommended that you enable the Microsoft Defender for Cloud service to enhance the security features.

- *Multifactor authentication (MFA)*: Enable multifactor authentication for all users and admins in Azure AD to improve Azure Virtual Desktop security while accessing Azure Virtual Desktop over the Internet.

- *Enable conditional access*: Enabling conditional access lets you manage risks before you grant users access to your Azure Virtual Desktop environment. Conditional access allows you to consider who the user is, how they sign in, and which device they're using while granting AVD access.

- *Audit/diagnostic logs*: Enable the audit log to allow you to view user and admin activity related to Azure Virtual Desktop.

- *Using RemoteApps*: You can provide remote users with access to entire virtual desktops or only selected applications. Remote applications, or RemoteApps, provide a seamless experience as the user works with apps on their virtual desktop. RemoteApps reduce risks by only letting the user work with a subset of the remote machine exposed by the application.

- *Monitor usage with Azure Monitor*: Monitor your Azure Virtual Desktop service's usage and availability with Azure Monitor. You can create service health alerts for the Azure Virtual Desktop service to receive notifications whenever there's a service-impacting event.

- *Enable endpoint protection*: To protect your deployment from known malicious software, we recommend enabling endpoint protection (Windows Defender or a third-party tool) on all session hosts. Make sure you are excluding FSLogix VHD files (user profile) so that the endpoint protection will not impact the user performance.

- *Patch software vulnerabilities in your environment*: Once you identify a vulnerability, you must patch it. It's recommended to patch your base images monthly to ensure that newly deployed machines are as secure as possible.

- *Establish maximum inactive time and disconnection policies*: Signing users out when they're inactive preserves resources and prevents access by unauthorized users. Disconnecting long-running applications that continue to run if a user is idle, such as a simulation or CAD rendering, can interrupt the user's work and may even require restarting the computer.

- *Set up screen locks for idle sessions*: You can prevent unwanted system access by configuring an Azure Virtual Desktop to lock a machine's screen during idle time and requiring authentication to unlock it.

- *Establish tiered admin access*: Granting admin access to virtual desktops is not recommended. If you need software packages, we recommend you make them available through configuration management utilities such as Microsoft Endpoint Manager. In a multisession environment, we recommend you don't let users install software directly.

- *Consider which users should access which resources*: By default, session hosts can connect to any resource on the Internet. There are several ways you can limit traffic, including using Azure Firewall, network virtual appliances, or proxies. If you need to limit traffic, make sure you add the proper rules so that Azure Virtual Desktop can work properly.

- *Windows Defender Credential Guard*: Windows Defender Credential Guard uses virtualization-based security to isolate and protect secrets so that only privileged system software can access them. This prevents unauthorized access to these secrets and credential theft attacks, such as pass-the-hash attacks.

- *Network security group*: Apply NSG rules to the subnet and make sure the traffic is limited and restricted only for required resources.

There are some additional security recommendations by Microsoft that you should consider implementing in your Azure Virtual Desktop environment. Refer to `https://docs.microsoft.com/en-us/security/benchmark/azure/baselines/virtual-desktop-security-baseline` for more detail about AVD security.

# Summary

In this chapter, you learned how to create an Azure Virtual Desktop host and host pools using the Azure portal, PowerShell, the command-line interface (CLI), and Azure Resource Manager templates.

# CHAPTER 9

# Install and Configure Apps on a Session Host

In this chapter, you will learn about the Azure Virtual Desktop application publishing options, including MSIX app attach, application masking, and application RemoteApp groups. All these options are different from each other, so we will explain each option in detail so that you can decide which option is better for your organization's requirements.

Additionally, you will see how to set up common applications such as Teams, OneDrive, and browsers of your choice for Internet access.

Let's get started with the MSIX app attach and other application options.

## Configure Dynamic Application Delivery by Using MSIX App Attach

In this section, you'll learn how to configure dynamic application delivery.

## What Is MSIX App Attach?

MSIX is a packaging format that offers many features to improve the application packaging experience for all Windows apps. MSIX app attach is different from regular MSIX because it's made to work better for Azure Virtual Desktop. MSIX app attach is a way to deliver MSIX applications to both physical and virtual machines. Let's learn what MSIX app attach is and what it can do for you.

What application delivery options are available in Azure Virtual Desktop? Azure Virtual Desktop provides different options to deliver applications to users as follows:

- Add the app in a master image so that it will be available on all session hosts.

© Arun Sabale and Balu N Ilag 2022
A. Sabale and B. N. Ilag, *Microsoft Azure Virtual Desktop Guide*,
https://doi.org/10.1007/978-1-4842-8063-8_9

- Use app masking to allow specific users to access applications from a full desktop implementation.

- Use RemoteApp application groups to publish applications on Azure Virtual Desktop instead of a full desktop.

- Use tools like SCCM or Intune for the central management of applications.

- Use dynamic app provisioning with AppV, VMware AppVolumes, or Citrix AppLayering.

- Create custom tools or scripts using Microsoft and third-party tools.

MSIX app attach is the best out of all of these options, as it's designed for Azure Virtual Desktop, and it provides apps dynamically to users at runtime and allows admins to centrally manage all applications.

## What Does MSIX App Attach Do?

In an Azure Virtual Desktop deployment, MSIX app attach can create a separation between user data (profile), the operating system, and apps by using MSIX containers, which means you don't need any configuration in the profile or operating system to attach specific applications at runtime and detach them once the user session ends. App attach does not require application repackaging when delivering applications dynamically. This option significantly reduces the time it takes for a user to sign in and reduce additional infrastructure costs for the application.

## How to Create a Package with the MSIX Packaging Tool?

The MSIX Packaging tool is a Microsoft tool that allows you to repackage your existing desktop applications to the MSIX format. It offers both an interactive UI and a command line for conversions and gives you the ability to convert an application without having the source code. The MSIX Packaging tool is now available from the Microsoft Store, or you can download it from `https://www.microsoft.com/p/msix-packaging-tool/9n5lw3jbcxkf`. You can run your desktop installers through this tool and obtain an MSIX package that you can install on your machine.

The MSIX Packaging tool enables you to create an MSIX application package from MSI, EXE, ClickOnce, App-V, Script, and a manual installation. The MSIX Packaging tool currently supports App-V 5.1, but if you have a package with App-V 4.x, then you can use the source installer to convert it to MSIX.

Let's go through the steps to capture the MSIX package using the MSIX Packaging tool. Once you install the MSIX Packaging tool, you will be prompted to provide consent to send telemetry data at first launch. Click "Application package" to create a new package. This tool also provides the ability to modify existing packages. See Figure 9-1.

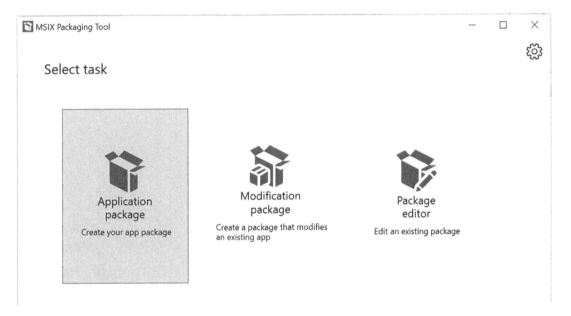

***Figure 9-1.*** *MSIX packaging tool*

Select a packaging method on the second screen and click Next. The following are the options you will use in the packaging method:

- If you are already working in a clean environment, select "**Create package on this computer.**"

- If you want to connect to an existing virtual or remote machine, select "**Create package on a remote machine.**"

- If you have a local virtual machine on your local VM that you want to convert, select "**Create package on a local virtual machine.**" Please note that we support only Hyper-V virtual machines; if you want to use another virtualization product, you can connect using the remote machine option. See Figure 9-2.

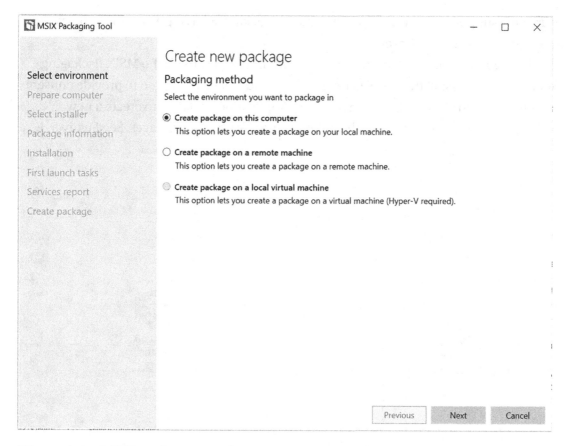

*Figure 9-2.*  *MSIX packaging tool, creating a new package*

MSIX will prepare the computer on the next screen. The **MSIX Packaging tool driver** is required, and the tool will automatically try to enable it, if it is not already enabled. The tool will first check with DISM to see if the driver is installed. Also, it will show some recommendations such as disabling Windows Update or Windows Search, so you can select the checkbox and click "Disable selected." See Figure 9-3.

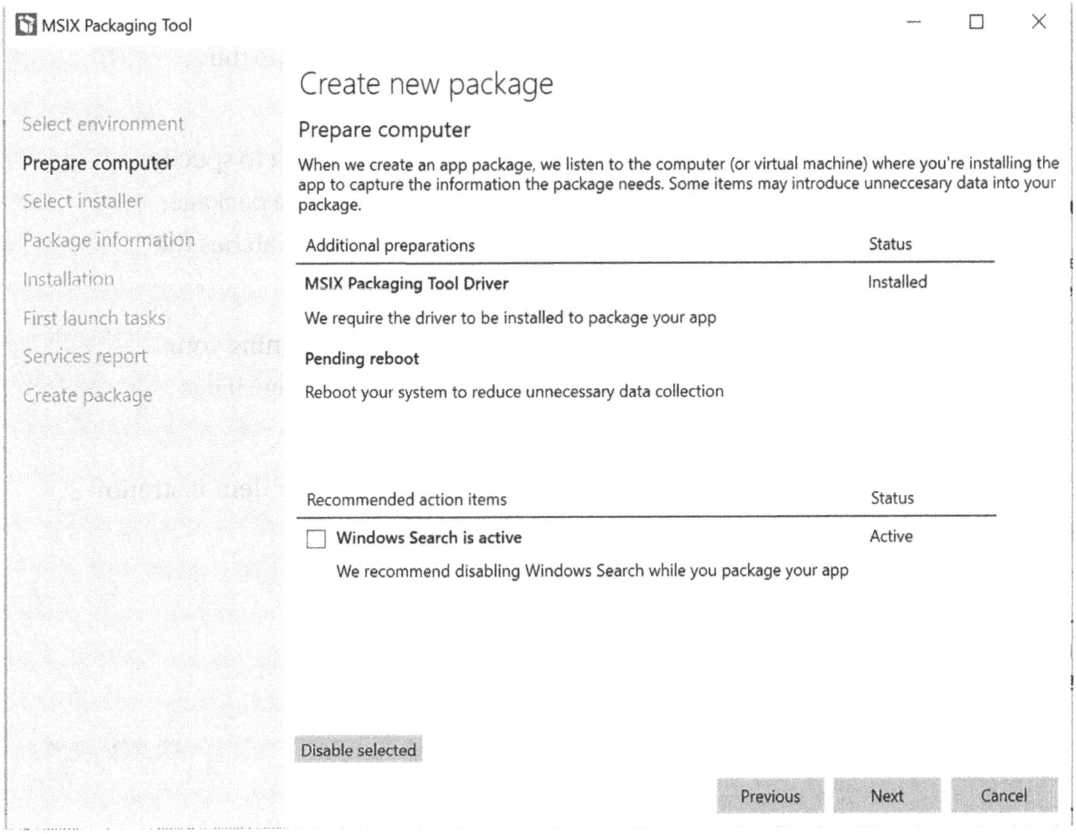

**Figure 9-3.** *MSIX packaging tool, preparing the computer*

You can select an existing installer in case you already have MSI, App-v, EXE, ClickOnce, or script files; otherwise, you can click Next and the MSIX Packaging tool will create the installer file for you, and then you can install the application manually during the installation phase.

If you have any installer arguments, you can enter the desired argument(s) in the "Specify installer arguments" field. This field accepts any string.

You also must specify the **signing preference**. The following are the signing options available, and you can select any one of them:

- ***Sign with Device Guard signing:*** This option allows you to sign into your Microsoft Active Directory (AD) account that you have configured to use with Device Guard signing, which is a signing service that Microsoft provides where you don't need to provide your own certificate.

- ***Sign with a certificate (.pfx):*** Browse to and select your `.pfx` certificate file. If the certificate is password protected, type the password in the password box.

- ***Specify a .cer file (does not sign):*** This option allows you to specify a `.cer` file. This is useful when you don't want to sign the package, but you want to ensure that the publisher information matches the subject of the certificate that will be used for signing.

- ***Do not sign package:*** Select this option if you will be signing your package later, because you cannot install an MSIX package if it is not signed.

I will be using the VLC MSI installer and self-sign certificate for demonstration purposes. See Figure 9-4.

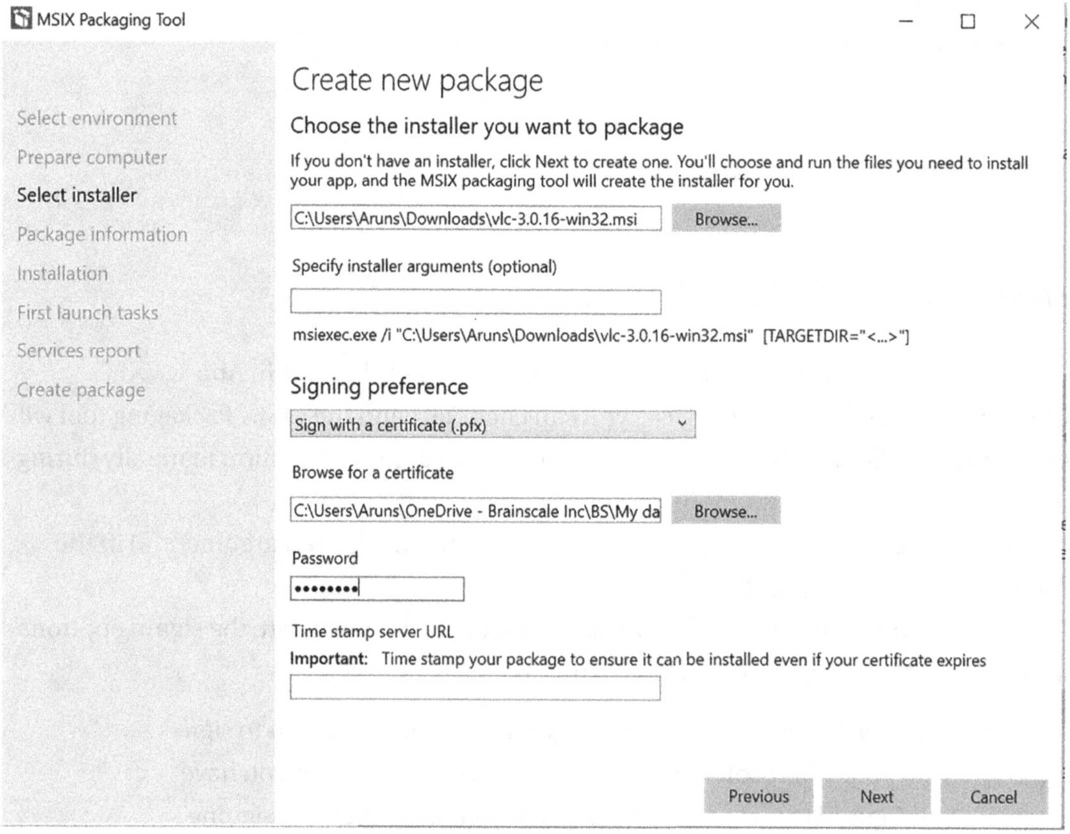

*Figure 9-4. MSIX packaging tool, choosing an installer*

After you choose to package your application on an existing virtual machine, you must provide information about to the app. The tool will try to autofill these fields based on the information available from the installer. If not, then you must provide all the information on the package information page. See Figure 9-5.

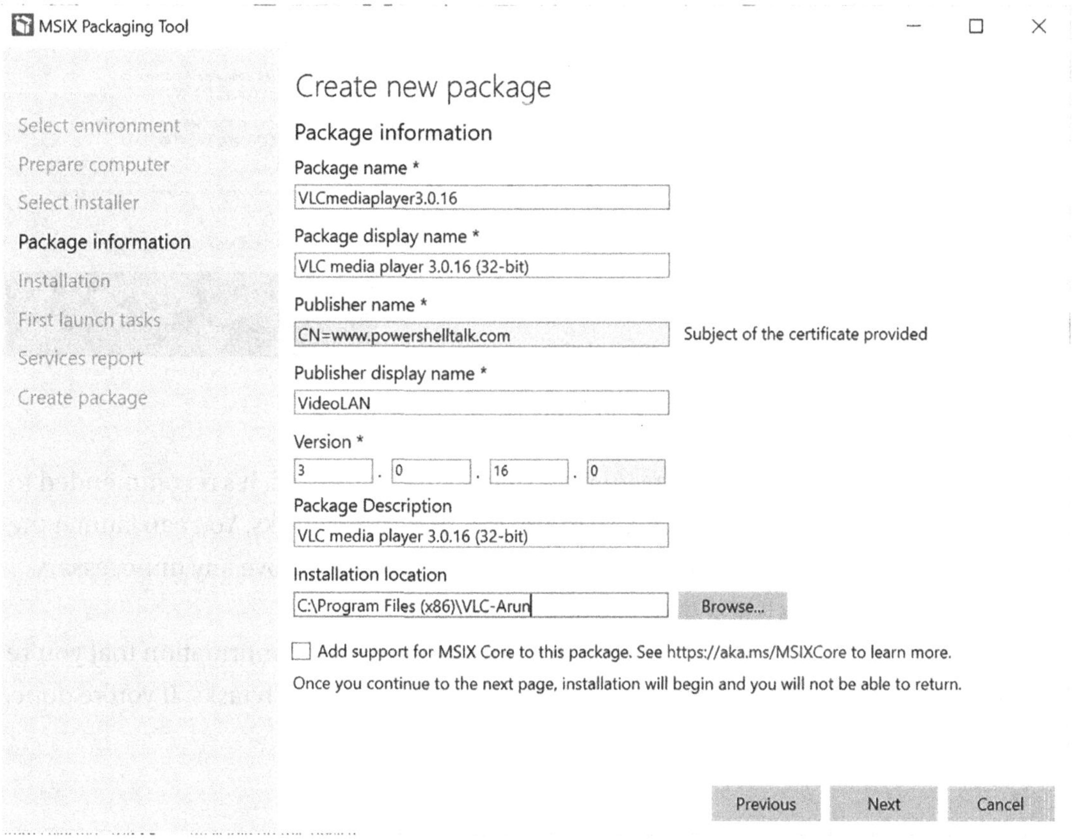

*Figure 9-5.* *MSIX packaging tool, package information*

This is the installation phase where the tool is monitoring and capturing the application install operations. The tool will launch the installer in the environment that was specified previously, and you'll need to go through the installer wizard to install the application. Make sure the installation path matches what was defined earlier in the package information page. See Figure 9-6.

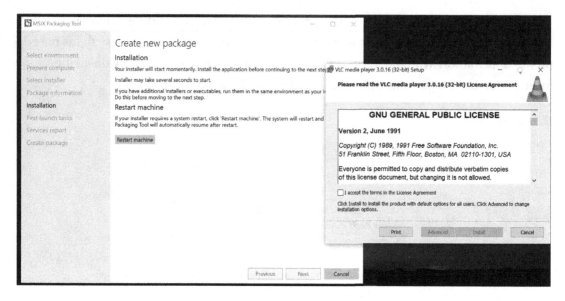

***Figure 9-6.*** *MSIX packaging tool, restarting*

This page shows application executables that the tool captured. It's recommended to launch the application at least once, to capture any first launch tasks. You can launch the executable by selecting it and then clicking Run. You can also remove any unnecessary entry points by selecting it and then clicking Remove.

Click Next, and you'll be prompted with a pop-up asking for confirmation that you're finished with the application installation and managing first-launch tasks. If you're done, click "Yes, move on." See Figure 9-7 and Figure 9-8.

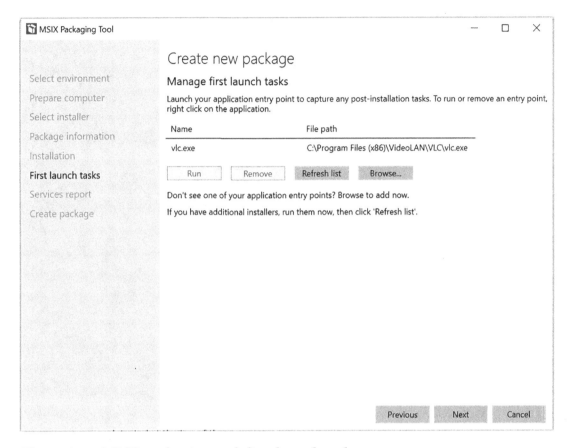

*Figure 9-7.  MSIX packaging tool, first-launch tasks*

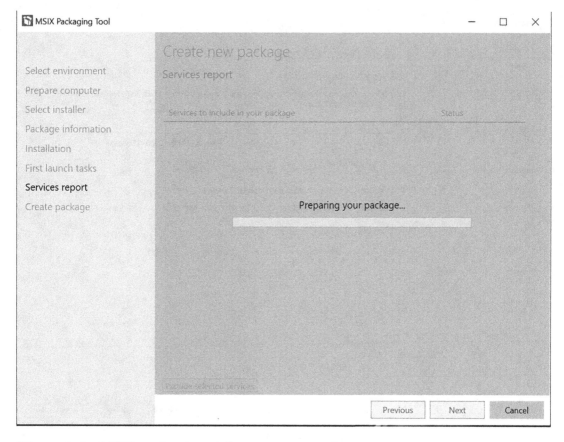

**Figure 9-8.** *MSIX packaging tool, preparing package*

The MSIX Packaging tool can convert an installer with services, and it will be visible on the Services report page. If no services were detected, you will still see this page, but it will be empty with a message that "No services were detected" at the top of the page.

In my case, I am using VLC, which does not install any services, so no service was detected. See Figure 9-9.

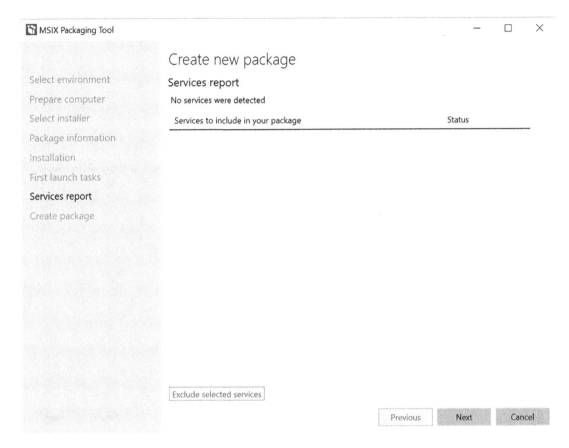

*Figure 9-9.* *MSIX packaging tool, service report*

Provide a location for saving the MSIX package. Click **Create** to create the MSIX package. See Figure 9-10.

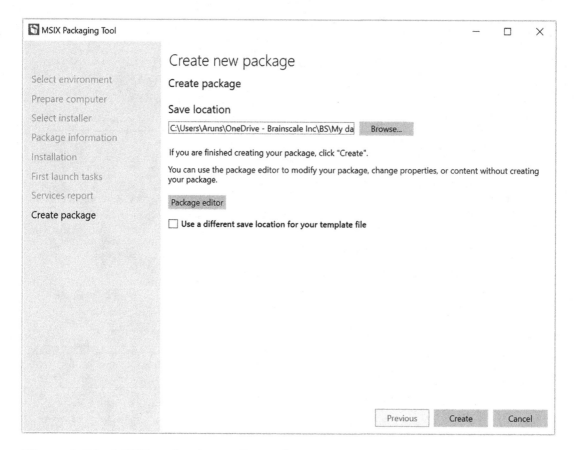

*Figure 9-10. MSIX packaging tool, save location*

You'll be presented with a pop-up when the package is created. This pop-up will include the save location, linked to the file location of the newly created package. See Figure 9-11.

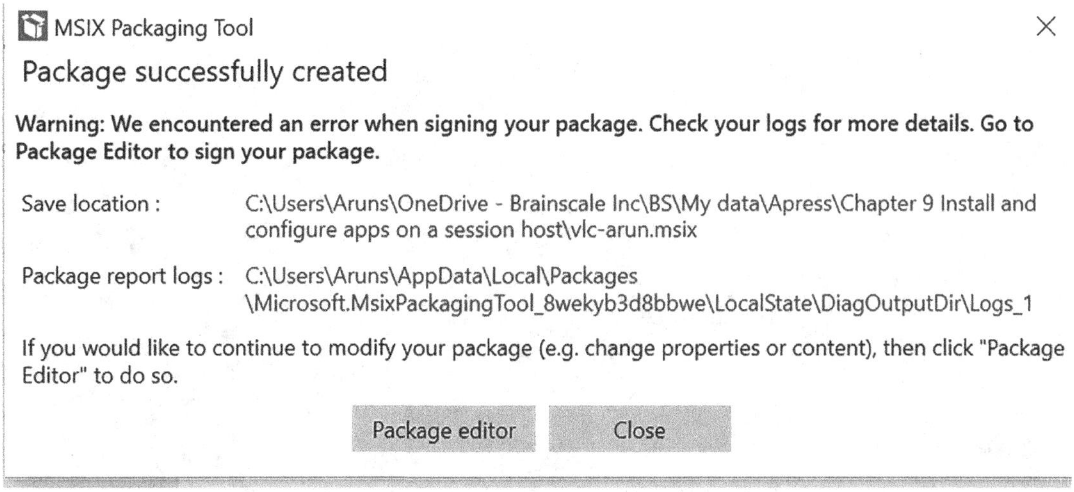

**Figure 9-11.**  *MSIX packaging tool, package status*

The next step is to unpack the MSIX package to a `.vhd` or `.vhdx` file so that you can upload the VHD file to a share folder, where it will be accessible from all Azure Virtual Desktop VMs (read permission). The unpack operation can be performed by the MSIXMGR tool, and it can be downloaded from `https://aka.ms/msixmgr`. See Figure 9-12.

Open a command prompt in elevated mode and run the following command in the command prompt to create an MSIX image:

```
msixmgr.exe -Unpack -packagePath "C:\Users\Aruns\OneDrive - Brainscale
Inc\BS\My data\Apress\Chapter 9 Install and configure apps on a session
host\vlc-arun.msix" -destination "C:\Users\Aruns\OneDrive - Brainscale
Inc\BS\My data\Apress\Chapter 9 Install and configure apps on a session
host\vlc-arun.vhdx" -applyacls -create -vhdSize 200 -filetype "vhdx"
-rootDirectory apps
```

Here is the command syntax:

```
msixmgr.exe -Unpack -packagePath <path to package> -destination <output
folder> [-applyacls] [-create] [-vhdSize <size in MB>] [-filetype <CIM |
VHD | VHDX>] [-rootDirectory <rootDirectory>]
```

*Figure 9-12.  MSIX packaging tool, unpack to VHDX*

Now that you have created the image, go to the destination folder, and make sure you successfully created the MSIX image (.vhdx). The next step is to upload the .vhdx file to be file share accessible from all Azure Virtual Desktop session hosts with read access.

Once the package is ready in .vhdx and uploaded to a file share, then you can add the MSIX package to the Azure Virtual Desktop by using the Azure portal or PowerShell.

## Recommendations to Avoid Issues with MSIX Packaging

Here are some tips:

- Make sure the certificate you are using for the MSIX signing is trusted in all Azure Virtual Desktop session hosts.

- If you are using a self-signed certificate for a proof of concept (POC), then make sure you add the certificate on all AVD session hosts so that the certificate will be trusted.

- Copy the final VHDX MSIX image to a file share that is accessible from all session hosts and have at least read permission on the .vhdx file.

# Set Up MSIX App Attach with the Azure Portal

Here are the steps to set up an MSIX image in Azure Virtual Desktop.

First, turn off automatic updates for MSIX app attach applications. You must disable automatic updates for MSIX app attach applications. Run the following commands in an elevated command prompt to disable updates:

```
rem Disable Store auto update:
reg add HKLM\Software\Policies\Microsoft\WindowsStore /v AutoDownload /t
REG_DWORD /d 0 /f
Schtasks /Change /Tn "\Microsoft\Windows\WindowsUpdate\Automatic app
update" /Disable
Schtasks /Change /Tn "\Microsoft\Windows\WindowsUpdate\Scheduled Start"
/Disable
```

```
rem Disable Content Delivery auto download apps that they want to promote
to users:
reg add HKCU\Software\Microsoft\Windows\CurrentVersion\
ContentDeliveryManager /v PreInstalledAppsEnabled /t REG_DWORD /d 0 /f
```

```
reg add HKLM\SOFTWARE\Microsoft\Windows\CurrentVersion\
ContentDeliveryManager\Debug /v ContentDeliveryAllowedOverride /t REG_DWORD
/d 0x2 /f
```

Add an MSIX image to the host pool. Next you will need to add the MSIX image to your host pool. Go to the Azure portal and browse the host pool on which you want to add the MSIX package. Follow these steps to add the MSIX image .vhdx file:

1. Go to the host pool where you want to add the MSIX package.

2. Select **MSIX packages** to open the data grid with all the **MSIX packages** currently added to the host pool.

3. Select **+ Add** to open the **Add MSIX package** tab.

4. In the **Add MSIX package** tab, enter the following values:

- For the MSIX image path, enter a valid UNC path pointing to the MSIX image on the file share (for example, `\\storageaccount.file.core.windows.net\msixshare\appfolder\MSIXimage.vhd`). When you're done, select Add to interrogate the MSIX container to check if the path is valid.

- For the MSIX package, select the relevant MSIX package name from the drop-down menu in case multiple packages exist in one image. This menu will be populated only if you've entered a valid image path in MSIX image path.

- For the package applications, make sure the list contains all the MSIX applications you want to make available to users in your MSIX package.

- Optionally, enter a display name if you want your package to have a more user-friendly name in your user deployments.

- Make sure the version has the correct version number.

- Select the registration type you want to use. Which one you use depends on your needs.

  - "On-demand registration" postpones the full registration of the MSIX application until the user starts the application. This is the registration type we recommend you use so that the application will be registered only if the user is going to use it and it will help to improve user performance.

  - "Log on blocking" registers only while the user is signing in. We don't recommend this type because it can lead to longer sign-in times for users.

5. For **State**, select your preferred state.

   - The Active status lets users interact with the package.

   - The Inactive status causes Azure Virtual Desktop to ignore the package and not deliver it to users.

6. When you're done, select **Add**. See Figure 9-13.

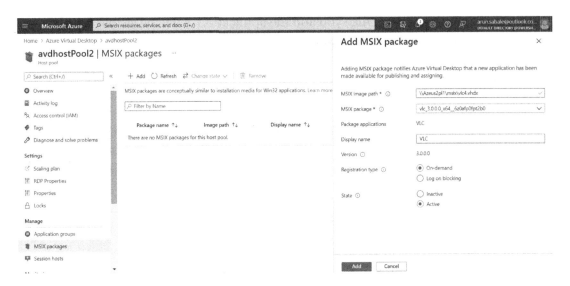

**Figure 9-13.** *MSIX packaging tool, adding a package from the file share*

Publish MSIX apps to an app group. Next, you'll need to publish the apps to the package. You'll need to do this for both desktop and remote app application groups. You can publish MSIX app to both fill the desktop and remote-app app group. See Figure 9-14.

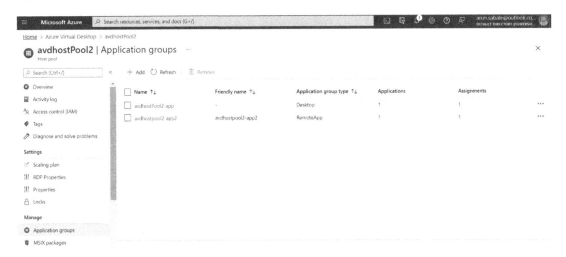

**Figure 9-14.** *MSIX packaging tool, publishing a package with an application group*

Select the full desktop application group and go to Applications. Click the Add button on the Application tab. The pop-up will allow you to select package from the

MSIX added to the host pool. Once you add the application, it will be visible for all users assigned on the full desktop application group. See Figure 9-15.

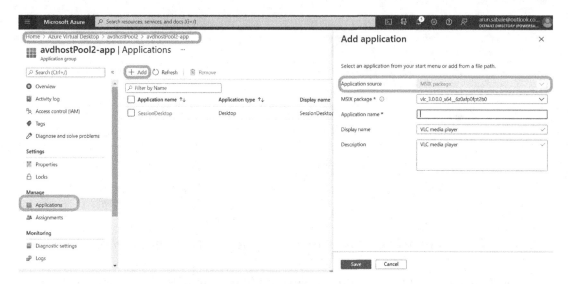

*Figure 9-15.* *MSIX packaging tool, publish package*

You can log in with a test user account to verify if the application is mounted on the VM. See Figure 9-16.

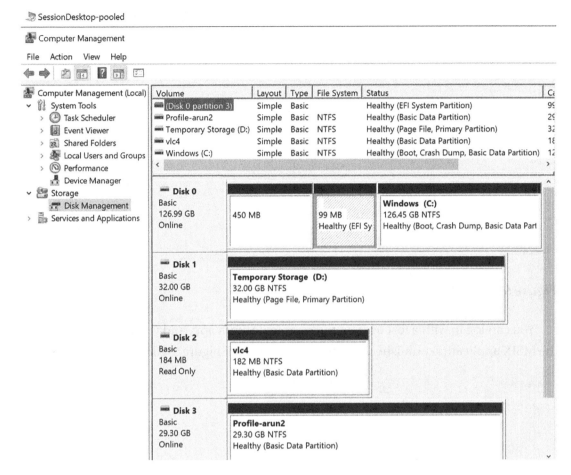

***Figure 9-16.*** *MSIX packaging tool, package test*

Select or create the remote app application group. You will be prompted to select the package from the MSIX package while adding the application in the remote-app application group. Once you add the application, it will be visible for all users assigned (under assignment) on the Remote-app application group. See Figure 9-17.

**Figure 9-17.** *MSIX packaging tool, remote-app*

You can log in with a test user on the remote desktop app, and you will be able to see the MSIX application published via the remote app. See Figure 9-18.

**Figure 9-18.** *MSIX packaging tool, remote-app test*

As you know, now that we can publish MSIX app on the host pool itself, there are a few other options available through which we can attach the MSIX app image at the time of user login scripts via Group Policy.

You can select the MSIX app attach option based on your requirements and complexity.

# Implement Application Masking

As you learned earlier, application masking is one of the options you can use to allow only specific groups of users to access specific applications in a pooled environment. The main challenge with a pooled full desktop is the application access if you have different set of applications needed by different groups of users. You can create different pooled host pools for different sets of applications, but it's not a cost-effective solution, and management will be difficult, so the best option is to have common host pools with multiple applications installed on all session hosts and restrict access by using the FSLogix app masking. Use application masking to manage user access of the installed components. Application masking may be used in both physical and virtual environments. Application masking is most often applied to manage nonpersistent, virtual environments, such as virtual desktops.

## Where to Use Application Masking?

Application masking can be used with full desktop pooled Azure Virtual Desktop instances where you need multiple small applications for different groups of users.

For example, let's consider you have 100 users out of which 50 users want Visual Studio Code, 50 users want Microsoft Office, but all 100 users want the Chrome browser. Now in this case you can create two different host pools, the first one with Visual Studio Code and Chrome for the first 50 users and Microsoft Office and Chrome for another set of 50 users, but you must create two different images, and host pools management will be difficult. Infrastructure costs will be higher, because you must keep a minimum number of VMs running in both pooled host pools.

The alternative is to create a single host pool and install all three applications, and you can add application masking to allow the first 50 users to access Visual Studio Code plus Chrome, and second group of 50 users to access Microsoft Office plus Chrome. By doing that you will be saving infrastructure costs, since there will be a single host pool and fewer VMs will be running during off business hours. Additionally, autoscaling will allow you to stop all VMs if they are not in use.

## How to Create Application Masking Rules?

You can apply application masking in the image itself, but you need the FSLogix rule editor to create an application masking rule. FSLogix Rules Editor setup comes

with the FSLogix download, so once you download the FSLogix zip file, you can run
FSLogixAppsRuleEditorSetup.exe to install the rule editor.

Make sure that the application you want to add in app masking is system centric and
not user centric. This applies for all applications you want to install on pooled desktops
as if the application is user centric; then the application setup will get stored in user
AppData, and other users will not be able to access it.

Once you install the rule editor, you can create app masking rules. Open the FSLogix
Rules Editor in elevated mode to create your first rule. Click New from the File menu (or
the New button in the top bar). See Figure 9-19.

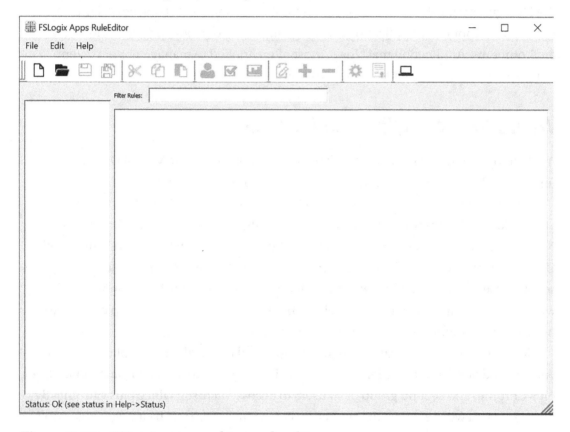

***Figure 9-19.***  *FSLogix app masking, rule editor*

Now enter a name for the rule and save it in C:\Program Files\FSLogix\Apps\
Rules. Now select an application from the list in the pop-up and click the Scan button.
See Figure 9-20.

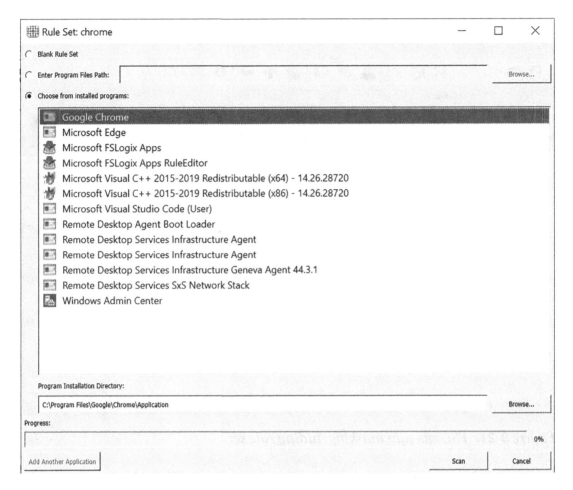

**Figure 9-20.** *FSLogix app masking, rule set*

FSLogix will find out all the dependencies for the selected application (called *hiding rules*) and show you them in the rule screen. See Figure 9-21.

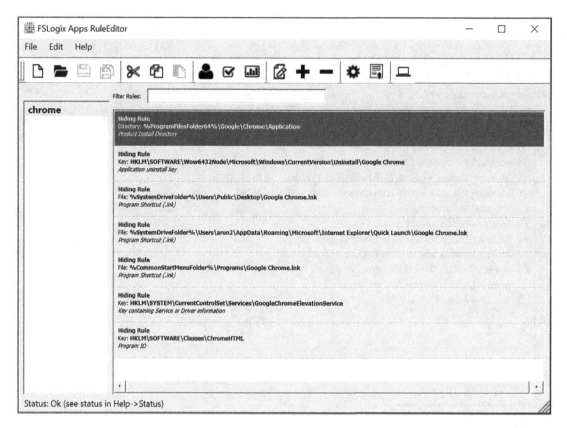

*Figure 9-21.*  *FSLogix app masking, hiding rule set*

Right-click the rule name and click "Apply rules to system." The rules that are within your rule set will be applied to your system. If your rule was a hiding rule on an application, the application will no longer be visible on the system. See Figure 9-22.

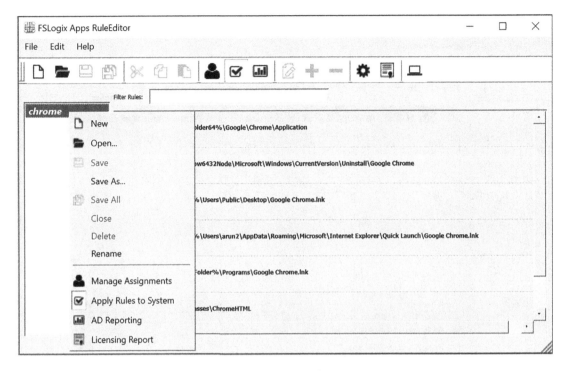

***Figure 9-22.*** *FSLogix app masking, hiding rule set test*

Rule set assignments specify how the rules in the rule set will be applied. To create and manage rule assignments, click File and then Manage Assignments. By default, everyone is set to No, which means everyone is allowed to access the selected application. See Figure 9-23. It's confusing, but here are the assignment access rules:

Everyone set to No (Not apply): all Allowed

Everyone set to Yes (apply): all deny

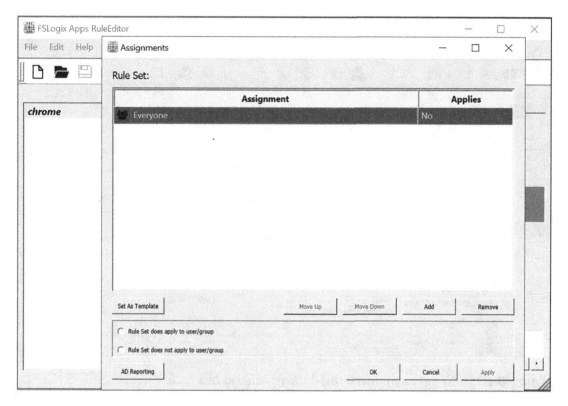

**Figure 9-23.** *FSLogix app masking, hiding rule set assignment*

The next step is to set everyone to Yes so it will block everyone and add the group that you want to allow access for and set it to NO. Click Add to create a new rule assignment, select : group for better assignment management, and set it to NO (Not Apply). See Figure 9-24.

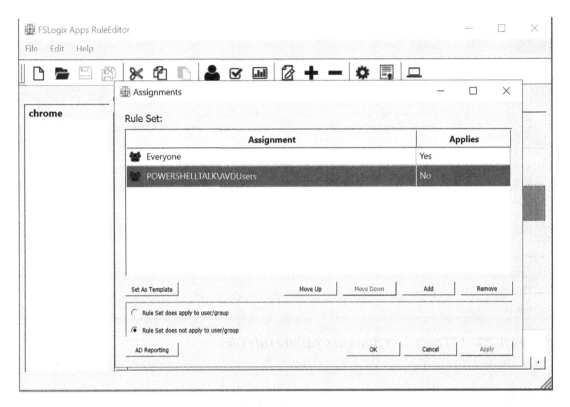

***Figure 9-24.*** *FSLogix app masking, hiding rule set assignment*

Create the same kind of rules for all different applications with different users' groups in the C:\Program Files\FSLogix\Apps\Rules folder on all session hosts. If you are creating rules in an image itself, then the rules will be there on all session hosts. Verify if there are two files for each rule, one for the rule and another for the assignment. See Figure 9-25.

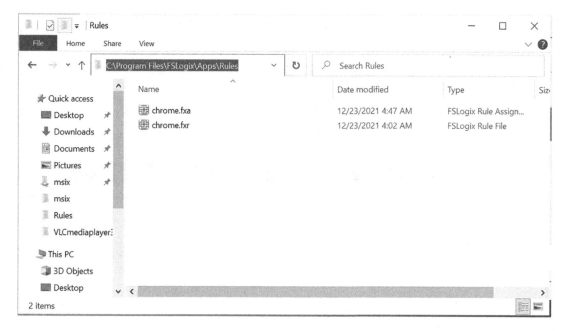

*Figure 9-25.* *FSLogix app masking, hiding rule files*

# Deploy an Application as a RemoteApp

RemoteApp is one of the best options to provide specific application access to specific sets of users without providing them with a full desktop. Azure RemoteApp helps you provide secure, remote access to applications from many different user devices. Azure RemoteApp basically hosts nonpersistent Terminal Server sessions in the cloud, and you get to use them and share them with your users. With Azure RemoteApp you can share apps and resources with users on almost any device.

A RemoteApp application group also needs a host pool and a session host in the back end. If you are using a pooled host pool for a RemoteApp with high availability, then you must install the application on all session hosts, before you publish the app with RemoteApp. You can create multiple RemoteApp application groups to publish different applications on one host pool and assign a different set of users on each RemoteApp.

Here we'll go over the simple steps to publish a specific application with RemoteApp application group.

You can follow the same steps mentioned in Chapter 8 to create a host pool, and then you can go to the application group to create a RemoteApp application group. See Figure 9-26.

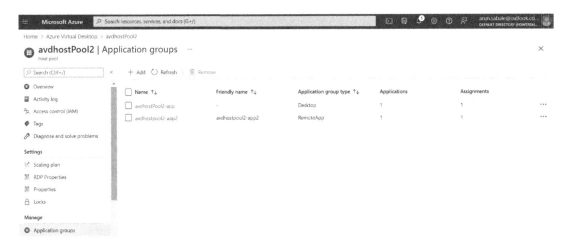

***Figure 9-26.***  *Deploying an application as a remote app, step 1*

Click the Add button and provide an application group name; make sure the application group type is RemoteApp and click the Applications tab. See Figure 9-27.

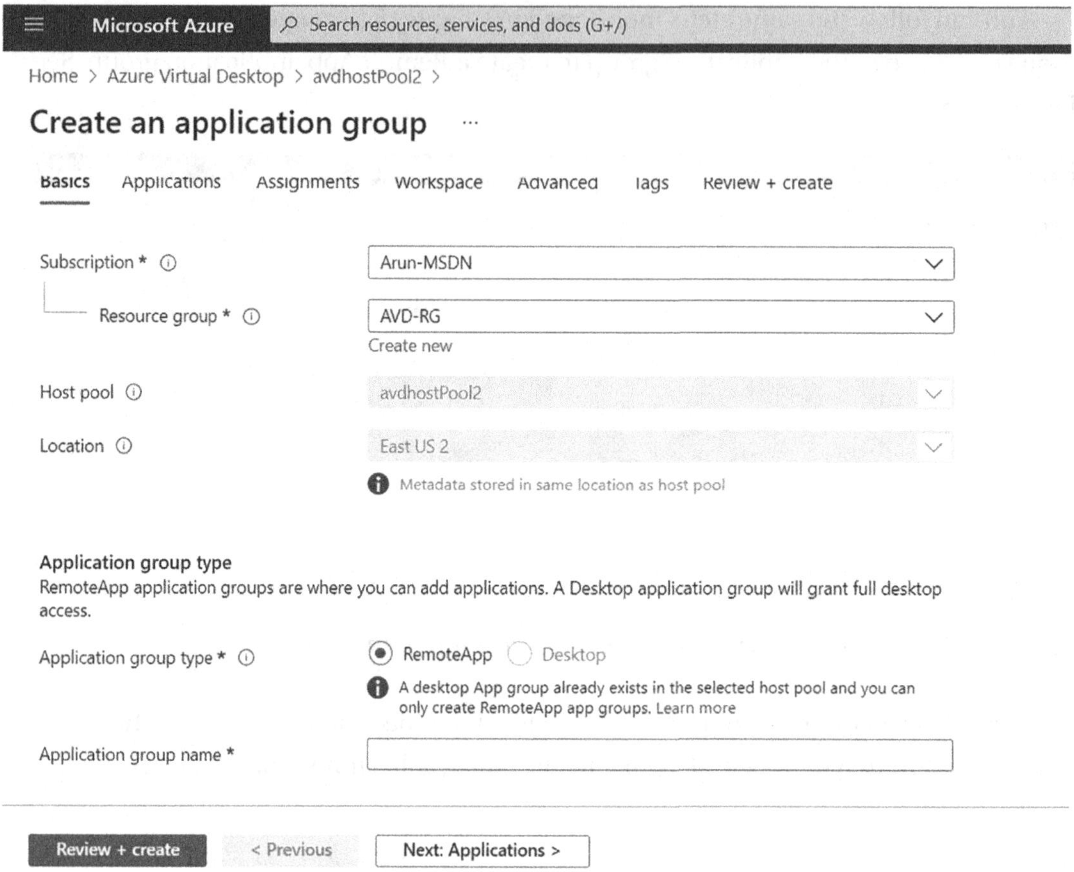

*Figure 9-27.* *Deploying an application as a remote app, step 2*

On the Applications tab, click "Add application" and provide the application details.

The application source can be a Start menu from a session host, a specific pile path from a session host, or an MSIX package. If you want to select the Start menu or file path, then make sure that the same application exists on all session hosts in a host pool.

Provide the application details in the pop-up and click Save. You can add multiple applications in one RemoteApp group. Once you add all applications, then click the Assignments button to go to the Assignments tab. See Figure 9-28.

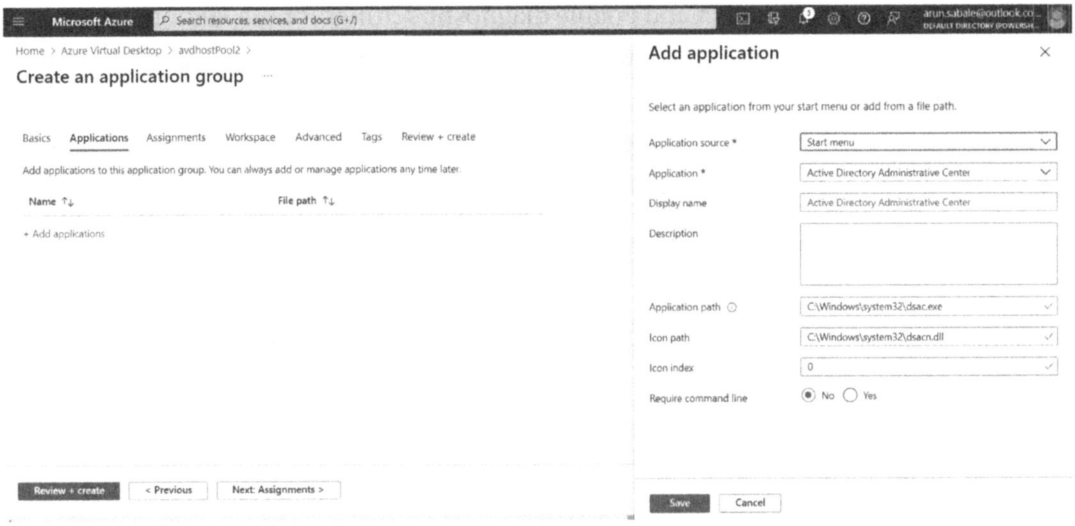

**Figure 9-28.** *Deploying a application as a remote app, step 3*

On the Assignments tab, add the group to allow access to the application selected on the earlier tab. You can also add individual users if you want, for testing especially, but it's always recommended to add groups for easy management. Click the Workspace button, select an existing workspace, and then click the Next button. See Figure 9-29.

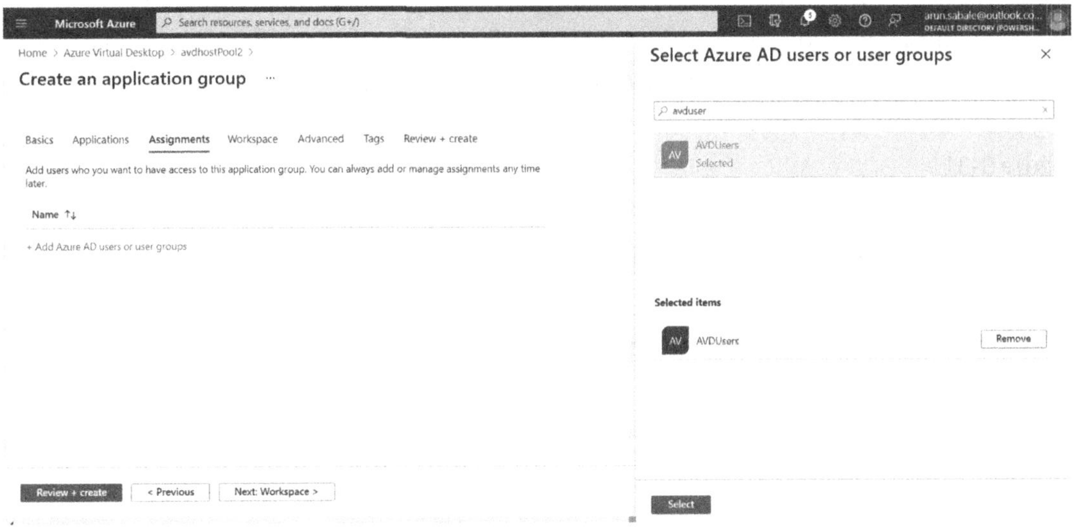

**Figure 9-29.** *Deploying an application as a remote app, step 4*

On the Advanced tab, select and enable diagnostic settings for the RemoteApp. Finally, click the "Review + create" button and then click Create to create the RemoteApp.

You can also verify the RemoteApp by logging in to the remote desktop client, and you will be able to see the application you published with RemoteApp. See Figure 9-30.

***Figure 9-30.*** *Deploying an application as a remote app, testing*

# Implement and Manage OneDrive for Business for a Multisession Environment

OneDrive is the Microsoft cloud service that connects you to all your cloud and local managed files. It lets you store and protect your files, share them with others, and access them from anywhere on any device. When you use OneDrive with an account provided by your company or school, it's sometimes called "OneDrive for work or school." See Figure 9-31.

# Apps and services

Create your best work on all your devices—from desktop to web—using the tools you need for home and business.

***Figure 9-31.*** *Microsoft 365 suite*

OneDrive is part of the Microsoft 365 suite that includes OneDrive, Teams, Word, Excel, PowerPoint, and many more apps. The licensing is available for personal, business, enterprise, and education. If you already have an E3, E5, or F1 license (Enterprise), then you just must assign the correct license to the user account so the user can access OneDrive.

By default, the Microsoft 365 suite will be installed on a multisession marketplace image with OneDrive, but the OneDrive sync app installs in per-user mode, meaning OneDrive.exe needs to be installed for each user account on the PC, below the %localappdata% folder. With the new per-machine installation option, you can install OneDrive in the Program Files (x86) or Program Files directory (depending on the OS architecture), meaning that all profiles on the computer will use the same OneDrive.exe binary. Other than where the sync app is installed, the behavior is the same.

The new per-machine sync app provides the following:

- Automatic transitioning from the previous OneDrive for Business sync app (Groove.exe)

- Automatic conversion from per user to per machine

- Automatic updates when a new version is available

The per-machine sync app supports syncing OneDrive and SharePoint files in Microsoft 365 and in SharePoint Server 2019.

# How to Install OneDrive in Per-Machine Mode?

The deployment steps are simple; you can download OneDriveSetup.exe from https://
www.microsoft.com/en-us/microsoft-365/onedrive/download and then run
OneDriveSetup.exe /allusers from a command prompt window (Elevated mode).
Alternatively, you can use the Microsoft Endpoint Configuration Manager to do this
on an all-session host or VM image. This will install the sync app in the Program Files
(x86)\Microsoft OneDrive directory. When setup completes, OneDrive will start. See
Figure 9-32.

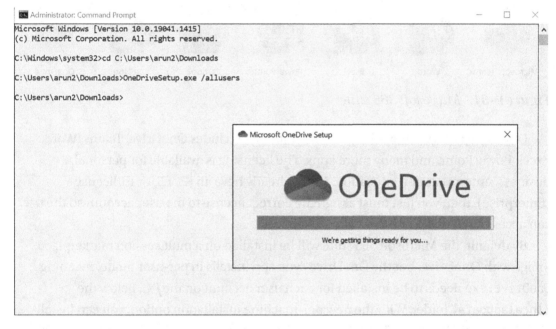

***Figure 9-32.*** *OneDrive installation*

If you are doing the setup on an existing session host, where you have users using
the Microsoft 365 suite and accounts were added on that computer, they'll be migrated
automatically.

# How to Redirect and Move Windows Known Folders to OneDrive?

There are two primary advantages of moving or redirecting Windows known folders (Desktop, Documents, Pictures, Screenshots, and Camera Roll) to Microsoft OneDrive for the users in your domain; first your users can continue using the folders they're familiar with. They don't have to change their daily work habits to save files to OneDrive, and saving files to OneDrive backs up your users' data in the cloud and gives them access to their files from any device.

Before you redirect known folders, make sure you are using the latest OneDrive build or upgrade to the latest available build before you deploy to decrease deployment issues.

OneDrive policies can be set using Group Policy, using Intune Windows 10 administrative templates, or configuring the Registry settings.

The following policy control the Known Folder Move feature:

- *Prompt users to move Windows known folders to OneDrive*: Use this setting to give the users a call to action to move their Windows known folders. See Figure 9-33.

*Figure 9-33.*  *OneDrive folder redirect*

If users dismiss the prompt, a reminder notification will appear in the activity center until they move all known folders. If a user has already redirected their known folders to a different OneDrive account, they'll be prompted to direct the folders to the account for your organization (leaving existing files behind).

# List of OneDrive Policies You Must Check

The following are the policies you must check:

- *AllowTenantList*: Allow syncing OneDrive accounts for only specific organizations.

- *AutomaticUploadBandwidthPercentage*: Limit the sync app upload rate to a percentage of throughput.

- *AutoMountTeamSites*: Configure team site libraries to sync automatically.

- *BlockExternalListSync*: Control list sync.

- *BlockExternalSync*: Prevent users from syncing libraries and folders shared from other organizations.

- *BlockKnownFolderMove*: Prevent users from moving their Windows known folders to OneDrive.

- *BlockTenantList*: Block syncing OneDrive accounts for specific organizations.

- *DefaultRootDir*: Set the default location for the OneDrive folder.

- *DehydrateSyncedTeamSites*: Convert synced team site files to online-only files.

- *DisableCustomRoot*: Prevent users from changing the location of their OneDrive folder.

- *DisableFirstDeleteDialog*: Hide the "Deleted files are removed everywhere" reminder.

- *DisableFRETutorial*: Disable the tutorial that appears at the end of the OneDrive setup.

- *DisableNucleusSilentConfig*: Control list sync.

- *DisableNucleusSync*: Control list sync.

- *DisablePauseOnBatterySaver*: Continue syncing when devices have battery saver mode turned on.

- *DisablePauseOnMeteredNetwork*: Continue syncing on metered networks.

- *DisablePersonalSync*: Prevent users from syncing personal OneDrive accounts.

- *DiskSpaceCheckThresholdMB*: Set the maximum size of a user's OneDrive that can be downloaded automatically.

- *DownloadBandwidthLimit*: Limit the sync app download speed to a fixed rate.

- *EnableAllOcsiClients*: Coauthor and share Office desktop apps.

- *EnableAutomaticUploadBandwidthManagement*: Enable automatic upload bandwidth management for OneDrive.

- *EnableHoldTheFile*: Allow users to choose how to handle Office file sync conflicts.

- *EnableODIgnoreListFromGPO*: Exclude specific kinds of files from being uploaded.

- *FilesOnDemandEnabled*: Use OneDrive files on demand.

- *ForcedLocalMassDeleteDetection*: Require users to confirm large delete operations.

- *GPOSetUpdateRing*: Set the sync app update ring.

- *KFMBlockOptOut*: Prevent users from redirecting their Windows known folders to their PCs.

- *KFMOptInNoWizard*: Silently move Windows known folders to OneDrive.

- *KFMOptInWithWizard*: Prompt users to move Windows known folders to OneDrive.

- *LocalMassDeleteFileDeleteThreshold*: Prompt users when they delete multiple OneDrive files on their local computer.

- *MinDiskSpaceLimitInMB*: Block file downloads when users are low on disk space.

- *PermitDisablePermissionInheritance*: Allow OneDrive to disable Windows permission inheritance in folders synced as read-only.

- *PreventNetworkTrafficPreUserSignIn*: Prevent the sync app from generating network traffic until users sign in.

- *SharePointOnPremFrontDoorUrl*: Specify the SharePoint Server URL and organization name. This setting is for customers who have SharePoint Server 2019. For information about using the new OneDrive sync app with SharePoint Server 2019.

- *SharePointOnPremPrioritization*: Specify the OneDrive location in a hybrid environment. This setting is for customers who have SharePoint Server 2019. For information about using the new OneDrive sync app with SharePoint Server 2019.

- *SilentAccountConfig*: Silently sign in users to the OneDrive sync app with their Windows credentials.

- *UploadBandwidthLimit*: Limit the sync app upload speed to a fixed rate.

- *WarningMinDiskSpaceLimitInMB*: Warn users who are low on disk space on One Drive.

# Implement and Manage Microsoft Teams AVD Redirect

Teams is the most used application by end users, and most organizations want teams on Azure Virtual Desktop as well. Microsoft Teams is supported on Azure Virtual Desktop personal and pooled desktops as well, but for a pooled desktop we need a different configuration. You have to use a remote desktop client if you want to use audio/video functionality. Teams has media optimization specially for a pooled desktop to enhance the audio and video functionality. Media optimization for Microsoft Teams is available only for the Windows Desktop client on Windows 10 machines. Media optimizations require Windows Desktop client version 1.2.1026.0 or later.

You have to prepare the image with Teams configuration for a pooled desktop as it is an easy option, and configuration will be the same from all session hosts. Implementing the configuration on all session hosts and making sure it's consistent across all session hosts are complicated tasks. To enable media optimization for Teams, open the Registry editor with elevated permission and add the `IsWVDEnvironment` DWORD key with the value 1, under `HKEY_LOCAL_MACHINE\SOFTWARE\Microsoft\Teams`.

```
[HKEY_LOCAL_MACHINE\SOFTWARE\Microsoft\Teams]
"IsWVDEnvironment"=dword:00000001
```

# Install the Teams WebSocket Service

Download and install the latest version of the Remote Desktop WebRTC Redirector Service on your VM image from `https://query.prod.cms.rt.microsoft.com/cms/api/am/binary/RWQ1UW`. See Figure 9-34.

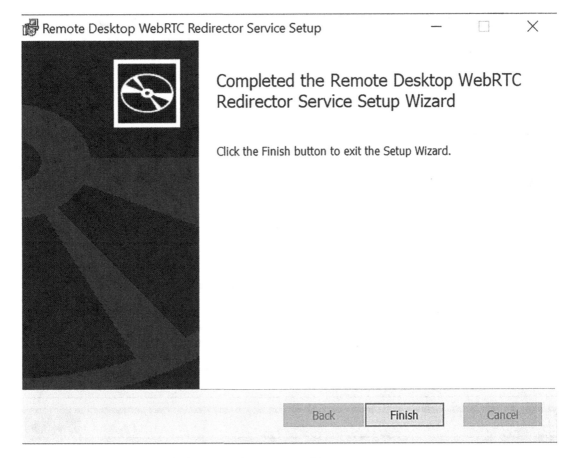

*Figure 9-34.*  *Remote desktop WebRTC installation*

# Install Microsoft Teams

The next step is to install Teams for all users; you can deploy the Teams desktop app using a per-machine installation. To install Microsoft Teams in your Azure Virtual Desktop environment, download the Teams package from https://teams.microsoft. com/downloads/desktopurl?env=production&plat=windows&arch=x64&managedInst aller=true&download=true. See Figure 9-35. Open a command prompt with elevated permissions and run the following commands to install the MSI to the host VM for per-machine installation:

```
msiexec /I c:\temp\Teams_windows_x64.msi /l*v c:\temp\teamslogs.txt
ALLUSER=1
```

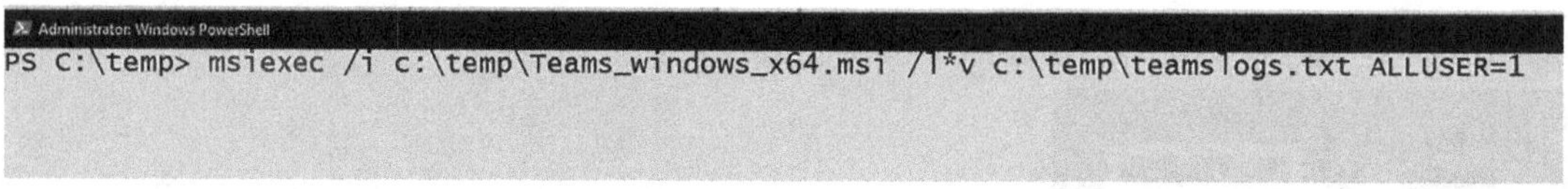

Administrator: Windows PowerShell
PS C:\temp> msiexec /i c:\temp\Teams_windows_x64.msi /l*v c:\temp\teamslogs.txt ALLUSER=1

***Figure 9-35.*** *Teams installation*

This installs Teams to the Program Files (x86) folder on a 32-bit operating system and to the Program Files folder on a 64-bit operating system. At this point, the golden image setup is complete. Installing Teams per machine is required for nonpersistent setups.

## Verify Media Optimizations Are Loaded

After installing the WebSocket Service and the Teams desktop app, follow these steps to verify that Teams media optimizations has been loaded (see Figure 9-36):

1. Quit and restart the Teams application.
2. Select your user profile image and then select About.
3. Select the version.

Search
You have Microsoft Teams Version 1.4.00.19572 (64-bit). WVD Media Optimized.

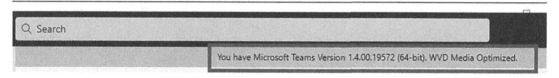

***Figure 9-36.*** *Teams for WVD optimized*

## Customize the Group Policies Properties of Your Session Host

It is recommended that you implement the following policy on the session host so that the app privacy allows Teams to use the camera and microphone. Implement the following settings in the GPO and apply it on all pooled session hosts:

1. Configure the following policies on the session host (Windows 10 multisession in Windows Virtual Desktop):

- Computer configuration\Administrative Templates\Windows Components\App Privacy\Let Windows apps access the Camera: Force Allow.

- Computer configuration\Administrative Templates\Windows Components\App Privacy\Let Windows apps access the microphone: Force Allow.

- Computer configuration\Administrative Templates\Windows Components\Remote Desktop Services\Remote Desktop Session Host\Devices and Resource Redirection\"Do not Allow Video Capture Redirection": Disable it.

## RDP Properties for a Host Pool to Enable Video and Audio

Make sure the audio and camera redirect is enabled on a host pool RDP properties for Microsoft Teams to work. You can go to the host pool RDP properties to change the settings.

- `audiocapturemode:i:1` enables audio capture from the local device and redirects audio applications in the remote session.

- `audiomode:i:0` plays audio on the local computer.

- `camerastoredirect:s:*` redirects all cameras.

## Implement and Manage Browsers and Internet Access for Azure Virtual Desktop Sessions

Most of the organizations allow end users to use a browser of their choice including Chrome, Edge, and Firefox. The question is how to add the additional browser on the session host. One of the best options is to install the browser in the image itself, but make sure that the installation is not user specific (per user). Alternatively, you can install the browsers using Intune or the configuration manager based on your organization setup.

Additionally, you can apply a Group Policy on all session hosts to control the browser behaver and restrict specific functionality.

Internet access is always required for end users, but in case your organization policy does not allow Internet access from an AVD virtual desktop, you can block the Internet access on an NSG or firewall.

It is recommended to send all Internet traffic via a cloud firewall so that you can monitor/filter the traffic and if required you can easily control the Internet access for all host pool/session hosts from a single place. Figure 9-37 is a high-level flow for outbound Internet access from session hosts. There is no inbound access required for session hosts and the session hosts and user connections go over the AVD gateway/broker using a reverse connection.

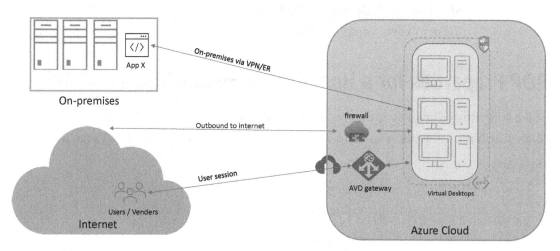

**Figure 9-37.** *Internet and on-premises access*

# Create and Configure an Application Group

An application group is the resource that allows you to add a user/group on the host pool. There are two different types of application groups that you can create in any host pool.

- *Desktop application group*: The desktop application group allows you to publish full desktops on any host pool, although you can create only one desktop application group in any host pool.

- *RemoteApp application group*: RemoteApp application groups allow you to publish application (like VLC, Visual Studio Code, MS Word)

on Azure Virtual Desktop without publishing the full desktop so that
users can access direct application without logging into a desktop.
This allows an organization to minimize security risk.

# How to Create an Application Group?

You can log in to the Azure portal and go to a Azure Virtual Desktop and select the host
pool where you want to create the application group. Click the Add button, provide the
application group name, and make sure to select the correct application group type
(RemoteApp/Desktop); then click the Next button to go to the next tab. See Figure 9-38.

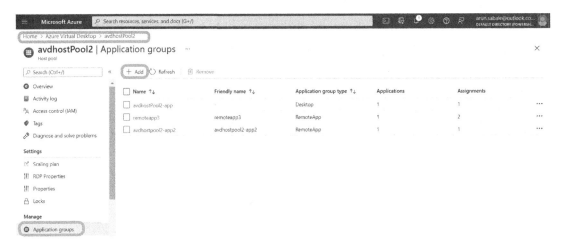

*Figure 9-38.* *AVD application group*

- *Application tab*: The next tab is Application. If you are creating a
  desktop application group, then you don't have to select anything
  here, but if you are creating a RemoteApp, then you must select
  the application source (MSIX/Start menu/file path) and provide
  the application information. Click the Next button and go to the
  Assignment tab.

- *Assignment tab*: On the Assignment tab, add a user/group that you
  want to access the desktop or RemoteApp. Click the Next button and
  go to the Workspace tab.

- *Workspace tab*: On the Workspace tab, select an existing workspace if you have already created one, or you can create a new workspace on this tab.

Once you add all the information, click the "Review + create" button to create the application group.

Refer to the RemoteApp section for more details about the RemoteApp application detail and steps.

# Summary

In this chapter, you learned all about the options to publish applications in Azure Virtual Desktop, including MSIX app attach, RemoteApp, and app masking. Additionally, you learned about the most common applications such as OneDrive, Teams, and browsers, as well as the steps to implement them in Azure Virtual Desktop.

Now that you know all the options to publish an application in Azure Virtual Desktop, you must select the correct options for your organization for better performance.

# CHAPTER 10

# Plan and Implement Business Continuity and Disaster Recovery

In this chapter, you will learn about planning and implementing disaster recovery for Azure Virtual Desktop and about designing and configuring a backup strategy for personal desktops. You'll also learn about FSLogix user profiles, MSIX packages, golden images, and restore options for all the backed-up components.

Backup and disaster recovery are different options; backup can be performed in the same region to recover/restore data from a specific point, and disaster recovery allows you to recover the infrastructure in another region in the case of a primary region outage.

Let's get started with disaster recovery for pooled and personal desktops.

## Plan and Implement a Disaster Recovery Plan for Azure Virtual Desktop

In this section, you'll learn how to implement a disaster recovery plan.

## What Is Disaster Recovery?

Disaster recovery is an organization's method of regaining access and functionality to its IT infrastructure in a secondary location/region after events like a disaster in the primary region. A variety of disaster recovery (DR) methods can be part of a disaster recovery plan. DR is one aspect of business continuity. Applications/infrastructure must be replicated to a DR region so that they can be made available during a disaster.

© Arun Sabale and Balu N Ilag 2022
A. Sabale and B. N. Ilag, *Microsoft Azure Virtual Desktop Guide*,
https://doi.org/10.1007/978-1-4842-8063-8_10

To keep your organization's data safe, you may need to adopt a business continuity and disaster recovery (BCDR) strategy. A sound BCDR strategy keeps your apps and workload up and running during planned and unplanned service or Azure outages.

Azure Virtual Desktop offers BCDR for the Azure Virtual Desktop service to preserve customer metadata during outages. When an outage occurs in a region, the service infrastructure components will fail over to the secondary location and continue functioning as normal. You can still access service-related metadata, and users can still connect to available hosts. End-user connections will stay online as long as the tenant environment or hosts remain accessible.

To make sure users can still connect during a regional outage, you need to replicate their virtual machines (VMs) in a different location. During outages, the primary site fails over to the replicated VMs in the secondary location. Users can continue to access apps from the secondary location without interruption. On top of VM replication, you'll need to keep user identities accessible at the secondary location. If you're using profile containers, you'll also need to replicate them. Finally, make sure your business apps that rely on data in the primary location can fail over with the rest of the data.

To summarize, to keep your users connected during an outage, you'll need to do the following things in this order:

1. Replicate the VMs in a secondary location.

2. If you're using profile containers, set up data replication in the secondary location.

3. Make sure the user identities you set up in the primary location are available in the secondary location.

4. Make sure any line-of-business applications relying on data in your primary location are failed over to the secondary location. See Figure 10-1.

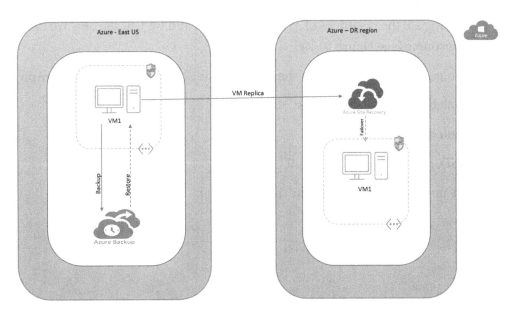

***Figure 10-1.*** *Disaster recovery*

Disaster recovery relies upon the replication of data and the computers in a secondary location not being affected by the disaster. When servers go down because of a natural disaster, equipment failure, or cyberattack, a business needs to recover lost data from a second location where the data is backed up. Ideally, an organization can transfer its computer processing to that remote location as well to continue operations.

Most Azure resources come with the option to set the data replication to another region, so you must plan the disaster recovery during Azure Virtual Desktop implementation so that data replication can be enabled for all required resources during the implementation phase. Different resources are involved in pooled and personal desktops, and planning DR for each type of desktop is different.

Let's see how we can plan and set up disaster recovery for each type of desktop.

# Disaster Recovery for Pooled Desktops

Pool desktops are nonpersistent desktops, and that's the reason we must use FSLogix to store the profile on a remote file share/storage. Since we already learned about all the pooled desktop concepts, you know that there are multiple resources we create as part of the pooled desktop creation, and you must plan disaster recovery for all the required resources.

315

The following are the resources of a pooled desktop, and we will see how we can plan DR for each resource (see Figure 10-2):

- Pooled user profile (DFS file share/Azure File Share Storage/Azure NetApp)

- Pooled host pool session host

- Pooled image

- MSIX package storage account

- On-premises connectivity and authentication

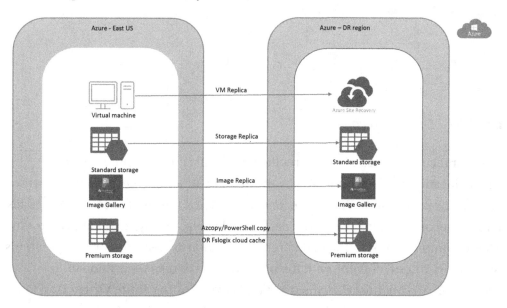

***Figure 10-2.*** *Disaster recovery for pooled desktop*

As you know, user profile storage is the most important resource in a pooled desktop, and it keeps all user profile data on a remote file share. There are multiple options to store user profiles like DFS file shares or Azure storage or Azure NetApp, and each resource has different options for DR.

- *DFS/Windows file share*: If you are using a DFS file share, then you must configure a file share replica on the file server in the DR region, and DFS will take care of the file replication to this DR region. Since you will be using a common workspace name, the DFS file share will be available with the same share name (workspace) from the DR region in the case of a disaster in the primary region. See Figure 10-3.

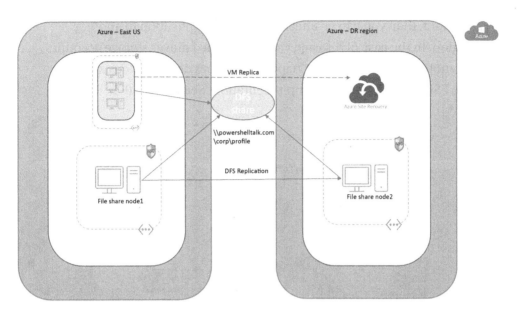

**Figure 10-3.** *Disaster recovery for pooled desktop with DFS*

Windows stand-alone file shares are a not recommended solution
for a Azure Virtual Desktop user profile, and I don't see any reason
to use this option as we have much better options available for user
profile storage. Anyway, if you are using a stand-alone file share, then
you should know that it does not allow the replication feature, and
you have to use robocopy/PowerShell to copy files to the file share in
another region as well as manage the file share DNS names so that
you don't have to change the FSLogix user profile registry every time.

- *Azure File Share storage*: File share storage is the most often used
solution for the FSLogix user profile because it's Azure native and
easy to integrate with other services like Azure AD, ADDS, and a
private endpoint with a virtual network. There are two options in
Azure storage: premium and standard storage.

  *Standard storage*: This comes with replication and a failover option
to another region, but this is not recommended for a production
workload because it can impact AVD performance due to limited
IOPS on the standard storage. Premium storage provides more IOPS
compared to standard storage, but if you are using a standard storage

account, then you can go ahead and enable replication to another region. In the case of disaster, you can set the failover storage account to another region. Refer to Chapter 5 for more detailed steps about the FSLogix VHDLocation implementation. See Figure 10-4.

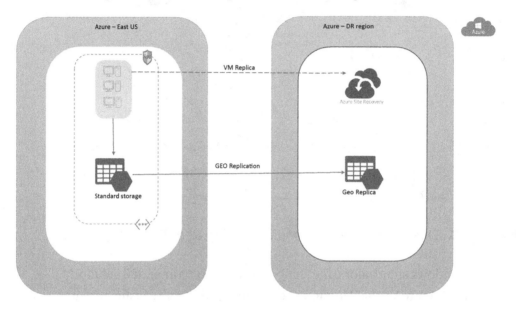

**Figure 10-4.**  *Disaster recovery for pooled user profile*

Make sure you are setting the redundancy to GRS or ZGRS if you want to use standard storage so it will allow you to enable georeplication. See Figure 10-5.

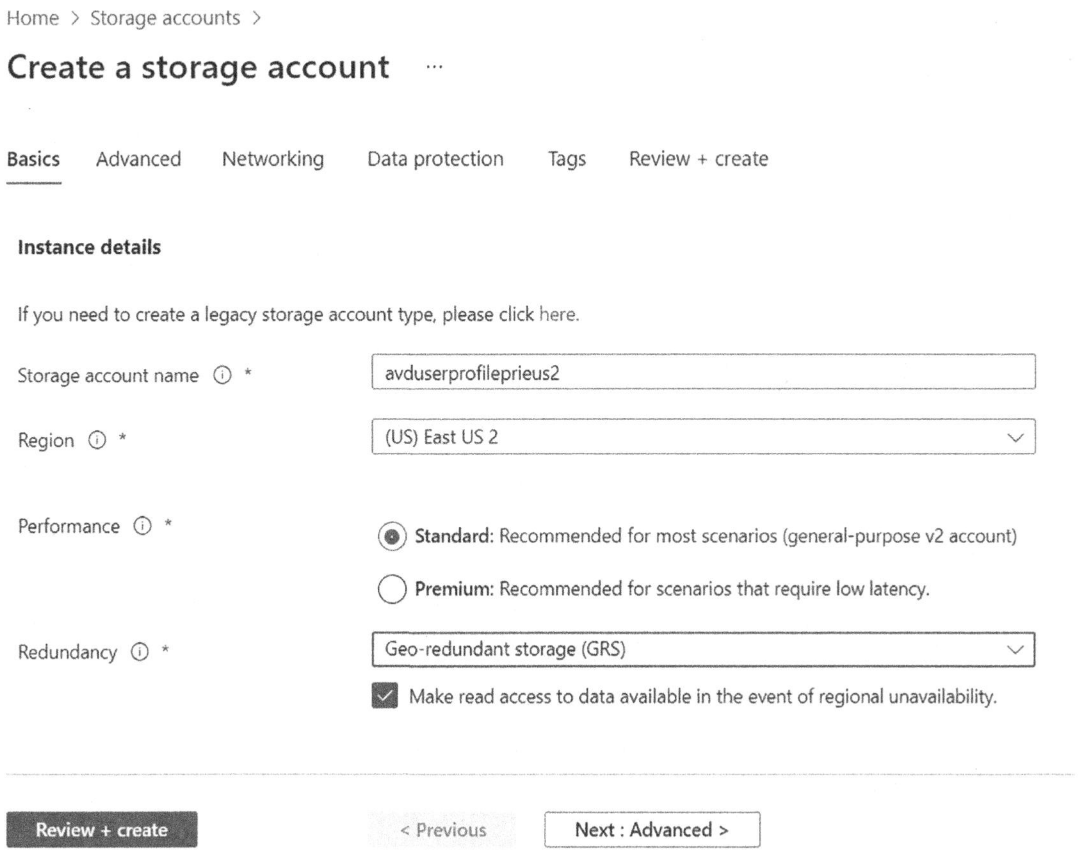

Home > Storage accounts >

# Create a storage account    ···

Basics    Advanced    Networking    Data protection    Tags    Review + create

**Instance details**

If you need to create a legacy storage account type, please click here.

Storage account name  ⓘ  *          avduserprofileprieus2

Region  ⓘ  *          (US) East US 2          ⌄

Performance  ⓘ  *          (⦿) **Standard**: Recommended for most scenarios (general-purpose v2 account)

                          ( ) **Premium**: Recommended for scenarios that require low latency.

Redundancy  ⓘ  *          Geo-redundant storage (GRS)          ⌄

                          ☑ Make read access to data available in the event of regional unavailability.

────────────────────────────────────────────

[ Review + create ]          < Previous          [ Next : Advanced > ]

***Figure 10-5.*** *Pooled user profile storage account creation*

Figure 10-6 shows the redundancy options available for a standard storage account.

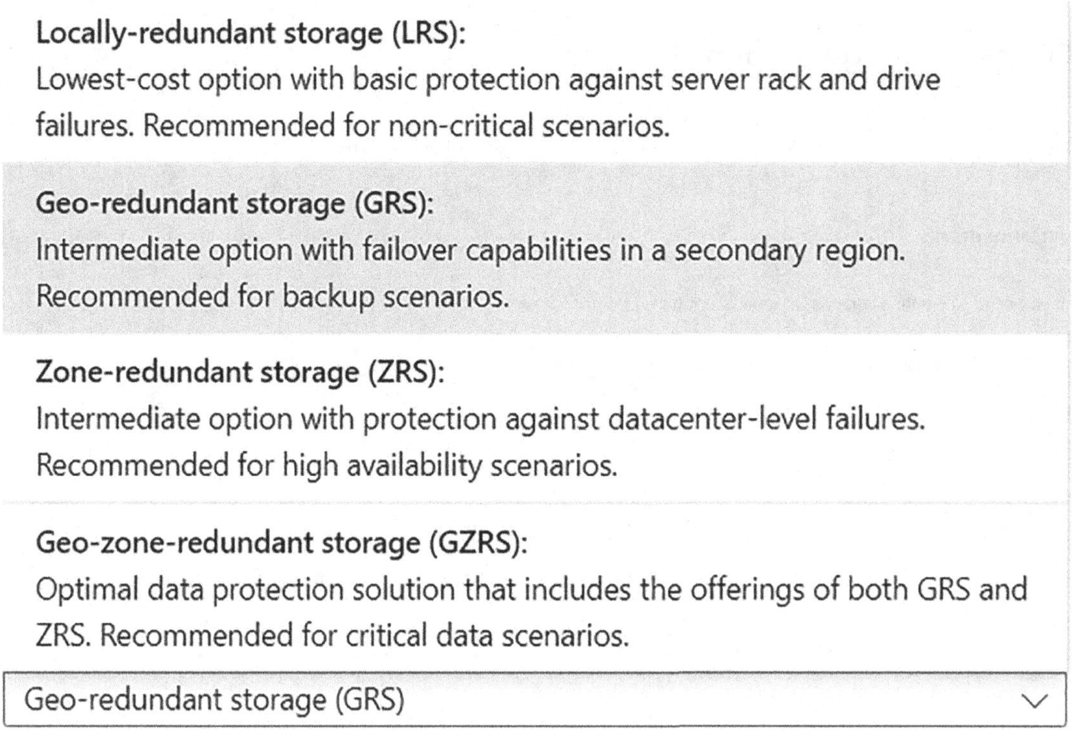

**Locally-redundant storage (LRS):**

Lowest-cost option with basic protection against server rack and drive failures. Recommended for non-critical scenarios.

**Geo-redundant storage (GRS):**

Intermediate option with failover capabilities in a secondary region. Recommended for backup scenarios.

**Zone-redundant storage (ZRS):**

Intermediate option with protection against datacenter-level failures. Recommended for high availability scenarios.

**Geo-zone-redundant storage (GZRS):**

Optimal data protection solution that includes the offerings of both GRS and ZRS. Recommended for critical data scenarios.

| Geo-redundant storage (GRS) |  |
|---|---|

***Figure 10-6.*** *Storage redundancy*

You can see the georeplication by going into the georeplication option in the user profile storage account. You will be able to see the replication status as the data center type (primary/secondary), and you can do failover in case of a disaster by clicking "Prepare for failover." See Figure 10-7 and Figure 10-8.

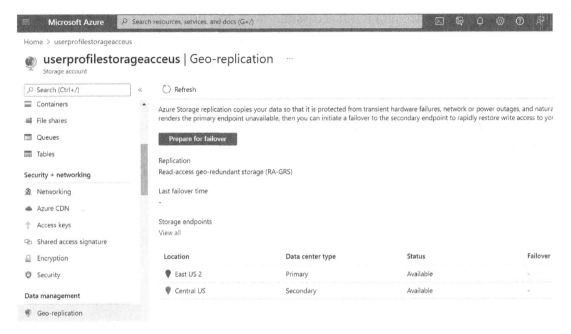

**Figure 10-7.**  *Storage georeplication*

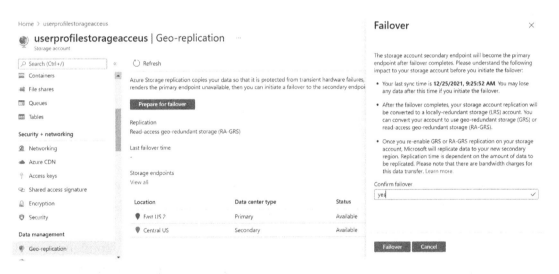

**Figure 10-8.**  *Storage georeplication and failover*

Premium storage does not allow for replication, but since premium storage is recommended for production workloads, you can use the FSLogix cloud cache, which will allow you to replicate the user profile to multiple storage accounts in a different region. By doing this you will be able to use the secondary storage account automatically if the primary storage account is not accessible/available. Primary and secondary storage are both dependent on the sequencing in the CCDLocation registry key, and both the storage accounts will be in sync. A CCDLocation overrides a VHDLocation, if they are both set.

The main advantage of using a cloud cache with premium storage is that you will get a high IOPS storage, which is recommended for production workloads; in addition, you will have profile data in two regions, and no manual intervention is required for failover or failback for the user profile in the case of a disaster in the primary region. See Figure 10-9.

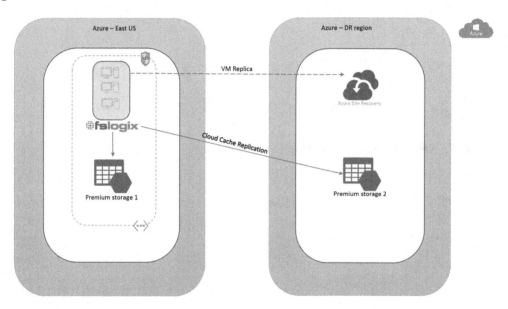

*Figure 10-9.* *FSLogix cloud cache*

In Figure 10-9 you can see that FSLogix is syncing the user profile data to both storage accounts using a cloud cache. Refer to Chapter 6 for more details about the cloud cache.

Azure NetApp also has a disaster recovery option, and you can easily configure replica in a supported cross region. The Azure NetApp Files replication functionality provides data protection through cross-region volume replication. You can asynchronously replicate data from an Azure NetApp Files volume (source) in one region to another Azure NetApp Files volume (destination) in another region. This capability enables you to fail over your critical application in the case of a region-wide outage or disaster. There are certain cross-region replication pairs to which you can replicate a

NetApp file volume, so it's recommended to check the Microsoft site for an updated list of supported cross-region replica pairs.

Another important resource you should consider in a DR plan is your golden image stored in the image gallery. The Azure image gallery has a replication future, which allows you to replicate images to a specific region and use the LRS/ZRS storage accounts to store the replicated image in a secondary region. Refer to Chapter 5 for more details. In the case of a disaster in a primary region, you don't have to perform any action to fail over the images, and the image copy will be available in the secondary region to create a VM from. See Figure 10-10.

*Figure 10-10.*  *Image gallery replication*

The limitation with image gallery replications is that you can create a limited number of VMs from a replicated image (20 VMs per replicated VM as of December 2021), and if you want to create hundreds of VMs in a replicated region, then you have to consider an alternative to storing an image in another region using the Azure image builder.

A pooled host pool is nonpersistent, and we can store all user profile data to the remote storage. Additionally, you can have pooled hostpool image with all application/configuration ready to deploy, so DR is not really required for a pooled host pool session host but definatly required for user profile storage and operating system image. You can simply create a new session host in the DR region using a pooled image, and it will come up with all the applications, FSLogix configuration inside new session host in DR region that will use the user profile from the fslogix cloud cache secondary location.

If you still want to protect your pooled session host from disaster, then you can use the Azure Recovery Services Vault (ASR) to protect the pooled session host, and you can fail over the session host during the disaster in a primary region. The following are the detailed steps to protect the session host as well as to fail over.

Creating a recover service vault in Azure is a one-time activity and can be part of your Azure Virtual Desktop deployment. You have to create a recovery vault in a secondary region to protect the session host from the primary region. Follow these steps to do this:

1.  Log in to the Azure portal and select the correct subscription. Search for *recovery service vault* on the top search bar in the Azure portal and click "Recovery Services vaults." See Figure 10-11.

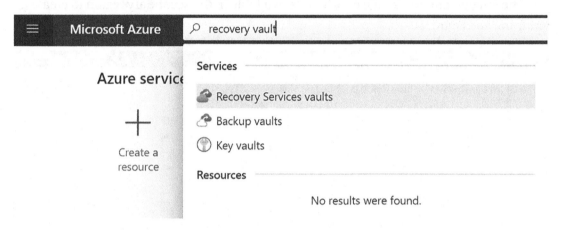

***Figure 10-11.***  *Recovery service vault search*

2.  Click the Create button under the recovery service vault. See Figure 10-12.

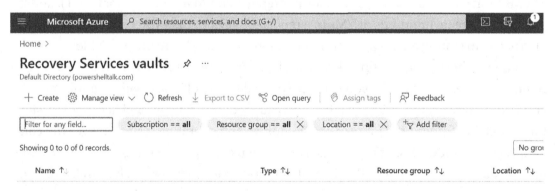

***Figure 10-12.***  *Creating the recovery service vault*

3.  On the create **recovery service vault** page, fill in the mandatory details such as the subscription, resource group name, vault

name, and region for vault creation. Make sure you select the
secondary region to create the vault so that you can protect
the session host from the primary region and the vault will be
available during disaster in the primary region. See Figure 10-13.

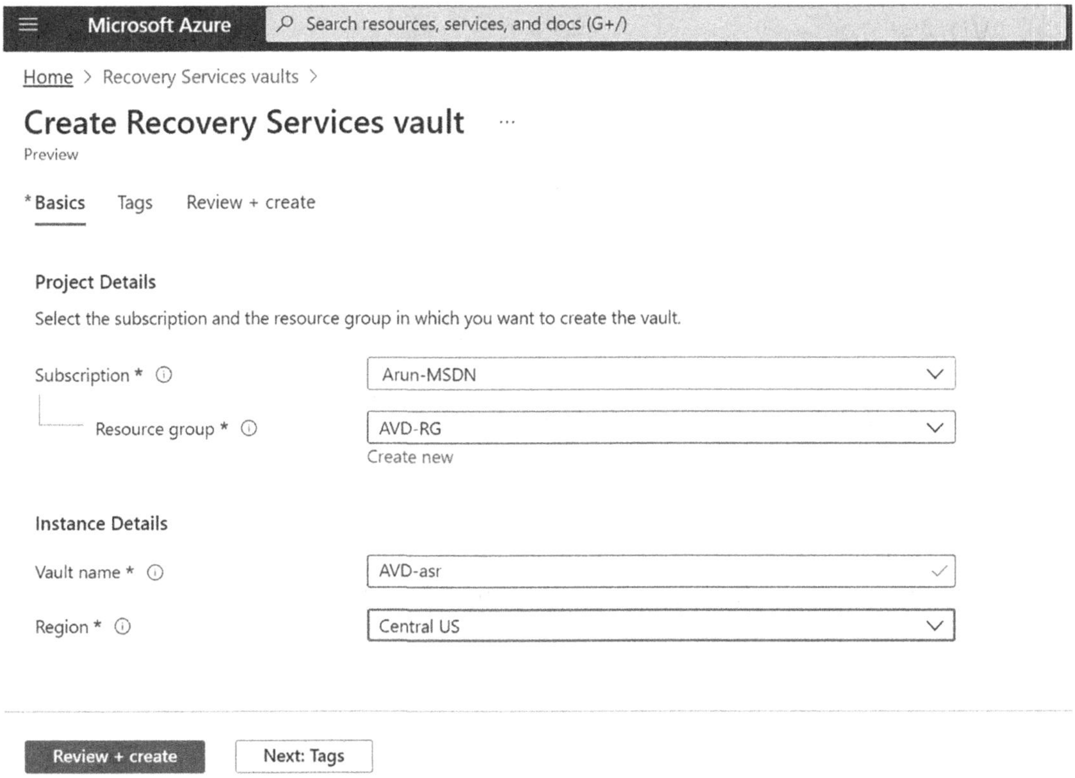

**Figure 10-13.**  *Creating a recovery service vault, Basics tab*

4. Verify all the vault properties once the recovery service vault is
   created successfully.

Enabling replication/protection for AVD virtual machines is again a one-time activity
at the time of Azure Virtual Desktop creation, but you might want to repeat it if you
add additional session hosts of the host pool in your environment. You can automate
the additional session host protection by using the PowerShell Az.RecoveryServices
module. Follow these steps to protect the AVD session host using ASR:

1. Open newly created recovery service vault, click + Enable Site
   Recovery, and fill in the source virtual machine details, source

virtual machine location, and source VM resource group location.
See Figure 10-14.

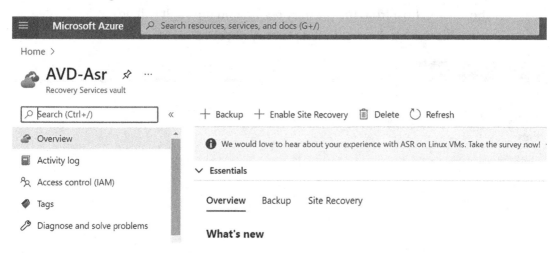

***Figure 10-14.***  *Recovery service vault, Overview tab*

2.  Note that the recovery vault and the recovery vault resource group
    should be in the secondary region and select the correct source
    primary region while protecting the Azure Virtual Desktop session
    host. See Figure 10-15.

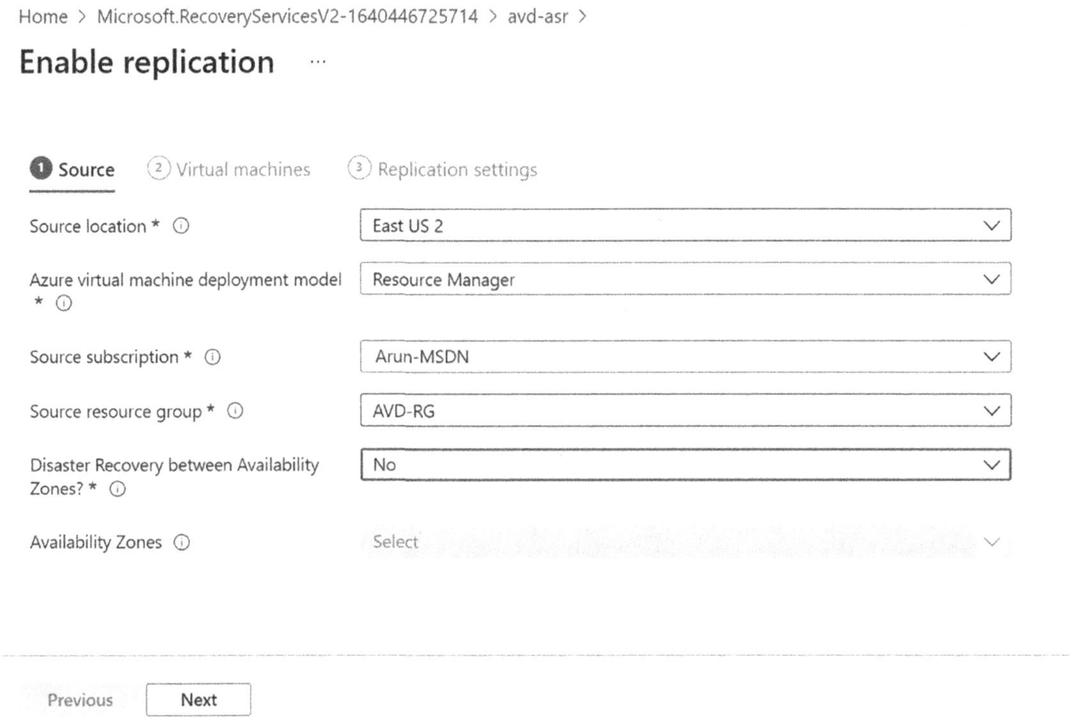

Home > Microsoft.RecoveryServicesV2-1640446725714 > avd-asr >

# Enable replication   ...

① **Source**      ② Virtual machines      ③ Replication settings

| | |
|---|---|
| Source location * ⓘ | East US 2 ⌄ |
| Azure virtual machine deployment model * ⓘ | Resource Manager ⌄ |
| Source subscription * ⓘ | Arun-MSDN ⌄ |
| Source resource group * ⓘ | AVD-RG ⌄ |
| Disaster Recovery between Availability Zones? * ⓘ | No ⌄ |
| Availability Zones ⓘ | Select ⌄ |

Previous    Next

***Figure 10-15.** Recovery service vault, enabling replication*

    3.    Select the virtual machines we want to replicate. See Figure 10-16.

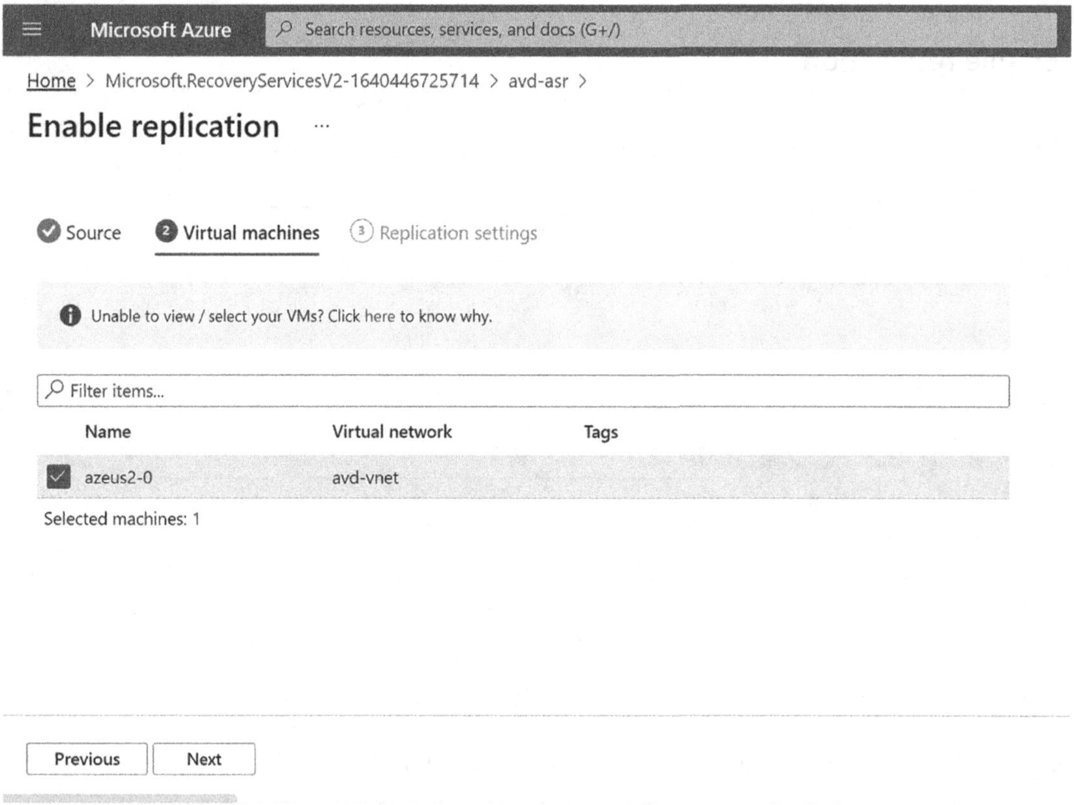

*Figure 10-16.* *Recovery service vault, selecting the virtual machine*

4.  Make sure you select the correct target region and subscription
    for the DR on the "Enable replication" tab. Also verify the target
    resource group, network, storage, and availability setting and
    click Customize in case you want to modify the target naming (DR
    region) settings. See Figure 10-17.

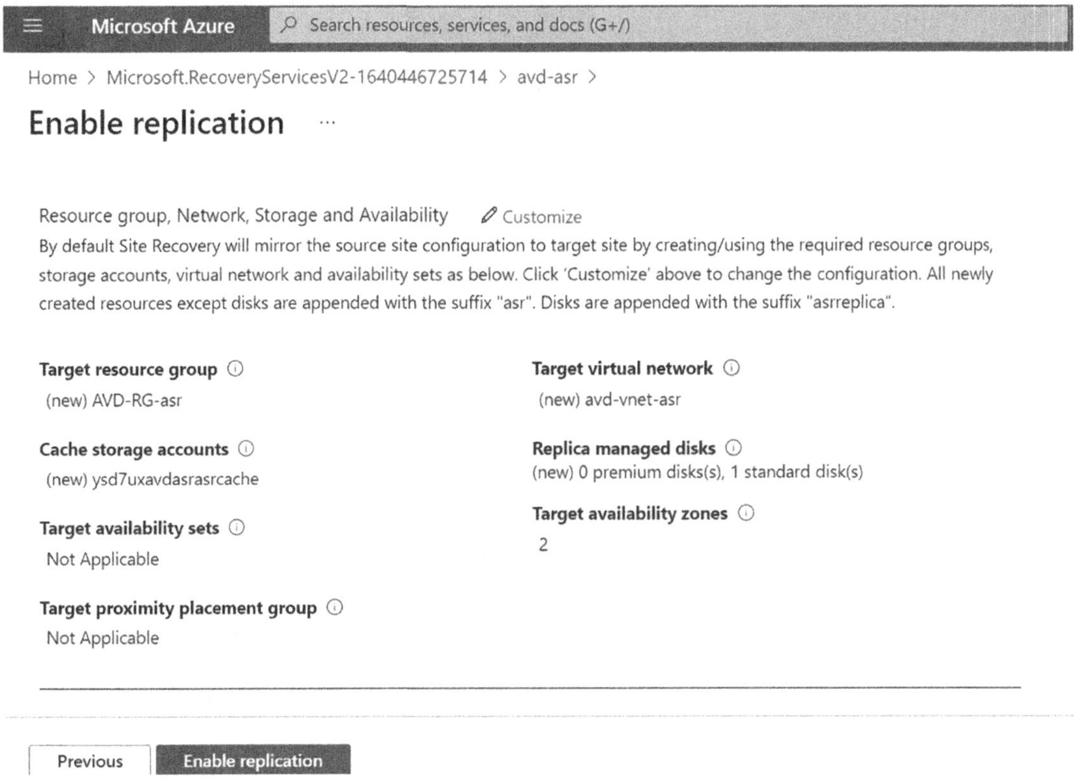

**Figure 10-17.**   *Recovery service vault, target resources*

5.  Verify and modify the replication policy as per your needs. By
default, recovery point retention will be 24 hours, and snapshot
frequency will be 4 hours. See Figure 10-18.

Replication Policy    ✎ Customize

**Name:** 24-hour-retention-policy
**Recovery point retention:** 24 hour(s)
**App consistent snapshot frequency:** 4 hour(s)
**Replication group:** None

Extension settings    [+] Show details

Site Recovery manages site recovery extension updates for all your replicated items. 1 new automation account will be created.

| Previous | **Enable replication** |

***Figure 10-18.*** *Recovery service vault, replication policy*

6.  Click "Enable replication" to start the replication of the selected virtual machines. Click the Notification icon (from the top bar) to monitor the enabling replication job status. See Figure 10-19.

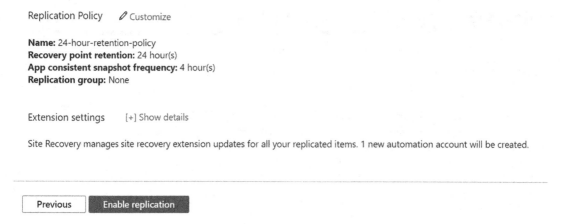

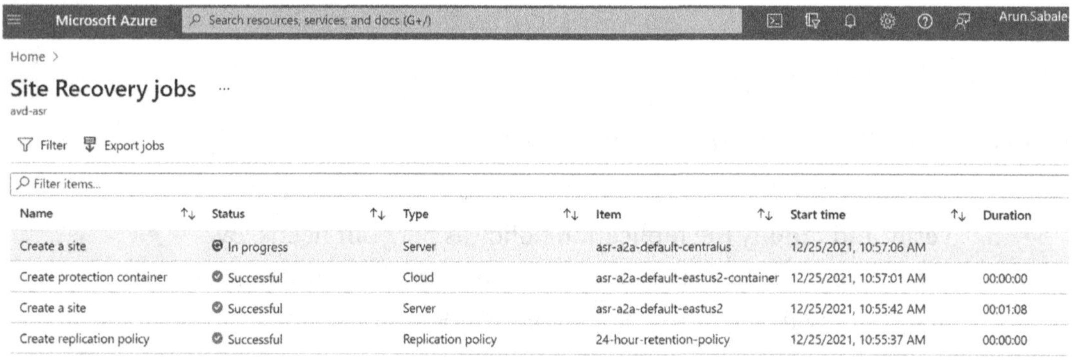

***Figure 10-19.*** *Recovery service vault, site recovery job*

7.  To check replication status of the virtual machines, go to the recovery service vault that was selected to enable replication and click the "Replicated items" tab. See Figure 10-20.

**Figure 10-20.**  *Recovery service vault, replicated items*

8.  We can monitor the replication status of each virtual machine in the same blade. See Figure 10-21.

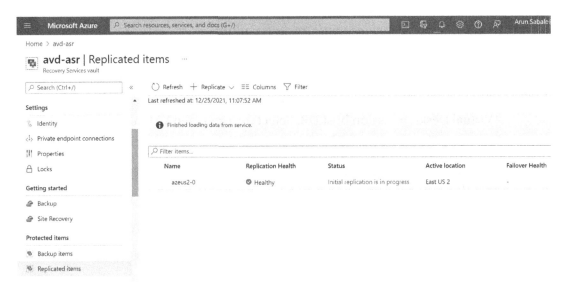

**Figure 10-21.**  *Recovery service vault, replicated items status*

Adding virtual machines to the recovery service plan is a one-time activity to group multiple protected VMs/session hosts in the recovery plan so that you can fail over all the VMs together.

1.  Go to the Azure portal and select the recovery service vault we created for the Azure Virtual Desktop session host. Click the Recovery Plans tab. See Figure 10-22.

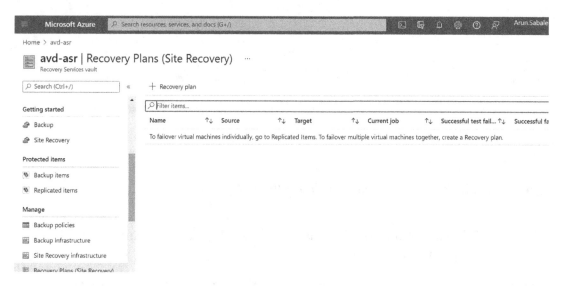

**Figure 10-22.**  *Recovery service vault, recovery plan*

2.  Click "+ Recovery plan" to add a new recovery plan. Make sure you are selecting the correct source and target for the Azure Virtual Desktop session host DR. Select the protected VM in the recovery plan. You can add 100 protected VMs in the recovery plan (as of December 2021), so prepare the recovery plan accordingly. See Figure 10-23.

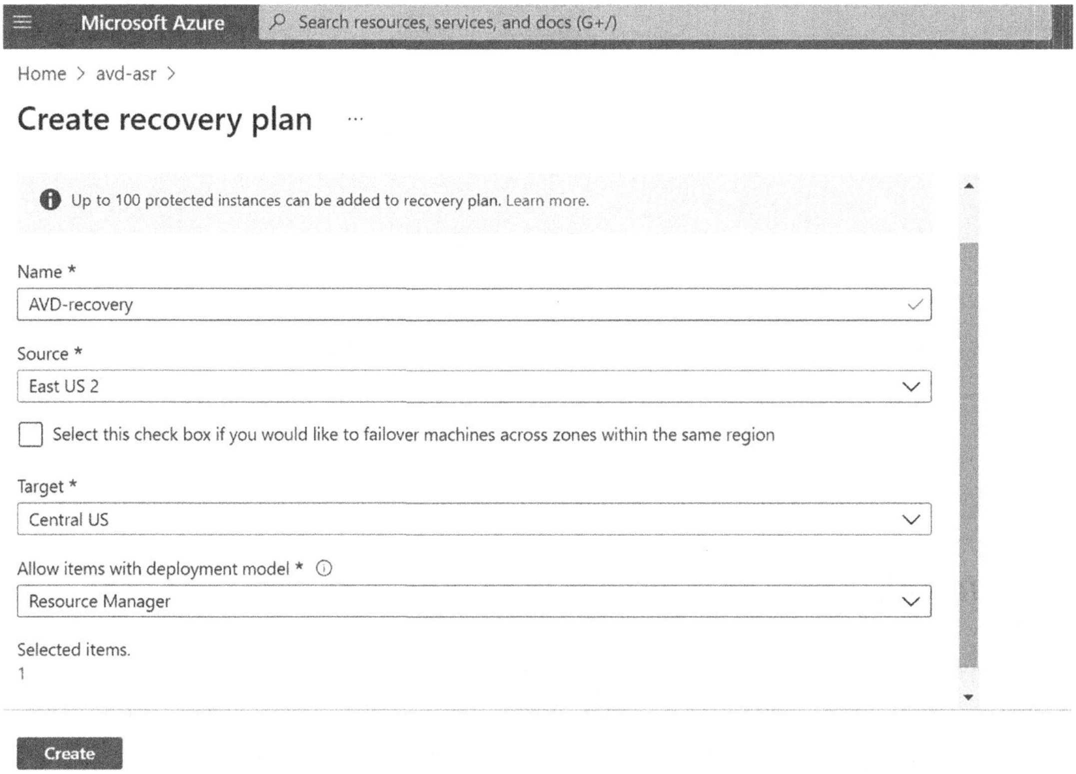

≡    **Microsoft Azure**    🔎 Search resources, services, and docs (G+/)

Home > avd-asr >

# Create recovery plan    ...

ℹ️ Up to 100 protected instances can be added to recovery plan. Learn more.

Name *

AVD-recovery                                                                    ✓

Source *

East US 2                                                                        ⌄

☐ Select this check box if you would like to failover machines across zones within the same region

Target *

Central US                                                                       ⌄

Allow items with deployment model * ⓘ

Resource Manager                                                                 ⌄

Selected items.
1

Create

***Figure 10-23.***  *Recovery service vault, creating a recovery plan*

3.  Click the Create button to create the recovery plan. Once the
    recovery plan is ready, verify the source session host is showing in
    the recovery plan. See Figure 10-24.

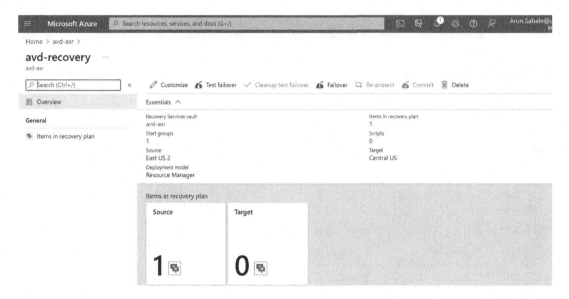

***Figure 10-24.*** *Recovery service vault, recovery plan overview*

It's always recommended to test the failover every quarter to make sure that the session hosts are protected and that DR is working fine with the correct RTO and RPO as per your organization's requirement. The following are the steps to test failover:

1.  Log in to the Azure portal and go to recovery vault created in the secondary region. Click the recovery plan name on the recovery server vault and click "Cleanup test failover." See Figure 10-25.

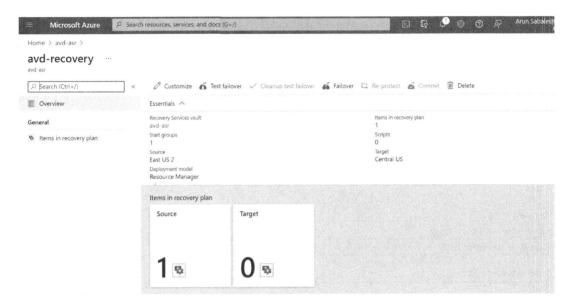

*Figure 10-25.* *Recovery service vault, recovery plan overview*

2.  Select "Latest processed (low RTO)" under Recovery Point, select
    the target failover virtual network, and click OK. If you choose
    the Latest option, the failover will be triggered after processing
    all the data sent to the service. The time taken will depend on the
    number of unprocessed logs. Check the time of the latest crash-
    consistent recovery point to get an estimate of the unprocessed
    logs so you can select the latest processed. See Figure 10-26.

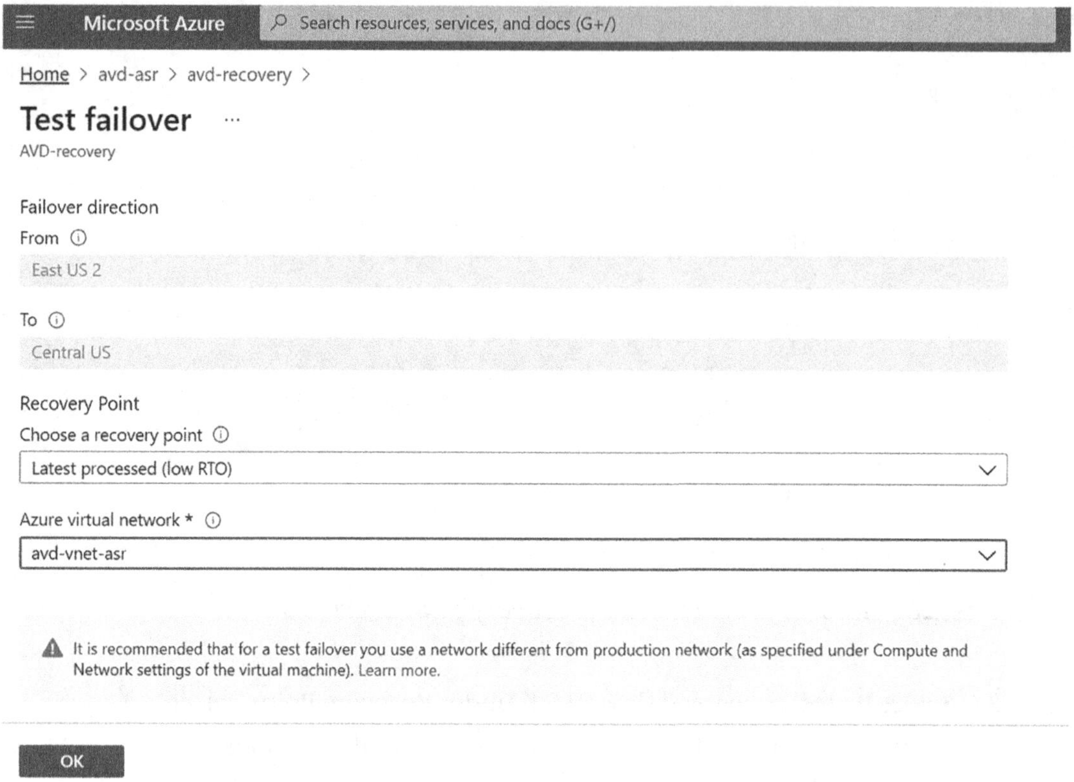

**Figure 10-26.** *Recovery service vault, test failover*

3.  You can monitor the status by clicking the notification icon on the
    top bar. See Figure 10-27.

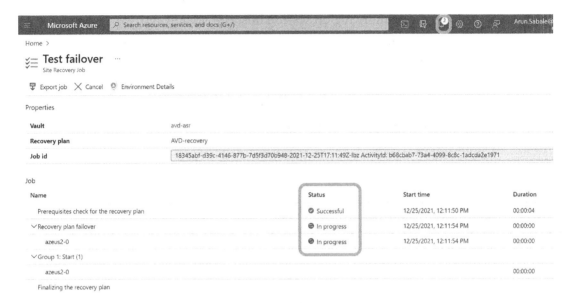

***Figure 10-27.*** *Recovery service vault, test failover job*

4. Wait until Azure completes the failover tasks. Test failover is completed. See Figure 10-28.

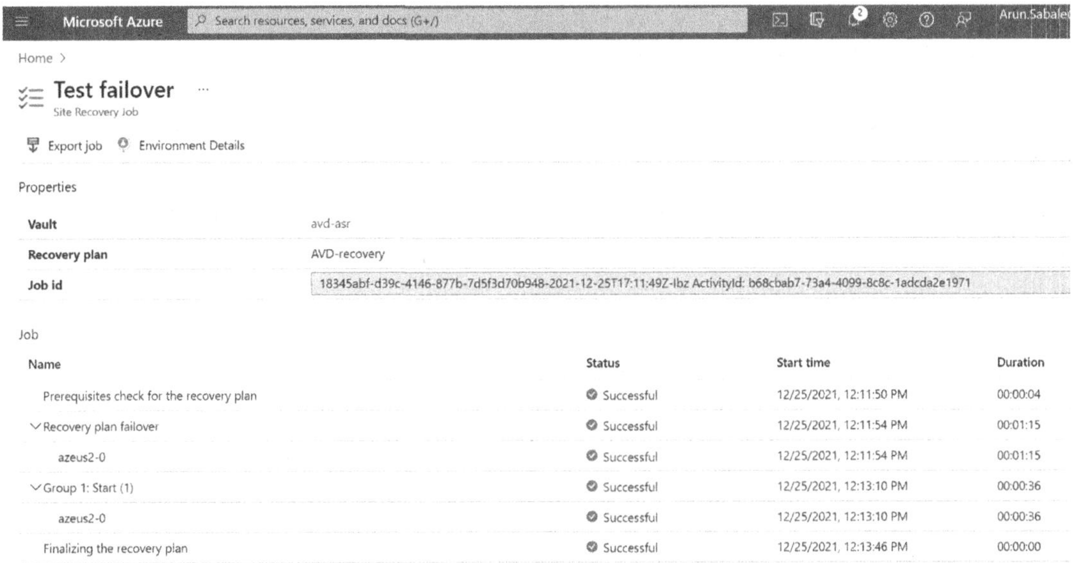

***Figure 10-28.*** *Recovery service vault, test failover job status*

5. Shut down the primary region session hosts for testing and check if the host pool session host is available and allowing user sessions. If the host pool allows sessions on the DR region session host, it means the test failover is working fine, and you can start the primary region session host and then clean the test failover and revert the host pool/session host to the primary region. See Figure 10-29.

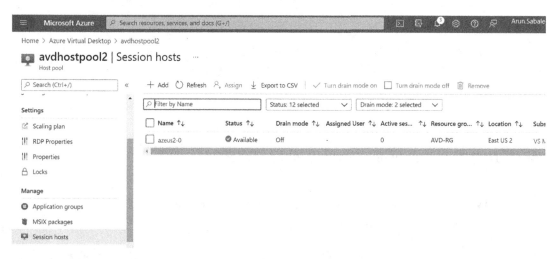

***Figure 10-29.*** *Test failover validation*

As we discussed, it's mandatory to test the failover to make sure Azure Virtual Desktop is protected. Once you are done with testing the failover, you have to clean the test failover so that the primary region session host will be back in action. You can follow these steps to clean the test failover, and it will delete the test resources/VMs created in the secondary region.

1. Log in to the Azure portal and go to the recovery vault where you performed the test failover. Select the recovery plan and click the "Cleanup test failover" option. See Figure 10-30.

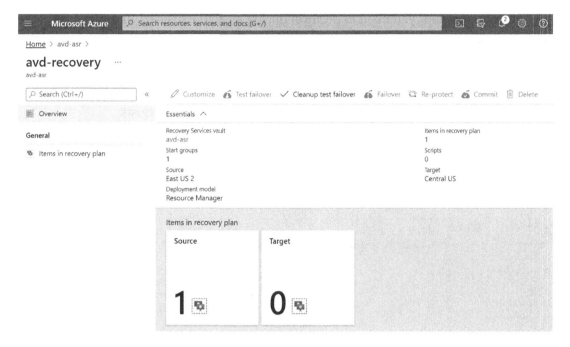

***Figure 10-30.*** *Test failover cleanup*

2.   Wait until the cleanup is completed. See Figure 10-31.

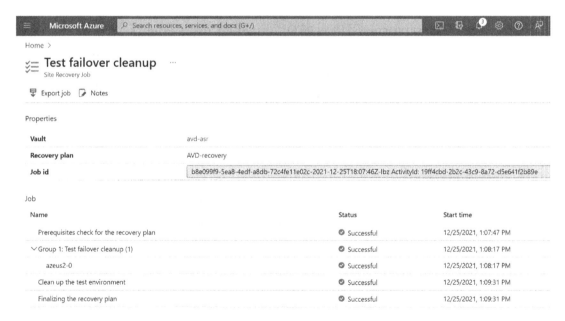

***Figure 10-31.*** *Test failover cleanup job status*

These are the steps you need to perform during an actual disaster in the primary region:

1. Log in to the Azure portal and go to the recovery vault. Click Recovery Plans (Site Recovery) under your recovery service vault. Next click the Failover menu item to fail over the session hosts from the recovery plan. See Figure 10-32.

***Figure 10-32.***  *Failover, recovery plan*

2. Select "Latest processed (low RTO)" under Recovery Point, select "Shutdown machines before beginning failover," and click OK. You can also change directions in case you have an active/protected VM in the secondary region and you want it to fail back to the primary. See Figure 10-33.

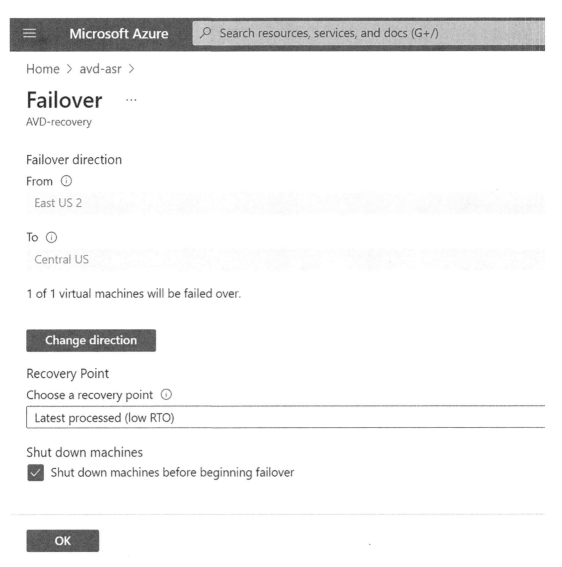

***Figure 10-33.*** *Failover, failover direction*

3.  Click the notification icon on the top bar to monitor the failover
    job status and wait until Azure completes the failover job. See
    Figure 10-34.

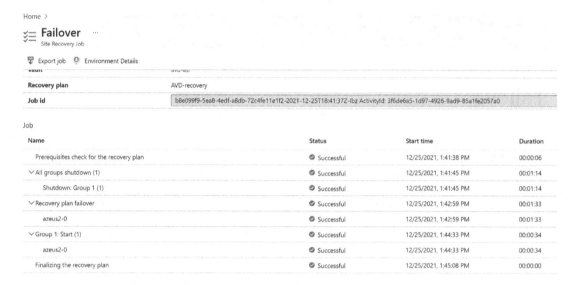

**Figure 10-34.** *Failover, failover job status*

4. Now you can see new virtual machines running in the DR region and the primary region VMs deallocated. See Figure 10-35.

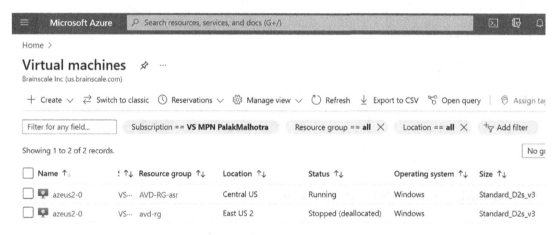

**Figure 10-35.** *Failover, VM status after failover*

5. The next step is to make sure the remaining Azure Virtual Desktop–dependent resources are also available in the DR region so that the user can start logging in using the secondary region. The Azure control plane (gate, broker) is available in multiple regions and managed by Microsoft, so you don't have to worry

about that. If you are using the FSLogix cloud cache (required only for pooled), then you don't need additional action to failover user profile storage, and once you fail over the session hosts, the user can access Azure Virtual Desktop from the DR region.

After the DR, you can fail back the session host to the primary region and protect the VMs again using ASR. When you fail over Azure VMs from one region to another using Azure Site Recovery, the VMs boot up in the secondary region, in an **unprotected** state. If you want to fail back the VMs to the primary region, do the following tasks:

1. Reprotect the VMs in the secondary region so that they start to replicate to the primary region.

2. After reprotection completes and the VMs are replicating, you can fail over from the secondary to primary region.

Let's see the detailed steps:

1. If you need to be fail back to the original primary region (in my case East US2) after DR, then click the Site Recovery tab under the recovery service vault and select the "Re-protect" option. See Figure 10-36.

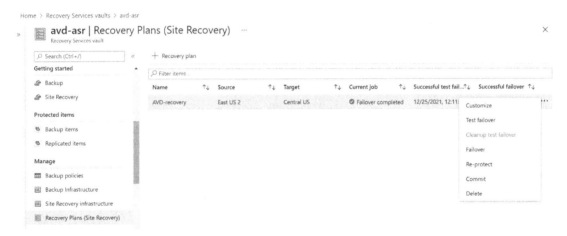

***Figure 10-36.*** *Failback to the original primary region*

2. Select all the correct details for the target (East US2 in my failback case) and click OK to re-protect the session host from the DR region to the original primary region. See Figure 10-37.

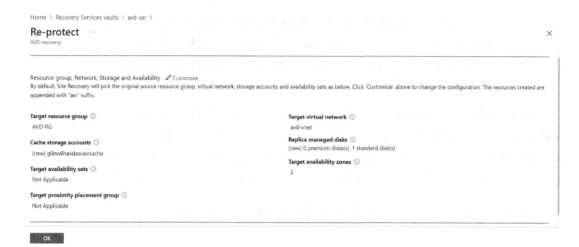

**Figure 10-37.**  *Failback, target resources*

3.   You can check the re-protect job status from a notification. See Figure 10-38.

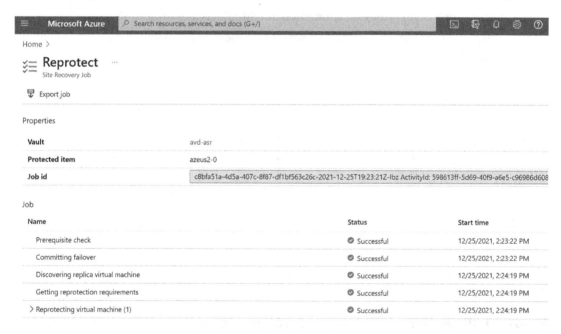

**Figure 10-38.**  *Failback, failback job status*

4.  Once reprotection is completed, you can change the network
    setting of the protected VM and initiate failover from the DR
    region to the original primary region. See Figure 10-39.

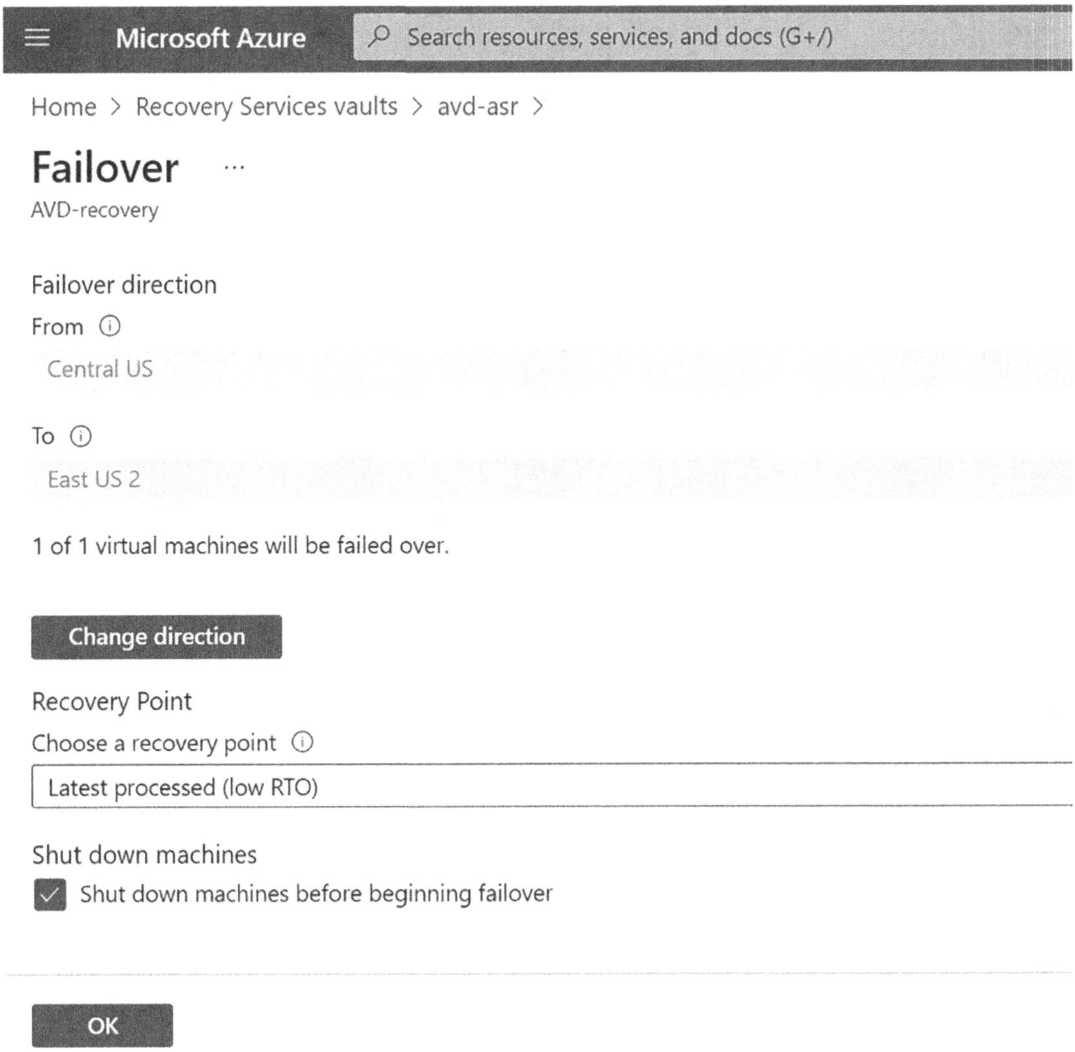

*Figure 10-39.* *Failback, failback direction*

5.  Wait for the failover job to complete and check the running
    VM. See Figure 10-40.

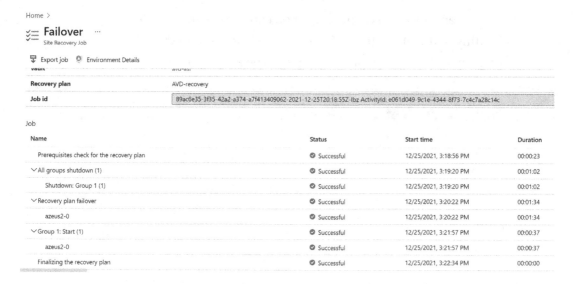

**Figure 10-40.** *Failback, failback job status*

6. You can see the changes in the running VM. Now the original primary VM is running, and the DR will be deallocated. See Figure 10-41.

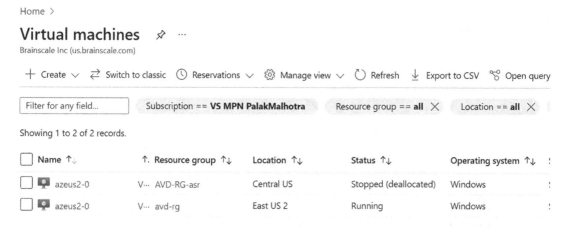

**Figure 10-41.** *Failback, VM status after failback*

7. The VMs will be unprotected now, so reprotect the VM from the original to the DR region again. See Figure 10-42.

***Figure 10-42.*** *Failback, re-protect VM*

What happens during reprotection? By default, the following occurs:

1. A cache storage account is created in the original primary region where the failed over VM is running. If the target storage account (the original storage account in the primary region) doesn't exist, a new one is created. The assigned storage account name is the name of the storage account used by the secondary VM, suffixed with `asr`.

2. If your VM uses managed disks, replica managed disks are created in the primary region to store the data replicated from the secondary VM's disks.

3. Temporary replicas of the source disks (disks attached to the VMs in the secondary region) are created with the name `ms-asr-<GUID>`, which are used to transfer/read data. The temp disks let us utilize the complete bandwidth of the disk instead of only 16 precent bandwidth of the original disks (that are connected to the VM). The temp disks are deleted once the reprotection completes.

4. If the target availability set doesn't exist, a new one is created as part of the reprotect job if necessary. If you've customized the reprotection settings, then the selected set is used.

5. *MSIX package storage account DR*: If you are using MSIX packages and if they are stored in Azure storage (standard/premium) or any other file share, then please refer to the "Azure File Share storage"

section in this chapter to plan and implement DR for MSIX packages.

6. *On-premises connectivity and authentication*: Make sure the ADDS service is available and reachable from the DR region as well so that if the primary is down, the VM authentication and name resolution will work with ADDS and DNS. Additionally, if you have some application needs on-premises connectivity, then you have to make sure that the same connectivity is there in the DR location with all the firewall rules.

# Disaster Recovery for Personal Desktops

Personal desktops are persistent desktops, which means the user data will be there on the same VM, and the user will be able to log in to the same VM every time. Since the user profile/data will be on the VM itself, you have to protect the VM using ASR. See Figure 10-43.

The following are the resources part of the personal desktop, and you have to plan the DR for each resource:

– Personal host pool session host

– Personal image

– MSIX package storage account

– On-premises connectivity and authentication

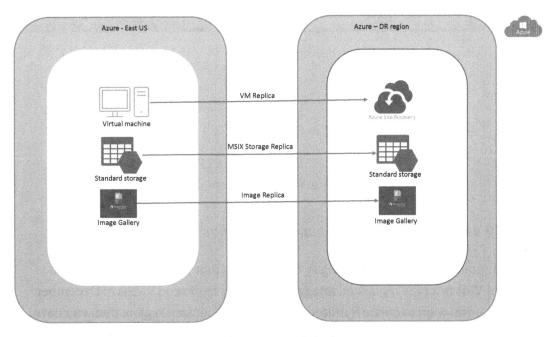

***Figure 10-43.*** *Disaster recovery for personal desktop*

- *Personal host pool session host DR plan and implementation*:
  Protecting a personal session host is the same as pooled VM
  protection using ASR. You can follow the same steps as the pooled
  host pool DR mentioned in the previous section.

- *Operating system image DR*: Another important resource you should
  consider in a DR plan is your golden image stored in the image
  gallery. The Azure image gallery has a replication feature that allows
  you to replicate images to a specific region and use LRS/ZRS storage
  accounts to store the replicated image in the secondary region.
  Please refer to Chapter 7 for more details.

In the case of a disaster in a primary region, you don't have to perform any action
to fail over the images, and the image copy will be available in the secondary region to
create the VM from. See Figure 10-44.

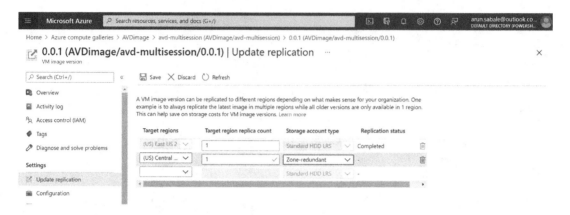

***Figure 10-44.*** *Azure image gallery, image replication*

The limitation with the image gallery replication is that you can create a limited number of VMs from the replicated image (20 VMs per replicated VM as of December 2021), and if you want to create hundreds of VMs in a replicated region, then you have to consider an alternative to store the image in another region using the Azure Image Builder.

- *MSIX package storage account DR*: If you are using MSIX packages and if they are stored on Azure storage (standard/premium) or any other file share, then please refer to the "Azure File Share storage" section in this chapter to plan and implement DR for MSIX packages.

- *On-premises connectivity and authentication*: Make sure the ADDS service is available and reachable from the DR region as well so that if the primary is down, the VM authentication and name resolution work with ADDS and DNS. Additionally, if you have some application needs on-premises connectivity, then you must have to make sure that the same connectivity is there in DR location with all firewall rules.

# Design a Backup Strategy for Azure Virtual Desktop

A backup is required if you want to retrieve old data or accidentally deleted data. As we discussed earlier, the backup and disaster both are different. Disaster allows you to continue service access during disaster in your primary region, but it will not allow you to retrieve old data in case something goes wrong with the user data. Backups can be taken in the same region using the Azure native service called Azure Backup.

You can protect your data by taking backups at regular intervals, via a backup policy. Azure Backup creates recovery points that can be stored in georedundant recovery vaults. See Figure 10-45.

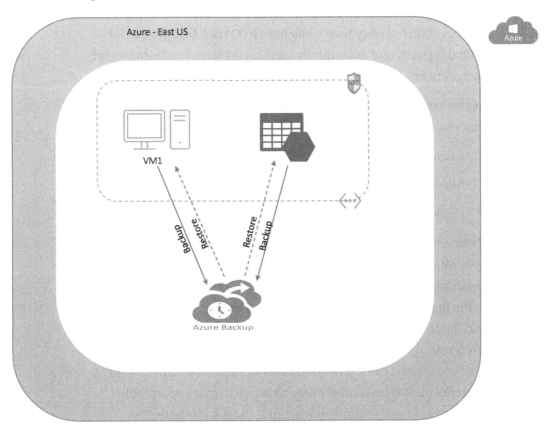

***Figure 10-45.*** *Azure Backup*

A comprehensive backup strategy is an essential part of an organization's cyber safety. It can be defined as an administrator's plan to ensure critical organizational data is backed up and available for restore in the case of a data loss event. A backup strategy, along with a disaster recovery plan, is a better business continuity plan, which allows an organization to recover with zero-to-minimal damage to the business, data, and reputation.

Here we'll detail four steps to develop a backup strategy for the enterprise.

1. ***Determine what data has to be backed up***: **When it comes to data**, "everything" will probably be your answer. However, the level of data protection will vary based on how critical it is to

restore that data. Your organization's recovery time objective (RTO), which is the maximum acceptable length of time required for an organization to recover lost data and get back up and running, is a reliable benchmark when forming your backup strategy. The recovery time objective (RTO) can be different for each data type, and accordingly you should form your strategy for each data set.

Assess and group your applications and data into the following so that you can decide your priority:

- *Existentially-critical* for the business

- *Mission-critical* for the organization to operate

- *Optimal-for-performance* for the organization to thrive

2. **Determine how often data has to be backed up:** The frequency with which you back up your data should be aligned with your organization's recovery point objective (RPO), which is defined as the maximum allowable period between the time of data loss and the last useful backup of a known good state. Thus, the more often your data is backed up, the more likely you are to comply with your stated RPO. As a good rule of thumb, backups should be performed at least once every 24 hours to meet acceptable standards of most organizations, but if the data is more/less important, then you should define your backup schedule strategy accordingly.

3. **Identify and implement a suitable backup and recovery solution:** Based on your organization's requirements, you need to identify a suitable backup solution as part of your backup strategy. Azure Backup is the most preferred and suitable solution when it comes to Azure Virtual Desktop or any other cloud service backup, but if you already have backup solution, then make sure it's compatible and suitable for Azure Virtual Desktop.

4. **Test and monitor your backup system:** Once your backup system is in place, check that the backup is successful, and the restore is smooth and accurate.

There are two major components you must have to consider in your backup plan:

- Personal desktop VM backup

- Pooled FSLogix user profile storage

A personal desktop needs to be backed up as users can store data on personal desktop and it should be protected with any backup tool.

For pooled desktops, VMs are not required to be backed up, because user data will be there in the user profile storage, so you have to plan a backup option for the user profile data for pooled desktops.

# Configure Backup and Restore for FSLogix User Profiles and Personal Virtual Desktop Infrastructures

You now know why backup is important for Azure Virtual Desktop, so let's go ahead and see how to configure a backup for a personal desktop and FSLogix user profile (pooled desktop).

Azure backups can be created through the Azure portal. This method provides a browser-based user interface to create and configure Azure backups and all related resources. You can protect your data by taking backups at regular intervals. Azure Backup creates recovery points that can be stored in georedundant recovery vaults.

A recovery services vault is a logical container that stores the backup data for each protected resource, such as Azure VMs. When the backup job for a protected resource runs, it creates a recovery point inside the recovery services vault. You can then use one of these recovery points to restore data to a given point in time.

1. To set up a backup on a session host, log in to the Azure portal and go to the personal desktop session host. Click the Backup option under the session host. You can use an existing vault or create a new one on the Backup page. See Figure 10-46.

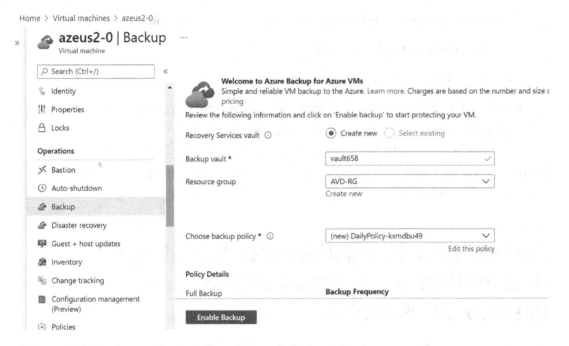

***Figure 10-46.*** *Azure Backup for personal desktop*

2.  By default, backup frequency will be daily, and it will retain data
    for 30 days, but you can click the Edit button and change the
    backup frequency as per your organization's need. Once you
    verify all details, then click "Enable backup." See Figure 10-47.

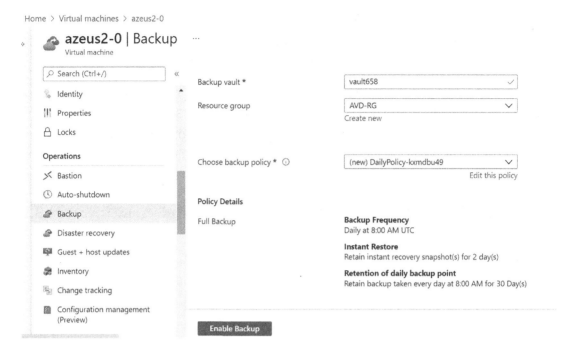

***Figure 10-47.*** *Azure Backup, VM backup setting*

3.  Once the backup is enabled, you will be able to see the VM backup in the vault under "Backup items." See Figure 10-48.

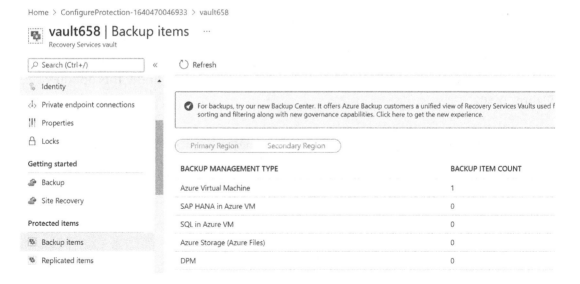

***Figure 10-48.*** *Azure Backup, backup items*

4.  Repeat the same steps for all personal session hosts. Alternatively, you can create automation using PowerShell/CLI to enable backups on multiple personal desktop session hosts.

Restoring a session host/VM is possible from the recovery vault or from the VM page in the Azure portal. You can log in to Azure and go to the session host you want to restore and click the Backup option. You will be able to see the backup status of the session host under the Backup option, and you can see two different restore options. See Figure 10-49.

***Figure 10-49.*** *Azure Backup, backup status*

You can restore a full VM to a specific restore point, you can overwrite the disk, or you can also create new a VM from the restore point you selected under this option. See Figure 10-50.

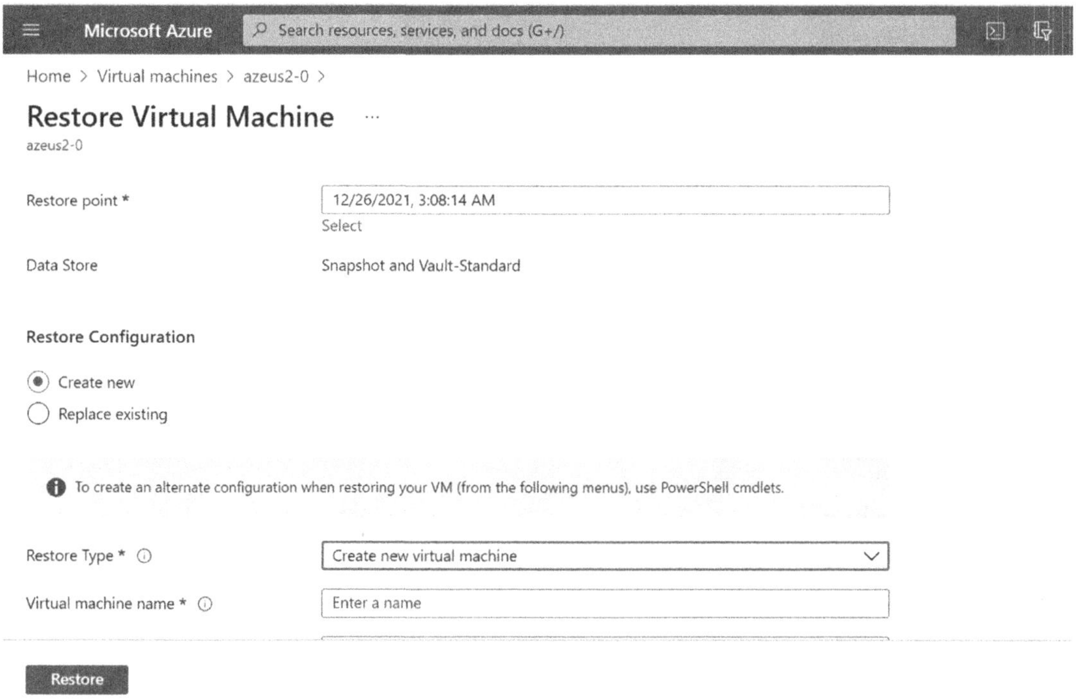

***Figure 10-50.*** *Azure Backup, restore a VM*

File recovery allows you to download the executable and run it on the VM where you want to restore data. Once you execute the file, then it will attach the disk to the VM, and you can recover specific files from the backup. See Figure 10-51.

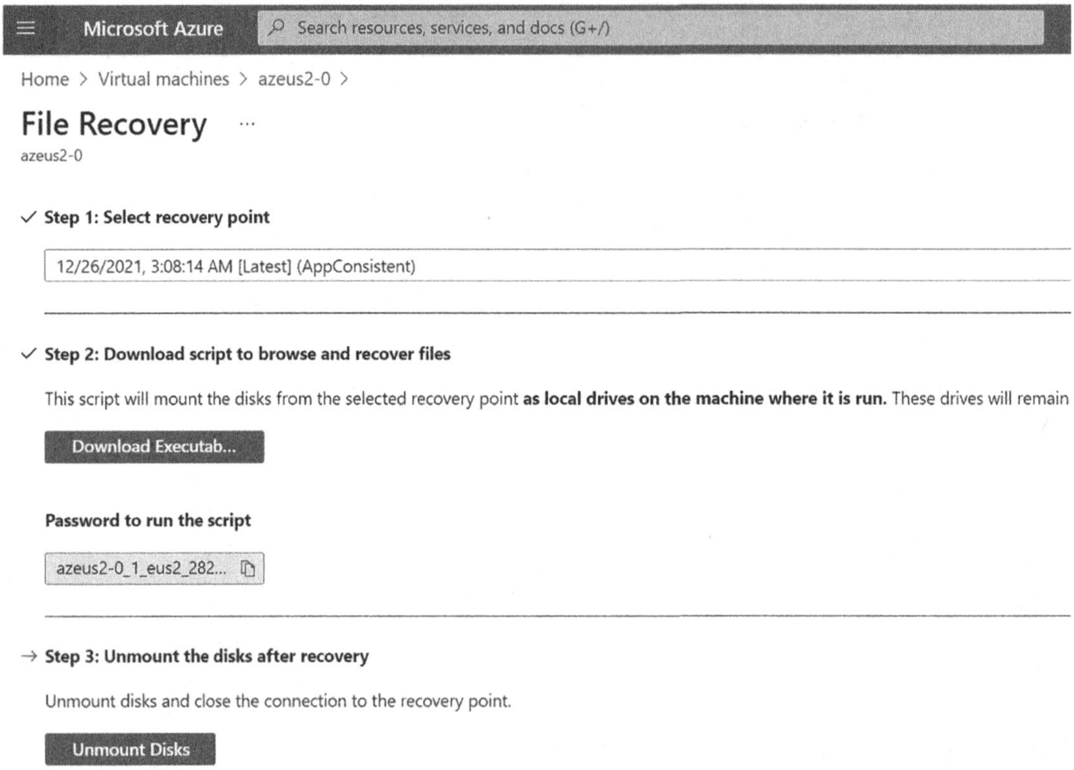

**Figure 10-51.** *Azure Backup, restoring specific files from backup*

Pooled desktops use FSLogix to store user profile/data to a remote storage, so it is important to take backups of the user profile storage. You can protect the user profile data by taking backups at regular intervals. Azure Backup creates recovery points that can be stored in georedundant recovery vaults.

Azure file share backup is a native, cloud-based backup solution that protects your data in the cloud and eliminates additional maintenance overheads involved in on-premises backup solutions. The Azure Backup service smoothly integrates with Azure File Sync and allows you to centralize your file share data as well as your backups. This simple, reliable, and secure solution enables you to configure protection for your enterprise file shares in a few simple steps with an assurance that you can recover your data in any disaster scenario.

# Key Benefits of Azure File Share Backup

Here are the key benefits:

- **Zero infrastructure**: No deployment is needed to configure protection for your file shares.

- **Customized retention**: You can configure backups with daily/weekly/monthly/yearly retention according to your requirements.

- **Built-in management capabilities**: You can schedule backups and specify the desired retention period without the additional overhead of data pruning.

- **Instant restore**: Azure file share backup uses file share snapshots, so you can select just the files you want to restore instantly.

- **Alerting and reporting**: You can configure alerts for backup and restore failures and use the reporting solution provided by Azure Backup to get insights on backups across your file shares.

- **Protection against accidental deletion of file shares**: Azure Backup enables the soft delete feature on a storage account level with a retention period of 14 days. Even if a malicious actor deletes the file share, the file share's contents and recovery points (snapshots) are retained for a configurable retention period, allowing the successful and complete recovery of source contents and snapshots with no data loss.

- **Protection against accidental deletion of snapshots**: Azure Backup acquires a lease on the snapshots taken by scheduled/on-demand backup jobs. The lease acts as a lock that adds a layer of protection and secures the snapshots against accidental deletion.

These are the steps to enable user profile storage backup:

1. Log in to the Azure portal and go to the user profile storage account and file share. Click the file share name under the file share option.

2. Go to the backup option on the file share and select an existing vault or create a new vault if you don't have one. The vault must be in the same region. Also verify the backup policy and backup frequency to proceed. Once you verify everything, then click "Enable backup." See Figure 10-52.

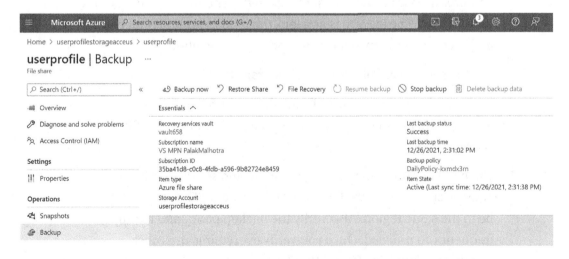

*Figure 10-52.* *Azure Backup, backing up Azure storage file share*

You can restore specific files or all data from the Azure storage account file share backup. Go to the file share and click Backup to restore the full share or file recovery. See Figure 10-53.

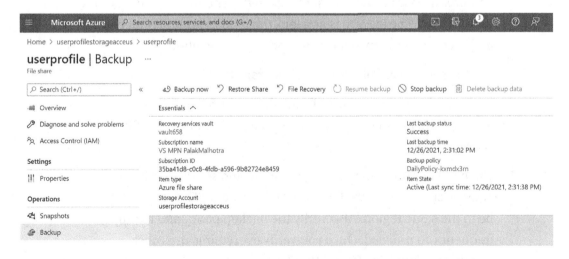

*Figure 10-53.* *Azure Backup, Azure storage file share restore options*

# Summary

In this chapter, you learned about planning and implementing disaster recovery for Azure Virtual Desktop including pooled and personal desktops. You also learned about the difference between backup and disaster recovery. Backup is also important to protect the user data in same region, so you learned how to back up user profile data for pooled and personal session host VMs.

# CHAPTER 11

# Monitor and Manage Performance and Health

In this chapter, you will learn how to monitor Azure Virtual Desktop by using the Azure Monitor native tool and see all the different components you can monitor. Additionally, you will see some recommendations for how to use Azure Advisor for Azure Virtual Desktop (AVD).

You can customize Azure Monitor workbooks for Azure Virtual Desktop monitoring and create dashboards with the customized view required for your monitoring team.

Let's get started with Azure Monitor for Azure Virtual Desktop.

## Monitor Azure Virtual Desktop by Using Azure Monitor

Azure Monitor is a full-stack monitoring service that provides a complete set of features to monitor your Azure resources, including Azure Virtual Desktop. You don't need to directly interact with Azure Monitor, though, to perform a variety of monitoring tasks, because its features are integrated with the Azure portal for the Azure services that it monitors.

When you have critical applications and business processes that rely on Azure resources, it's important to monitor those resources for their availability, performance, and operation. Azure Virtual Desktop is an application used by multiple end users, so you must monitor and set up alerts for Azure Virtual Desktop.

Some services in Azure display customized monitoring experiences in Azure Monitor. These experiences are called *insights*, and they include prebuilt workbooks

© Arun Sabale and Balu N Ilag 2022
A. Sabale and B. N. Ilag, *Microsoft Azure Virtual Desktop Guide*,
https://doi.org/10.1007/978-1-4842-8063-8_11

and other specialized features for that service. Azure Virtual Desktop also provides a customized experience with insights, and you can customize them per your requirements.

There are two things you must enable monitoring for.

- Session host virtual machines

- Host pool diagnostic logs.

Let's see why the session host monitor is important and what you can monitor.

## Monitoring Virtual Machine Data

Azure virtual machines collect the same kinds of monitoring data as other Azure resources, which are described in the article "Monitoring Data from Azure Resources." Azure Monitor provides a basic level of monitoring for Azure virtual machines at no cost and with no configuration. Platform metrics for Azure virtual machines include important metrics such as the CPU, network, and disk utilization with no additional configuration. You can onboard machines to VM insights, which deploys required agents and begins collecting data from the guest operating system. Follow these steps to enable insights on each session host:

1. Log in to the Azure portal and go to the session host on which you want to enable insights.

2. Click Insights on the left and then the Enable button. See Figure 11-1.

***Figure 11-1.*** *Azure virtual machine insights*

Once you enable the Insights option, then you will be able to see the performance, map, and health of the VM on the Insights page.

On the Performance tab, you can see the disk attached and its usage as well as its CPU usage. See Figure 11-2.

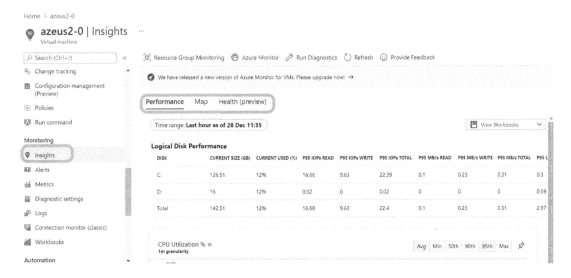

***Figure 11-2.*** *Azure virtual machine insights, Performance tab*

On the second tab, Map, you can see the process running and the connection to remove the server/host with the port details. You can also see VM properties, log events, alerts, connections, and changes on the right. See Figure 11-3.

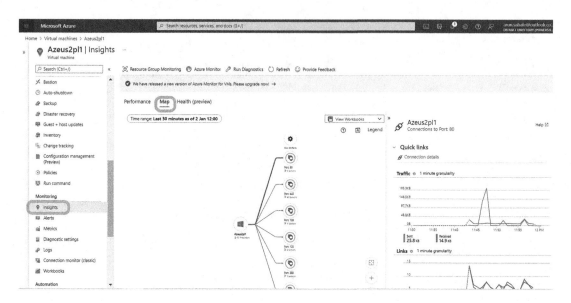

***Figure 11-3.*** *Azure virtual machine insights, Map tab*

Additionally, VM monitoring can be done from the Overview page as well, and you can see all the key metrics on the Monitoring tab. This tab contains the CPU, network, memory, and disk usage for the last 30 days or less. See Figure 11-4.

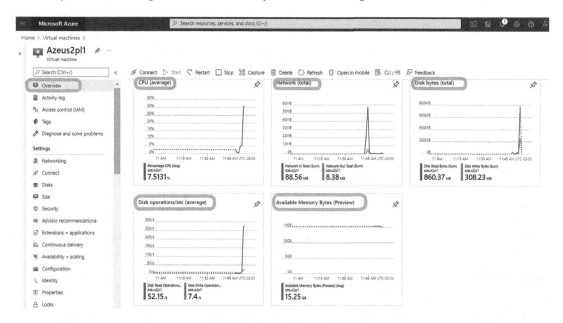

***Figure 11-4.*** *Azure virtual machine insights, Overview*

# Analyze Logs

Data in the Azure Monitor logs is stored in a Log Analytics workspace, where it's separated into tables, each with its own set of unique properties.

VM insights store the collected data in logs, and the insights provide performance and map views that you can use to interactively analyze the data. You can work directly with this data to drill down further or perform custom analyses. To analyze other log data that you collect from your virtual machines, use the log queries in Log Analytics. Several built-in queries for virtual machines are available to use, or you can create your own. You can interactively work with the results of these queries, include them in a workbook to make them available to other users, or generate alerts based on their results.

# Alerts

Azure Monitor alerts proactively notify you when important conditions/issues are found in your monitoring data. These alerts can help you identify and address issues in your system before your customers notice them or have a big outage. You can set alerts on metrics, logs, and the activity log.

# Create Alerts from the Azure Portal

The following procedure describes how to create a metric alert rule in the Azure portal:

1.  Log in to the Azure portal, and go to the session host on which you want to create the alert. Alternately, you can create an alert from Azure Monitor that consolidates all your monitoring settings and data in one view.

2.  Click Alerts, expand the "+ Create menu" item, and select "Alert rule." See Figure 11-5.

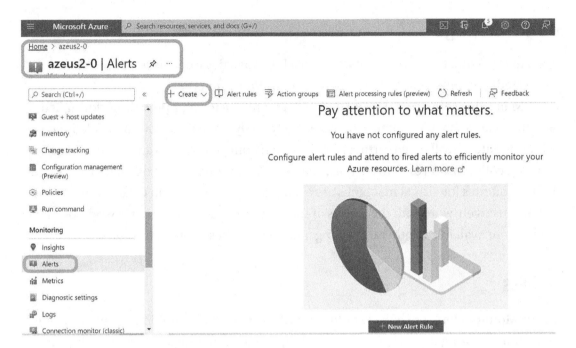

**Figure 11-5.** *Azure Monitor, adding an alert*

3. On the **next** page you will add the **scope, condition, and actions**.
   See Figure 11-6.

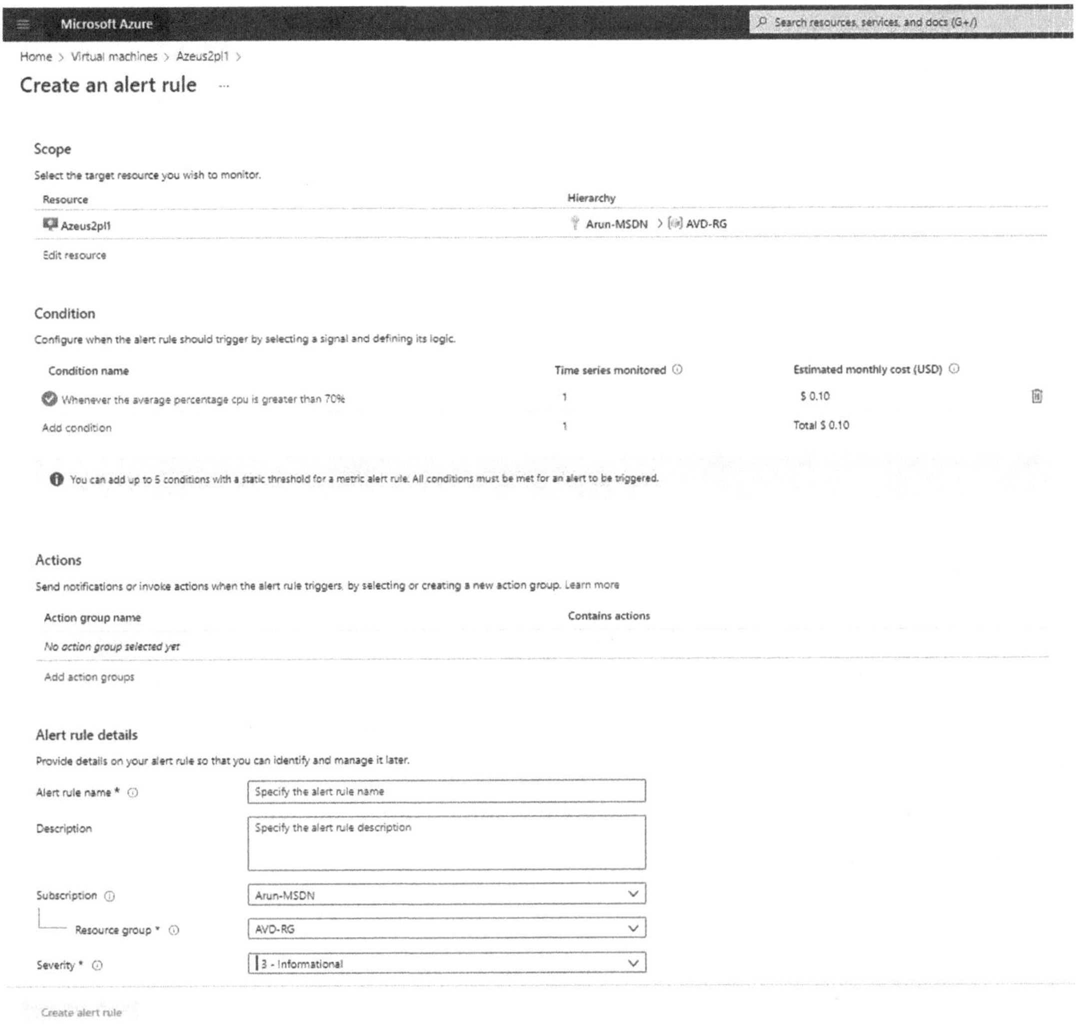

**Figure 11-6.** *Azure Monitor, Add Alert page*

The alert scope, condition, and action are part of alert creation page, so let's see what exactly each represent.

*What is an alert scope?* The scope is the target resource(s) that you want to alert on. You can **filter by subscription**, **by resource type**, and **by location** drop-downs to find the resource you want to monitor. You can also use the search bar to find your resource. If the selected resource has metrics that you can create alert rules on, the **available signal types** on the bottom right will include metrics. Once you have selected a target resource, click **Done**. See Figure 11-7.

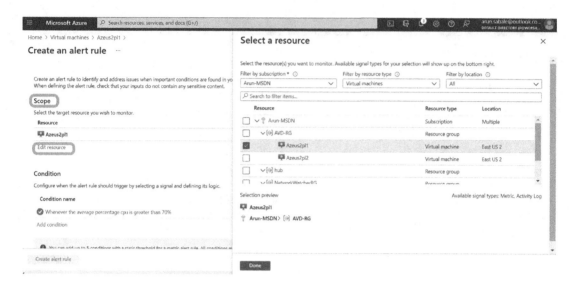

***Figure 11-7.*** *Azure Monitor, Scope option*

*What is an alert condition?* Select the condition on which you want the alert to get triggered. Under the Condition option, you will see a list of signals supported for the resource. Select the metric you want to create an alert on. You will see a chart showing the metric's behavior for the last six hours. Use the "**Chart period**" drop-down to see a longer history for the metric. If the metric has dimensions, you will see a dimensions table presented. Optionally, select one or more values per dimension. See Figure 11-8.

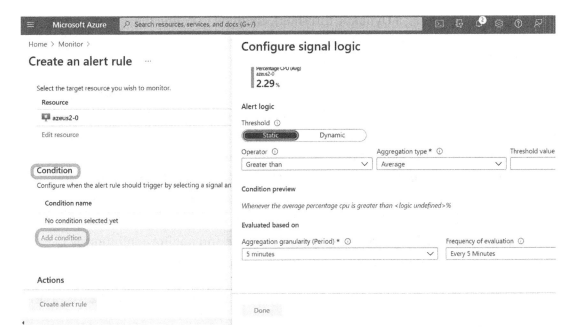

***Figure 11-8.*** *Azure Monitor, Condition option*

- The displayed dimension values are based on metric data from the previous day.

- If the dimension value you're looking for isn't displayed, click "Add custom value" to add a custom dimension value.

- You can also choose "Select all current and future values" for any of the dimensions. This will dynamically scale the selection to all current and future values for the dimension.

The metric alert rule will evaluate the condition for all combinations of values selected.

Select the **threshold** type, **operator**, and **aggregation type**. This will determine the logic that the metric alert rule will evaluate.

- If you are using a Static threshold, continue to define a Threshold value. The metric chart can help determine what might be a reasonable threshold.

- If you are using a Dynamic threshold, continue to define the
  Threshold sensitivity. The metric chart will display the calculated
  thresholds based on recent data.

*What are alert actions?* You can define what actions and notifications are triggered
when the alert rule generates an alert. You can add an action group to the alert rule
either by selecting an existing action group or by creating a new action group. Proceed
to the **Details** tab. Under **Project details**, select the subscription and resource group
in which the alert rule resource will be saved. Under "**Alert rule details**," specify the
**severity** and **alert rule name**. You can also provide an **alert rule description**, select if
the alert rule should be enabled when created and if it should **automatically resolve
alerts** (which instructs the alert rule to maintain a state and not fire continuously if
there's already a fired alert on the same condition). See Figure 11-9.

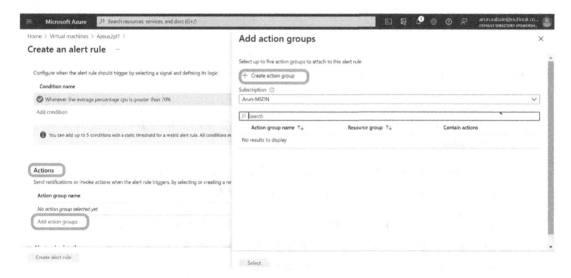

***Figure 11-9.*** *Azure Monitor, action groups*

1. Once you add the scope, condition, and action, then you can
   proceed further with the **Tags tab**, where you can set tags on the
   alert rule you're creating.

2. Proceed to the "**Review + create**" tab, where you can review
   your selections before creating the alert rule. A quick automatic
   validation will also be performed, notifying you in case any

information is missing or needs to be corrected. Once you're
ready to create the alert rule, click **Create**.

# Azure Monitor for Azure Virtual Desktop

Azure Monitor for Azure Virtual Desktop is a dashboard built on Azure Monitor
Workbooks that helps IT professionals understand their Azure Virtual Desktop
environments. This topic will walk you through how to set up Azure Monitor for Azure
Virtual Desktop to monitor your Azure Virtual Desktop environments. See Figure 11-10.

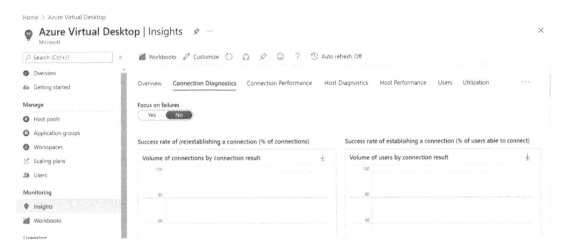

***Figure 11-10.*** *Azure Virtual Desktop, insights*

You can open Azure Monitor for Azure Virtual Desktop with one of the following
methods:

- Go to `aka.ms/azmonwvdi`.

- Search for and select Azure Virtual Desktop from the Azure portal;
  then select Insights.

- Search for and select Azure Monitor from the Azure portal. Select
  Insights Hub under Insights; then select Azure Virtual Desktop. Once
  you have the page open, enter the subscription, resource group, host
  pool, and time range of the environment you want to monitor.

# Log Analytics Settings for AVD

To start using Azure Monitor for Azure Virtual Desktop, you'll need at least one Log Analytics workspace. Use a designated Log Analytics workspace for your Azure Virtual Desktop session hosts to ensure that performance counters and events are only collected from session hosts in your Azure Virtual Desktop deployment. If you already have a workspace set up, skip ahead to "Set Up the Configuration Workbook."

# Set Up the Configuration Workbook

If it's your first time opening Azure Monitor for Azure Virtual Desktop, you'll need set up Azure Monitor for your Azure Virtual Desktop environment. To configure your resources, follow these steps:

1.  Open Azure Monitor for Azure Virtual Desktop in the Azure portal at `aka.ms/azmonwvdi`, and select **configuration workbook**.

2.  Select an environment to configure under **Subscription**, **Resource Group**, and **Host Pool**.

The configuration workbook sets up your monitoring environment and lets you check the configuration after you've finished the setup process. It's important to check your configuration if items in the dashboard aren't displaying correctly or when the product group publishes updates that require new settings. See Figure 11-11.

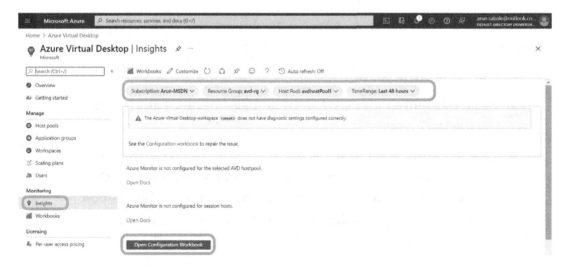

***Figure 11-11.***  *Azure Virtual Desktop, Configuration Workbook*

# Resource Diagnostic Settings

To collect information on your Azure Virtual Desktop infrastructure, you'll need to enable several diagnostic settings on your Azure Virtual Desktop host pools and workspaces (this is your Azure Virtual Desktop workspace, not your Log Analytics workspace).

To set your resource diagnostic settings in the configuration workbook, follow these steps:

1. Select the "**Resource diagnostic settings**" tab in the configuration workbook.

2. Select the **Log Analytics workspace** to send Azure Virtual Desktop diagnostics.

# Host Pool Diagnostic Settings

To set up host pool diagnostics using the "resource diagnostic settings" section in the configuration workbook, follow these steps:

1. Under "**Host pool**," check to see whether Azure Virtual Desktop diagnostics are enabled. If they aren't, an error message will appear that says, "No existing diagnostic configuration was found for the selected host pool." You'll need to enable the following supported diagnostic tables:

   - Checkpoint

   - Error

   - Management

   - Connection

   - HostRegistration

   - AgentHealthStatus

2. Select "**Configure host pool**." See Figure 11-12.

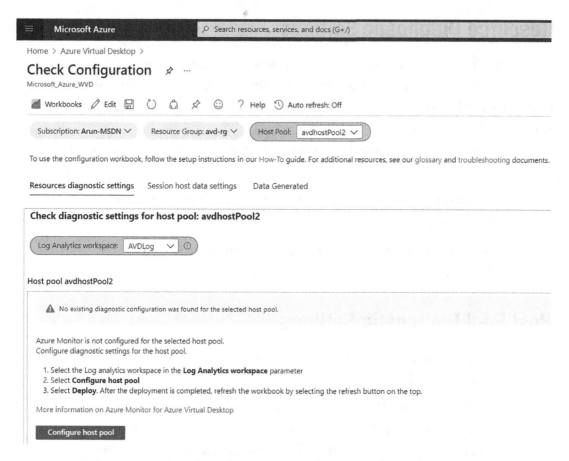

***Figure 11-12.***  *Azure Virtual Desktop, hostpool diagnostic setting*

3.   Select **Deploy**.

4.   Refresh the configuration workbook. See Figure 11-13.

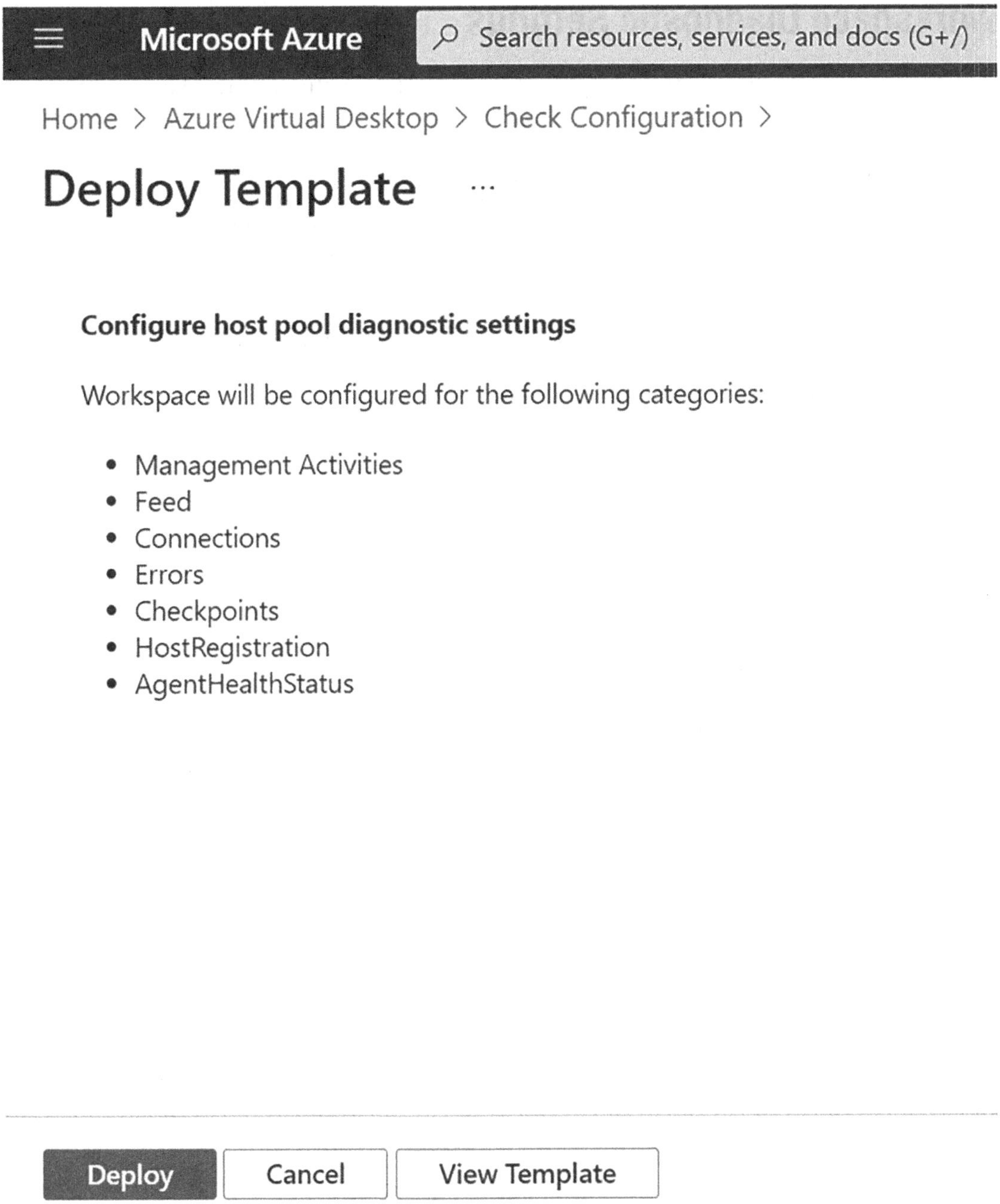

≡    **Microsoft Azure**    🔍 Search resources, services, and docs (G+/)

Home > Azure Virtual Desktop > Check Configuration >

# Deploy Template ⋯

### Configure host pool diagnostic settings

Workspace will be configured for the following categories:

- Management Activities
- Feed
- Connections
- Errors
- Checkpoints
- HostRegistration
- AgentHealthStatus

Deploy    Cancel    View Template

***Figure 11-13.*** *Azure Virtual Desktop, hostpool diagnostic setting deployment*

# Workspace Diagnostic Settings

To set up workspace diagnostics using the "resource diagnostic settings" section in the configuration workbook, follow these steps:

1.  Under **Workspace**, check to see whether Azure Virtual Desktop diagnostics are enabled for the Azure Virtual Desktop workspace. If they aren't, an error message will appear that says "No existing diagnostic configuration was found for the selected workspace." You'll need to enable the following supported diagnostics tables:

    -   Checkpoint

    -   Error

    -   Management

    -   Feed

2.  Select "**Configure workspace.**"

3.  Select **Deploy**.

4.  Refresh the configuration workbook. See Figure 11-14.

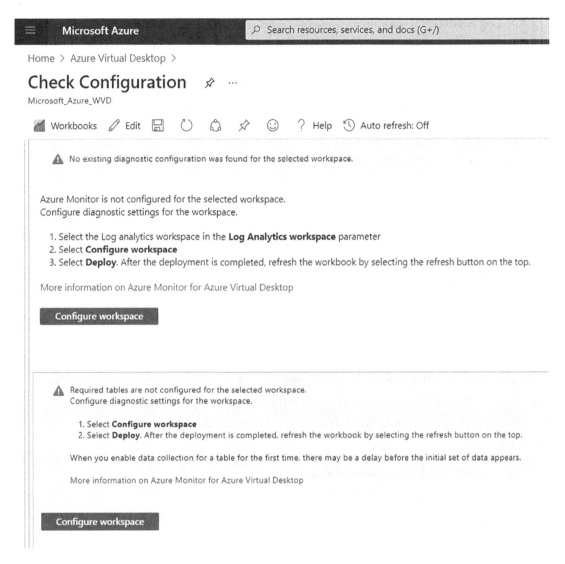

**Figure 11-14.** *Azure Virtual Desktop, workspace diagnostic setting*

# Session Host Data Settings

To collect information on your Azure Virtual Desktop session hosts, you'll need to install the Log Analytics agent on all session hosts in the host pool, make sure the session hosts are sending to a Log Analytics workspace, and configure your Log Analytics agent settings to collect performance data and Windows Event Logs.

The Log Analytics workspace you send session host data to doesn't have to be the same one you send diagnostic data to. If you have Azure session hosts outside of your Azure Virtual Desktop environment, we recommend having a designated Log Analytics workspace for the Azure Virtual Desktop session hosts.

To set the Log Analytics workspace where you want to collect session host data, follow these steps:

1.   Select the **session host data settings** tab in the configuration workbook.

2.   Select the **Log Analytics workspace** you want to send session host data to.

## Session Hosts

You'll need to install the Log Analytics agent on all session hosts in the host pool and send data from those hosts to your selected Log Analytics workspace. If Log Analytics isn't configured for all the session hosts in the host pool, you'll see a "Session hosts" section at the top of the session host data settings with the message "Some hosts in the host pool are not sending data to the selected Log Analytics workspace."

To set up your remaining session hosts using the configuration workbook, follow these steps:

1.   Select "**Add hosts to workspace**."

2.   Refresh the configuration workbook.

## Optional: Configure Alerts

Azure Monitor for Azure Virtual Desktop allows you to monitor Azure Monitor alerts happening within your selected subscription, in the context of your Azure Virtual Desktop data. Azure Monitor alerts are an optional feature of your Azure subscriptions, and you need to set them up separately from Azure Monitor for Azure Virtual Desktop. You can use the Azure Monitor alerts framework to set custom alerts on Azure Virtual Desktop events, diagnostics, and resources.

# Monitor Azure Virtual Desktop by Using Azure Advisor

Here's how to use Azure Advisor.

## Use Azure Advisor with Azure Virtual Desktop

Azure Advisor can help users resolve common issues on their own, without having to file support cases. The recommendations reduce the need to submit help requests, saving you time and costs.

Let's see how to set up Azure Advisor in your Azure Virtual Desktop deployment to help your users.

## What Is Azure Advisor?

Azure Advisor analyzes your configurations and telemetry to offer personalized recommendations to solve common problems. With these recommendations, you can optimize your Azure resources for reliability, security, operational excellence, performance, and cost.

## How to Start Using Azure Advisor

First, open the Azure portal at `https://portal.azure.com/`, and then select Advisor under Azure Services, as shown in Figure 11-15. You can also enter **Azure Advisor** into the search bar in the Azure portal.

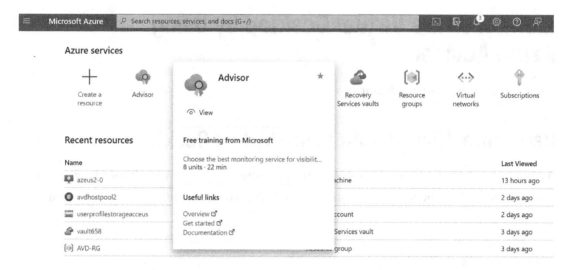

**Figure 11-15.** *Azure Virtual Desktop, Advisor*

When you open Azure Advisor, you'll see five categories (see Figure 11-16).

- Cost

- Security

- Reliability

- Operational Excellence

- Performance

***Figure 11-16.*** *Azure Virtual Desktop, Advisor overview*

When you select a category, you'll go to its active recommendations page. On this page, you can view which recommendations Azure Advisor has for you, as shown in Figure 11-17.

***Figure 11-17.*** *Azure Virtual Desktop, Advisor recommendation*

## Additional Tips for Azure Advisor

Here are some additional tips:

- Make sure to check your recommendations frequently, at least more than once a week. Azure Advisor updates its active recommendations multiple times per day. Checking for new recommendations can prevent larger issues by helping you spot and solve smaller ones.

- Always try to solve the issues with the highest priority level in Azure Advisor. High-priority issues are marked with red. Leaving high-priority recommendations unresolved can lead to problems down the line.

- If a recommendation seems less important, you can dismiss it or postpone it. To dismiss or postpone a recommendation, go to the Action column, and change the item's state.

- Don't dismiss recommendations until you know why they're appearing and are sure it won't have a negative impact on you or your users. Always select "Learn more" to see what the issue is. If you resolve an issue by following the instructions in Azure Advisor, it will automatically disappear from the list. You're better off resolving issues than postponing them repeatedly.

- Whenever you come across an issue in Azure Virtual Desktop, always check Azure Advisor first. Azure Advisor will give you directions for how to solve the problem, or at least point you toward a resource that can help.

# Summary

In this chapter, you learned about monitoring Azure Virtual Desktop resources such as the session host, host pool, and workspace. You also learned about setting up alerts for different resources with different conditions.

You checked how to use Azure Advisor and how it can help you to improve your AVD environment by providing recommendations.

Now you know everything about Azure Virtual Desktop, so you are good to design and set up the AVD environment and optimize it based on your requirements. If you are preparing for AZ-140, then good luck for the exam, and if you want to implement the AVD service in production, then I recommend you set up a lab to test Azure Virtual Desktop and verify all the options. Microsoft always keeps updating the cloud services, so check the recent changes in the service and test them before you implement them in production.

# Glossary

AVD - Azure Virtual Desktop

WVD - Windows Virtual desktop

VNET - Virtual network

RG - resource group

VM - Virtual machine

AD - Active directory

DNS - domain naming service

AAD DS - Azure Active directory domain services

AD DS - Active directory domain services

RDP - Remote Desktop Protocol

TLS - Transport Layer Security

TCP - Transport Control Protocol

ADC - Active Directory Connection

FQDNs - Fully Qualified Domain Names

UDR - User Defined Route

PaaS - Platform as a service

IaaS - Infrastructure as a service

VM - Virtual Machine

URI - Uniform Re source Identifier

GPU - Graphics Processing Units

© Arun Sabale and Balu N Ilag 2022
A. Sabale and B. N. Ilag, *Microsoft Azure Virtual Desktop Guide,*
https://doi.org/10.1007/978-1-4842-8063-8

# Index

© Arun Sabale and Balu N Ilag 2022
A. Sabale and B. N. Ilag, *Microsoft Azure Virtual Desktop Guide*,
https://doi.org/10.1007/978-1-4842-8063-8

Printed in the United States
by Baker & Taylor Publisher Services